# Fear, Faith, and Patience

## My fight for justice in an injustice system

Felecia S. Killings

*PowerFaithLove Publishing*

Editor: PFL Publishing, CA

Cover Design: Tyora Moody/Tywebbin.com

Photography: Ariel Killings of Ariel Kay Designs

FEAR, FAITH, AND PATIENCE: MY FIGHT FOR JUSTICE IN AN INJUSTICE SYSTEM

Copyright © 2012

Published by PowerFaithLove Publishing
Suisun City, CA 94585

Library of Congress Cataloging-in-Publication Data
ISBN 10: 0-984-83530-0
ISBN 13: 9-780984-835300

Printed in the United States of America

# Thematic Scripture

"He who dwells in the secret place of the Most High shall remain stable and fixed under the shadow of the Almighty [Whose power no foe can withstand]./I will say of the Lord, He is my Refuge and my Fortress, my God; on Him I lean and rely, and in Him I [confidently] trust!/For [then] He will deliver you from the snare of the fowler and from the deadly pestilence./[Then] He will cover you with His pinions, and under His wings shall you trust and find refuge; His truth and His faithfulness are a shield and a buckler./You shall not be afraid of the terror of the night, nor of the arrow (the evil plots and slanders of the wicked) that flies by day./Nor of the pestilence that stalks in darkness, nor of the destruction and sudden death that surprise and lay waste at noonday./A thousand may fall at your side, and ten thousand at your right hand, but it shall not come near you./Only a spectator shall you be [yourself inaccessible in the secret place of the Most High] as you witness the reward of the wicked./ Because you have made the Lord your refuge, and the Most High your dwelling place,/There shall no evil befall you, nor any plague or calamity come near your tent./For He will give His angels [especial] charge over you to accompany and defend and preserve you in all your ways [of obedience and service]./They shall bear you up on their hands, lest you dash your foot against a stone./You shall tread upon the lion and adder; the young lion and the serpent shall you trample underfoot./**Because [she] has set [her] love upon Me, therefore I will deliver [her]; I will set [her] on** high, because [she] knows and understands My name [has a personal knowledge of My mercy, love, and kindness—trusts and relies on Me, knowing I will never forsake {her}, no never]./[She] shall call upon Me, and I will answer [her]; I will be with [her] in trouble, I will deliver [her] and honor [her]./With long life will I satisfy [her] and show [her] My salvation" (Psalms 91 AMP, emphasis added).

# TABLE OF CONTENTS

# Foreword

In her well-documented book, *Fear, Faith, and Patience: My fight for justice in an injustice system,* author Felecia S. Killings draws primarily on a dark, extended period of her life, offering the reader valuable insights to the reasons why—and the solutions to—the challenges that may come our way.

As an observer, I am amazed how God works through trials, tests, and heartaches to bring one to a place of triumph, victory, and success; but I have read how He does this in the pages of this extraordinary book. Killings does not sugar coat her anguish and suffering at the hands of a God-less system; nor does she make up excuses for what had befallen her. But she gives a step-by-step account of how she dealt with her accusers while learning one of life's greatest lessons: "Sometimes the conflicts that you go through are not necessarily about you; they may be for the deliverance and salvation of others" (excerpt from *Fear, Faith, and Patience*).

Killings is to be commended for her display of courage, tenacity, and resolve in this memoir. Bringing to light and exposing a system that embraces tyranny, she speaks with boldness and confidence as she becomes a voice crying out for truth and justice to a world that openly opposes transformation.

For those that are facing despair, gloom, and a hopeless situation, this is a highly-recommended text that will surely bring encouragement to your souls. It is truly an astonishing book worthy of your time.

Paulette-Harper Johnson
Award-winning, best-selling author of *That Was Then, This is Now* and *Completely Whole*
www.pauletteharper.com

# *Dedication*

*I* want to dedicate the first portion of my book to my heroes, my former scholars from April 2008: Nicolas Rogoff, Ally Rosemond, Roman Robinson, Nicole Terrell, Adam McCray, Sylver Wallace, Shalamar Jamerson, Lisa Mattis, and Tamika Scott. I promised you all that one day the world would know what you did for your school and the District, and here it is.

By my own definition, a scholar is one who possesses a great level of intelligence, and is not afraid to share that intelligence with the world. You nine epitomize that very essence of those words. I could have never made it through the 2008 school year without you. Your love, honor, and respect for each other—regardless of differences in gender, race, or ethnicity—were my inspiration and my hope. I pray that you learned as much from me as I learned from you, and may this portion of the book live with you in your hearts forever. Always remember that every movement has a leader, but it is the followers and supporters that make the movement a success. You all changed the nature of your school in the midst of intense heat and fear, and you loved and embraced my heart when others had abandoned me. Your demonstration of charity and courage was rare and unique, and for that I honor you.

To the parents of these fantastic scholars, your love and support for us brought so much hope and encouragement. I honor you as well. You have produced heroes unlike any other.

Lastly, I want to dedicate this entire book to all those who desire to be grand in this world, and for those who aspire to make a change in our society. The greatest act that we can accomplish in life is not that we become famous and make a name for ourselves. Neither is it having our image in the spotlight. Rather, our greatest moments come to us when we perform one thing: service to mankind. We must understand that looking beyond our own selfish needs and seeking to serve those who have no voice and who have no hope are our greatest feats. Jesus, our great Hope and Savior, said that if any desire to be first in the kingdom, he must be a servant (Mark 9:35). The greatest act of servitude is to love—to show love towards our family, our neighbors, and yes, even our enemies. Our love for others will cause us to do what is necessary to help those in need. This is what makes us great. It should be the desire of our hearts that when we are gone from this earth, our legacy of love towards others remains engraved in society for the next generation to follow. God has given us this authority to love, and we must never neglect such great power. When we recognize, appreciate, and apply this God-given endowment, then and only then will we become change makers and world shakers.

# Acknowledgements

$\mathcal{I}$ want to acknowledge the following people who have helped me become the woman I am today: my father (Pastor Henry Killings), step mother (Lusia Killings), and my mother (Paulette Harper-Johnson). Thank you for being a help, a shield, and a support during the most trying times of my life. May God continue to manifest His power and might through us all as we seek to become more like His dear Son, Jesus Christ.

To my friends and family members: Thank you for your immediate response of love and encouragement to me when I was at my lowest state.

To my sisters: Pumpkin and Sister (Fatima and Ariel). I love you both so much. I couldn't have asked for more supportive and protective guardian angels. It's strange how tragedies have a way of bringing some people closer together, but my situation did just that for all three of us.

To Sister, especially, thank you for being my voice at times when I could not speak directly to some folks when they personally

11

confronted me—like the lying student who saw us at the gas station. Thank you for never giving up on me, and for being my ace throughout the years. I don't think it is possible for any two sisters to become as close as we are; and I know that when God sent you to me, He knew you were exactly the kind of person I needed to get me through so many difficult situations. I cannot repay you enough, Sister, for the unconditional love you have shown me. Nothing in the world would ever make me love you any less, and I promise to do for you as you have done for me. **We are so the coolest sisters in the world!**

# Special Thanks

I want to send a special thanks to the representatives of the Fairfield-Suisun Unified Teachers Association. Your help and support over the last few years enabled me to face every challenge thrown my way while in the Fairfield School District and at Rodriguez High School. I pray that as you continue to provide protection and guidance to every teacher within this organization, God will strengthen you who work tirelessly for teachers' rights.

I also want to send a special thanks to the Fairfield chapter of the National Association for the Advancement of Colored People (NAACP). Thanks to the leaders and members who helped me and my scholars in 2008. Thank you for your support and diligence in getting the District to enact its official hate crime policy. It brought significant and profound change to an institution that would otherwise turn a blind eye to social justice. Thank you for being the "pressure" that we needed to create cultural activities and staff training initiatives that were lacking in the District. I pray that your efforts will continue to be influential as we seek to provide a more-excellent education for our children.

Also, I would like to thank my lawyer for working so diligently on my case, Thomas Maas. More importantly, thank you for believing me when others would not. I realize that my situation was not like anything you had ever heard, and I appreciate you taking the time to not only listen to me, but to also defend me against all odds.

In addition, I want to send another thanks to the countless scholars and parents who stood by me in heart and spirit during these last five years, especially during the 2010-2011 school year. It speaks of your unconditional love, and I could never repay you for your acts of kindness and generosity that you showed me throughout the years.

One family in particular is especially dear to my heart: To the Lewis family, thank you for what you shared with me after the passing of one of my dearest scholars, Kendrick J. Lewis. (I miss him dearly.) Just knowing that you and others recognized and appreciated my efforts to help this generation become more successful in education and God's kingdom was the only reward I needed as an educator. May God continue to favor you with His blessings.

And last, but certainly not least, to all the haters, backstabbers, liars, betrayers, negative bloggers/commentators, and lying students; to all those who had so much to say and who negatively prejudged the situation before knowing anything: When a tragedy strikes you as it did me, I pray that the same "courtesy" you have publicly shown me will be shown to you doubly. May the very nature and intent of your words return to you in your time of crisis. May God return to you the very words that you have thrown my way. May He grant you grace and patience to endure public humiliation and shame when you did not deserve it. And when those that you thought loved you the most and cared for you actually despised and rejected you, may you recall the past actions you committed against me. For when that moment arrives, I hope that you realize that **you have just reaped what you have sown.**

*"A tongue can accuse or carry bad news;*
*The seeds of distrust it will sow.*
*So unless you have made no mistakes in life,*
*Be careful of the stones that you throw."*

—Hank Williams

# *Introduction*

For months, I had been waiting for the moment to finally share what had been on my heart and in my mind for so long. It would seem as though every time I tried to speak up and defend myself against all the things that were negatively spoken against me, the Spirit of the Lord would silence me. For a while, it seemed like He had nearly taken me off the face of the earth because no one had heard from me in months. And anyone that knows me understands that if anything is directed towards me in a negative fashion, it is quickly met with a sharp or harsh word. But this was the first time that I had seen the Lord stand in front of me and declare, "This is My battle, and you will not have to fight."

I don't know how else to begin this book other than to give thanks and praise to the Lord of heaven and earth. I can't imagine what my life would be like had I never known the Lord. He has demonstrated such grace and mercy to me, and I know I would not have made it through any situation without Him.

We often question why the Lord allows us to go through some situations that we believe we did not deserve. Even when we don't understand everything, we must be confident in knowing that in all things, He has made us more than conquerors through Christ Jesus. Even in the midst of all hell, whether we opened the door to it through our sins or not, we are assured that God is faithful to cause all things to work together for our good. He is a reliable God, and He will prove His trustworthiness by forgiving us of all our sins and cleansing us from all unrighteousness (I John 1:9). Not only that, but He also promises us blessings and favor when we call upon His name and depend on Him in every situation.

I asked the Lord many times why He allowed this situation to happen; why He closed all other doors of teaching opportunities, and only opened the door for me to work at Rodriguez High. Why place me there if He knew all along what would happen to me? Why allow me to experience the worst situation in my life when I had faithfully loved and served Him throughout the years? His answer was the same as it is to anyone who suffers tragedies, and yet still loves Him: "My grace is sufficient for you. For in your times of weaknesses, I am made strong in you."

When I first made the decision to record the events that had happened to me within the last five years as an educator, I believed that I was doing it to simply keep record of things as a personal memoir. I always had a desire to write books and share with the world whatever God placed on my heart; but I did not envision that my first book would discuss the most trying and difficult times of my life. I never imagined that my name would be in headlines across the nation. I never once thought that people outside my sphere of influence would ever hear my voice; but over the years, my name became one that people admired, respected, praised, despised, or feared. I realize that all the things that I had been through thus far were future testimonies of God's saving grace and power, which would be used to help others in dire situations, and would also draw many to Christ.

There were a few people who told me that it was not a good idea to put my story out there because people would have something to judge me on once again. I heard their advice, and I asked the Lord what to do. I could have kept silent about my story and just let time erase all things, but I couldn't resist the unction to speak once again. It's like when Jeremiah told the Lord that he would not speak anymore because the people did not believe the Word given to him; but the message of God burned like an unquenchable fire in his soul. How do you contain such unction? How do you tell the Lord, "I won't speak anymore because it cost too much"? I tell you, it is virtually impossible to restrain such unction. And from that, I realized that it was not my job to worry or fear what others may think or say, but to do what I do best, and that is to speak out.

We often ask, "How can God use someone's weaknesses, failures, faults, mistakes, or bad situations to draw others to Christ?" In response to this question, I reflect on the life of Paul. Before God had changed his name, he was a persecutor of the church (Acts 8). He consented to imprison and destroy men and women who preached the Gospel of Jesus Christ. But one day, Jesus appeared before him and literally knocked him off his horse. From that supernatural encounter, he was convinced that Jesus was the Messiah, and God turned his life around completely. Paul would later become the greatest apostle that the Church ever knew, even though he was once a persecutor to Christians. But even he considered himself least worthy of such an honor because of his past. Nevertheless, God had a perfect plan for him. Because Paul was so consumed with the anointing and the power of God, he suffered so much; yet he did not allow his circumstances to keep him silent concerning the Gospel of Jesus Christ, even though it stirred controversy wherever he went. In that same fashion, neither can I be silent about matters that pertain to life and godliness. I cannot keep silent when evil works continue to destroy lives, and the very ones that we have in positions of authority and power are misusing and abusing their influence to bring a generation to hell. How can I keep silent?

By the time my book reaches the public, some will be searching for answers to questions they have regarding the allegations against me. Hundreds of thousands (possible millions now) will know me only by the reports from media and the Internet as the teacher who raped her students; and, well, I couldn't just sit back and let you all have the last words. You may have read the comments of so many people, many who argued that I was guilty of not only sleeping with one student, but a lot of them. You may have seen statements such as, "She deserves what she gets," or "She's been doing this for years;" but those people know very little and only speak evil of what they think they know. Whether people believe my story or not is up to them. I can't control that. But I hope that the information (and evidence) that I provide in this book will show the public that not everything is as it seems. There really are good people in this world who actually care for others and who believe strongly in righteousness and holiness within the public school system. While media won't promote this kind of story, all I can do is share my truth, and allow this moment to be an opportunity for others to see how magnanimous God can be when we allow Him to operate in our lives. More importantly, I want people to see that when an injustice has occurred, God promises to be our Vindicator and Deliverer. That's what He's been to me for the last five years, and what He has demonstrated with regards to this impossible situation.

The incident that most people are aware of is not an isolated moment, and I have attempted to share with the reader the context of everything to show how it all eventually led to my arrest on November 9, 2010. Because so much had happened within a few years, I have broken my story into three separate books. The first book provides some background information, and also tells the story of my first four years at Rodriguez High School in Fairfield, California through chronological narration; the second book, *Fear, Faith, and Patience: Letters to my Lord*, is divided into daily journal entries that record the events of my arrest and trial, and the emotions I went through while enduring that test. I conclude my story in my third and final book in this "series" called *Bouncing Back: Why Quitting is never an Option for a Believer*. Throughout these books, the reader will notice that I go from moments of fear to faith to patience. That's where the title comes from. At times, I am very confident and strong in my faith, and other times I express real fears that I had during the course of the years. But through it all, I had to **learn** to let patience have its perfect work in me. Patience shows that we are able to wait on God to do what only He can do. My patience is proof that I believe God to give me my breakthrough and my miracle at just the right time—His time.

Through my story, I want people to see how God's strength and power were with me immensely throughout these five years. Some will sympathize with the story; others will criticize. But ultimately I pray that my story will show how even when we are in our lowest state, we have someone fighting for us in our corner. Whenever we feel inept to affect change in our society and especially the schools, God gives us the wisdom and might to do what's right, even in the face of public scrutiny and professional backlash.

Surprisingly, my story is not new. There are thousands of others who are and have experienced similar incidents as I have; yet their stories have been hidden because many refuse to or are too afraid to speak up. For the longest time, I felt like I was alone. I wish I had someone else to talk to about my situations, but there was no one except the Lord. And as such, I write this book for all those silent, invisible individuals who feel they have no way out. The Lord is with you just as He was with me, and He is faithful to bring you out and help you overcome your situations as well.

To conclude this Introduction, I want to take this moment to say to the scholars (past and present) who embraced my heart and who loved me unconditionally: You are my pride and joy. You brought so much happiness and excitement to my life, and I will never forget you. Nothing that you could ever do, whether to me or to others, would ever make me hate or despise you. I still pray earnestly for your success and well-being; and while others may mock or ridicule me for the unyielding love I showed you, I know that ultimately I did exactly what I was supposed to do in guiding you to your next level. I pray that you will grow in strength, wisdom, and knowledge; but most of all, I pray that you will know the Lord and become a partaker in His divine kingdom. I pray that the blessings of the Lord will draw you closer to Him; and I pray that God will give me grace and mercy to see some of you again. May all that you do and say bring honor to the One Who made you and called you, and may His peace abide with you forever.

With unconditional love,

Ms. Killings

*"You will be a Queen Esther"*

# The Queen Esther Prophecy

*A prophetic word is spoken to an individual to give one a window or glimpse into that person's future. It serves as a roadmap that outlines God's perfect course and path for one's life. When we receive a prophetic word, God always intends for it to be fulfilled in its due time—at the right moment, at the right season. His word never returns to Him empty or unaccomplished. Rather, it comes back to Him, having completed what He desired.*

The Bible speaks of a young woman named Esther who became queen of an entire nation. Her beginnings were meek and mild; yet God raised her to become one of the Bible's most heroic female figures. She was an extremely beautiful young woman, and when the king of the land was looking to appoint a new queen, Esther became that one.

Before she was queen, Esther lived in humble dwellings with her cousin, Mordecai. When word spread around the kingdom that the king had a desire for a new queen (for he had divorced his first one), Mordecai, a worker in the palace, encouraged her to pursue that position. After much preparation, Esther was selected to be among the many handmaids, one of whom the king would later choose to be his next bride. While she lived in the palace, her cousin had instructed her not to reveal the nature of her ethnicity, for she was a Jew. For whatever reason, it was important to him that she did not convey this secret to anyone; and as such, she concealed it.

One day, the king promoted a prominent figure in his kingdom named Haman. As the Bible reads, the king "set [Haman's] seat above all the princes who were with him" (Esther 3:1). All the servants in the king's household were commanded to pay homage to Haman and to worship him because of his honor. But Mordecai, who loved the God of Israel, would not bow his knee to Haman. This outraged him, and from that point on, Haman not only hated Mordecai, but also made himself an enemy of the Jewish nation.

Out of his anger and frustration, Haman conspired to destroy the people who would not bow to him, and he convinced the king to sign a decree that would annihilate the Jewish people. As the Bible reads, "[Jewish] laws are different from all other people's, and they do not keep the king's laws. Therefore it is not fitting for the king to let them remain" (Esther 3:8). After the king heeded Haman's request, he agreed to the decree, and Haman made haste to kill the Jews (men and women, boys and girls) all in one day. As the judgment was being sent throughout the land, Mordecai, who quickly learned of Haman's plot, knew he needed to solicit the aid of their Jewish queen in hopes that she could save them from utter destruction.

When he finally delivered the message to Queen Esther, Mordecai demanded that she speak to the king immediately on behalf of her people. Esther, in her fear, told Mordecai that she could not do such a thing, for to come before the king without being summoned would warrant death. Mordecai then told her,

"Do not think in your heart that you will escape in the king's palace any more than all the other Jews. For if you remain completely silent at this time, relief and deliverance will arise for the Jews from another place, but you and your father's house will perish. Yet who knows whether you have come to the kingdom for such a time as this?" (Esther 4:13-14)

As these words pierced Esther's heart, she was persuaded to move on behalf of her people. She told Mordecai to have all the Jews who were in close proximity to fast and pray on her behalf for three days. He listened to her plea, and did as she asked.

When the time came for Esther to speak to her king before it was too late, fear gripped her heart and soul. Nevertheless, she presented herself before him; and because she had such grace and mercy from the king, he hardly considered killing her for breaking his law. Esther told him that she needed to speak to him, but that she wanted to do so with Haman present. The king agreed, and that same day, she prepared a banquet for the king and Haman. Initially, she anticipated sharing what was on her heart; but it would seem that in her fear, she could not explain the life-threatening matter at that moment. Instead, she told them that she wanted to hold another banquet the next day; and on that day, she would present her request. (Imagine sitting in front of the very man who has plotted to kill you and your people, and sitting in front of the king who had solidified the decree to murder the Jews. Wouldn't you be afraid?)

Now Haman had no idea that the queen was a Jew. He thought that because she requested his presence at both banquets, that she was showing favor towards him. Haman returned to his home, boasting to his family of the events that had just taken place. But when he returned to the palace for the second banquet, Haman soon learned that favor was not on her mind.

At the second meeting, the king asked Esther to make her request before them. Esther, with all her trust in God, boldly said, *If I have found favor in your sight, O king, and if it pleases the king, let my life be given me at my petition, and my people at my request. For we have been sold, my people and I, to be destroyed, to be killed, and to be annihilated. Had we been sold as male and female slaves, I would have held my tongue....* (Esther 7:3-4)

When the king heard this, he was outraged. He demanded that Esther reveal who had plotted to kill his queen and her people. Esther boldly pointed towards Haman and exclaimed, "The adversary and enemy is this wicked Haman!" At that moment, the king was blown away. He immediately left the banquet room out of wrath, and while he was gone, Haman attempted to plea with the queen to save his life (the irony). When the king returned, he saw how Haman placed himself so closely to the queen, and was further outraged because he believed Haman was attacking her. Immediately, the king ordered that Haman be taken away and hanged on the gallows—the very same ones that he tried to use against Mordecai. Not only that, but the king gave orders to allow the Jews to fight back and destroy those who set out to assassinate them. The queen, against all odds and in the midst of intense fear, saved the lives of her people. Her actions came solely as a result of her refusal to remain silent, even with death looming in her way.

Of all the stories that I have read from the Scriptures, it is this one that the Lord drew me to the most, beginning at a very early age.

When I was about eleven or twelve years old, I attended a youth conference with other youth leaders from my church. While we were there, God was working and speaking through one preacher in particular. Like many preachers, he had an altar call, and encouraged any youth to come up for prayer. So, I and the group with me went forward.

I remember standing at the altar with other youth leaders, waiting patiently for him to come over and pray for me. When he finally arrived, I was not expecting him to utter the words that would soon come out of his mouth. As he prayed, God gave him several words concerning my future, which indicated what God intended to do in my life. Among other prophecies given to me, he told me that God was going to cause me to be a Queen Esther in the earth. This word was very strange to me because it was not like anything I had ever heard before. But as he repeated that phrase over and over to me, I knew that God was going to do something great in and through me.

When we returned home, we were able to share that message with my father, and I remember him being so proud of that word. Over the years, my father watched over that word to make sure that nothing I or anyone else did prevented it from being fulfilled in its entirety. And even though we rejoiced in the uniqueness of that prophecy, it was unfortunately something that I never fully understood.

For years, I asked the Lord what He meant by the "Queen Esther prophecy;" but I never received a clear answer. All I knew was that this particular word was of great importance, and I just couldn't throw it by the wayside. In order to keep it at the forefront of my mind, I wanted that name to be on something that would serve as a daily reminder of that word spoken years ago. (My license plate reflects it: QN ESTR). I wanted God to know that while I did not fully understand what He meant by it, I was willing to let Him have His way in me. As far as I was concerned, I owed Him my life; and I was willing to do whatever He asked of me, no matter the cost. In essence, it was this prophecy that solidified my desires to become an educator. As I would later learn over the years, any time a prophet speaks over another person regarding being a "Queen Esther" in the land, it signifies God's intent for change to happen in an organization where lives are at stake, and where dramatic change is necessary and crucial.

# My Dreams

*Now Joseph had a dream, and he told it to his brothers;
and they hated him even more...And his brothers said to him,
'Shall you indeed reign over us? Or shall you indeed have
dominion over us? So they hated him even more for his dreams
and for his words. (Genesis 37:5, 8 NKJV)*

*There are times when God will give us prophetic dreams
to show us where He intends for us to be. Sometimes the desires
that we have for our own lives are God-given interests that
He embedded in our hearts. We must always be mindful and
careful of these dreams, and guard them with all diligence.
They give us purpose and illuminate our destiny.*

Dreams are far different than goals. Dreams are an overall
picture of how we see ourselves in our adult life. Goals are the roads
that we take in order to bring those dreams to pass. For me, my only
dream was to become a teacher.

When I was little, I thought being a teacher was the best
profession one could have. I loved how they could take a lesson and
make it fun for students. I loved how they would give out rewards
for good behavior; but I especially loved how they were the boss in

the classroom, and were paid for it. I wanted to be a teacher because I really did enjoy education; but I especially wanted that profession so that I could be a boss.

When I was little, I used to play school at my house. I would gather all my stuff animals and Barbie dolls, and give them lessons to learn. I used the books that we had in the house as the curriculum, and I would pretend to have them working on assignments for me to grade later. Because I knew what I wanted to do at a young age, my parents, especially my dad, made sure that I always performed well in school so that I could attend a prestigious university upon high school graduation. You see, it was not enough that I had a dream to do something great. I had to make sure that everything I did up until that point would somehow cultivate that dream. Doing exceptionally well in school was not an option. It was a requirement.

Of all the years I spent in school, I never struggled in the area of academics. For the most part, I had straight A's in most of my classes. During elementary, middle, and one year of high school, I attended two private Christian institutions (Shore Acres Christian School in Bay Point, California, and Christian Center in Pittsburg, California). And I always performed exceptionally well in every class. For some reason, the work and lessons came to me easily. A teacher only had to explain a concept to me once, and I mastered it immediately. I was a stellar student, and every year that we had honor ceremonies, I always came home with countless awards that centered on academic excellence.

Because the work came to me so easily, I found myself outperforming my school mates of my same grade level. When I was in the 8th grade, I was reading at college level (according to the assessments issued to me from the administrator), and proficient in mathematics at the same level as their average 10<sup>th</sup> grader. I had this issue, which remains with me today, that certain subject matters did not have the challenge that I needed to really produce the kind of intellectual results I was capable of. Unlike a lot of smart students who mess around because the work is too simple, I chose to take my education seriously because I knew that good grades and good behavior would be my tickets to immediate and life-long success. And even though I never fully experienced a challenge in school, I knew that success was my only option. I was addicted to it. And being the best at any and everything was my driving force. I don't know when I first felt the high of success; but whenever I did, it stayed with me, even as I transitioned to my first (and only) public school.

By my tenth grade year, I had transferred to Pittsburg High School in Pittsburg, California. I guess you could say I was tired of going to the private schools so much, and I wanted something different. A part of me actually believed that with the countless number of classes this school offered, I would finally find that challenge that I lacked everywhere else. I believed that by going to this public school, I would be given a lot more opportunities to participate in different types of classes, such as advanced placement courses, which would really prepare me for university-level work. Upon my transfer, I was already ahead of most of my grade-level classmates by the number of credits I had received from my former school. You see, at Christian Center, we were not bound by the regular six-class schedule. No, I had nine courses throughout the year, and the multiple credits I received from there were transferred to the public school. I had already accomplished so much by the time I reached the High that I even considered early graduation; but I dismissed that idea because I was in no rush to move through the educational system.

While at Pittsburg High, it was a dramatic change for me. I had never seen so many people in one area at one time. I went from seeing about 350 students at the private school to seeing over 2,000 students in this public school. My dad really helped me transition to this arena because he had worked for the Pittsburg Unified School District (another corrupt school district, but I won't get into that). I don't know what it is about parents who get heavily involved with their child's education; but whatever my father did during those years, he was truly influential in making sure that I always received the best. He made sure that I had the best counselor, the best teachers, and the best and most-challenging classes. During my junior year, he told my counselor, Adrian Brown (my other guardian angel), to place me in AP English, AP History, Honors Algebra II, Chemistry, and Physics; and to make my schedule a little easier, Physical Education just to relieve the academic stress. I remember thinking, "My father has gone crazy." But it was the first time that I had a challenge as a student; and as can be expected, I did very well in those courses also.

My time spent at the High was okay to say the least. A couple of the youth from the church went there, and they made sure to keep an eye on me. I met a couple of close female friends; but for the most part, I stayed very quiet and reserved. Everyone could tell that I was not from that area because I didn't speak like they did; I didn't dress like they did; and I took my education very seriously. This was not the common or stereotypical image of a Black female student, and in a way I stood out amongst the crowd. I was well received by my teachers and administrators, but a lot of students—female students—had issues with me. To say I had haters would be an understatement. I even had one female tell me that I was stuck up and conceited because I had my own hair (no weave). I can't count the number of the ridiculous comments I received in high school from so many females, and I never knew why. To this day, I still don't know why so many females hated me (or still do hate me). But it was only a stupid distraction to try and draw my focus off of what was real. I had better plans for my life anyways, plans that would be used to help others fulfill their goals and dreams. I didn't have time to deal with the petty drama of high school life.

Although I was heavily immersed in my education, I was also greatly involved with my church and youth organization. I would go to church every day except Tuesday. Since I was one of the Pastor's daughters, I found myself involved in any and everything. On Sunday, we had two church services. I would leave home by 8:30am and return by 8:00pm. On Mondays, I had dance practice; on Wednesdays, I had youth Bible study; on Thursdays, I had choir and praise and worship practice; on Fridays, I had either a youth night or intercessory prayer; and then Saturdays were spent either cleaning the church or having a youth leadership meeting or evangelism. By the age of 16, I was a full-time student and full-time ministry worker.

Ministry continued to be a huge part of my life. I wasn't the type of Pastor's daughter that simply attended church and helped out a little. Some Pastor's children do things because they feel forced or compelled. I, on the other hand, did it because I genuinely loved the Lord, and I had a real relationship with Him. I knew that God had anointed me to preach and teach His Word to His people. In fact, I preached my first message when I was 13 years old, and I spoke on Acts 1:8—the baptism of the Holy Ghost. That night, I prophesied the Word of the Lord to adults and youth, and it was certainly not the last time I did that. I knew that He had a calling on my life, which did not focus entirely on education. And I knew that the only way that the calling could come forth was if I put His gifts and talents to practice.

As addicted as I was to success and education, I was even more addicted to the Lord and His supernatural power. I wanted all of Him. I craved His presence and His anointing, so much so that I often feared that my love for education would take me away from my devotion to God. I didn't realize it then, but a youth who gets addicted to the Lord is a dangerous weapon to the enemy, Satan. A youth who not only wants better in life, but is entirely dependent on the Lord is deadly to the enemy's plan. And he made no small objections to it. I can't count the number of things he placed in my way to try and draw me away from God's plan and destiny. In high school, he tried to ruin my reputation and my good name (the same thing that is happening today). He placed people in my way that did not belong in my life. He raised hell in my family life. He did all kinds of things. But the Lord kept me, and I know it's because of the relationship I had with Him while I was a teenager. He helped me escape a lot of the traps that youth often fall into, including teenage pregnancy, promiscuity, alcoholism, drugs, prostitution, and the like. So many people, especially those in the church, were shocked when they realized that I had not become pregnant before graduating from high school, and still maintained my virginity into my adult life. (I guess chastity is not something that the Church expects from its youth…what a shame.) It was like the more I pressed into the things of God, the more I was attacked.

While under the leadership of my father and step mother, who were and are my spiritual parents, I developed a strong relationship with the Lord. God continued to use His servants to speak His Word over me concerning my future. Not only had God called me to be a Queen Esther in the earth, but also a prophet to the nations—someone who would proclaim God's Word to the world. Now, try to imagine hearing all these prophecies as a young girl and teenager. While most teens are enjoying life and doing what youth normally do, God was telling me that He had a plan for me that even I couldn't have imagined. He was consecrating me and setting me a part for His purpose. In fact, even when I tried to be a "normal" teenager, the Lord would ruin those plans, and draw me back to Him. I couldn't escape His presence, even if I tried. But as long as the Lord allowed me to continue pursuing my educational dreams, I had no problem serving Him and doing His will.

Albeit I was doing so much in the church and ministry, I was still focused on fulfilling my goals of becoming an educator. Being at the High helped me realize that working in the public school system was more necessary than working for a private school. I remember thinking how unfair it was that some families were able to send their children to the best schools, while other families had to settle for the weak public school education. I could tell the difference in the way the teachers worked with the students, and I always felt like our society was a promoter of inequitable education. I believed that the best way to help people become truly successful was not to work in a setting that was already thriving, but to go where my help was most needed. From there, I decided to become a public school English teacher, not because I liked English--which by the way I really hated in high school, especially those boring literature books--but because I wanted to help people in reading and writing. I always believed that those were the most important skills that everyone had to learn and master. It was also the one subject that I felt was universal enough to provide young people with lessons on life, morality, and more.

Making plans to fulfill my dream was so exciting. By my senior year, I had applied to five universities in California. Because I was in the top 5% of my class, the state guaranteed me a spot at one of their Universities; and with that, I was accepted into the University of California, Davis in the Fall of 2001. There was nothing more enthralling than seeing how my hard work and diligence paid off. My success was even recognized in our city's newspaper.

I could not wait to leave high school. Although it was an interesting experience, it was not what I had expected it to be. Looking back on it now, I think the best option would have been for me to have remained in the private school setting; but I am grateful that the Lord still used that experience to work in my favor. After all, it was because I went to a public school that I developed a heart for students who were forced to attend them. I believed that if a public school, with all its failures and what not, could have a good teacher in its organization, then there was hope for those students who had no choice in being there. This passion for the youth grew only stronger as I entered my undergraduate study at UC Davis.

In September 2001, I made my way to the first of a few college campuses that I would attend. For me, college was everything that high school was not. It was new and challenging. I was surrounded

**Ledger Dispatch**

Published Tuesday, June 19, 2001

# Outstanding teen deserves a salute

## BISHOP CURTIS A. TIMMONS

THIS WEEK'S profile of an outstanding East County African-American is Felecia Shareese Killings, a 2001 graduate of Pittsburg High School.

Felecia was born in Santa Clara and has lived in Pittsburg for 14 years. She attended the Christian Center School of Pittsburg through ninth grade and then transferred to Pittsburg High School, graduating with honors with a 3.79 GPA.

Her parents are the Rev. Henry Aaron and Paulette Killings. She has one sister, Ariel Latrice. Felecia is an active member of Shiloh Christian Center of Pittsburg, where her father is pastor. Felecia participates as a Sunday school teacher, youth group leader, praise and worship leader, and with the singles ministry and women's ministry. Her hobbies are playing volleyball and watching basketball.

She will attend UC-Davis in the fall, majoring in English. She hopes to earn a doctorate in literature and writing and someday she wants to write and publish books.

This young woman has received about a dozen scholarships totaling more than $12,000 from local organizations.

Join me in saluting this outstanding young woman.

with people who had worked hard to get there. Exceptional learning was the norm; and for the first time, I felt like I fit in with others. I was not surrounded with stupid females. I did not have to worry about high school boys and their drama. I was in a world where education, intelligence, and personal growth were as valuable as one's life. It was my home, where I belonged. And the more I explored new concepts and ways of thinking, the more I was convinced that education was truly the key to one's success.

Being in college did more for me than any other experience (except when I gave my life to the Lord). It opened up windows of opportunities for me that would not have been there had I never went. I was more convinced that being an educator was the right profession for me, because I needed to show others what education could do for them also. I knew that if I came out of this system with empowering tools for success, I could then demonstrate to others how they, too, could become more powerful than the average man. I was so consumed with learning that I spent so much time making sure that I got everything I possibly could within a four-year time frame. So, upon graduation in 2005, I left the UC Davis undergraduate program with a Bachelor's Degree in English and another in African American Studies. But I didn't stop there. I returned to the school, and enrolled in their School of Education program where I received my Teaching Credential and Master's Degree in Education—both within 15 months. By the age of 23, I was not only loaded down with academic degrees, but I had also received a full-time job as an English instructor. But I'm getting ahead of myself.

# Graduate School and My First Professional Conflict

*How can I curse those God has not cursed? Or how can I [violently] denounce those the Lord has not denounced...God is not a man, that He should tell or act a lie, neither the son of man, that He should feel repentance or compunction [for what He has promised]. Has He said and shall He not do it? Or has He spoken and shall He not make it good? You see, I have received His command to bless Israel. He has blessed and I cannot reverse or qualify it. (Numbers 23:8, 19-20 AMP)*

*When God chooses you, there is no one or nothing that can take His hand from you. For example, in spite of how Joseph's brothers treated him, it did not take away from his destiny in God. Rather, what his brothers had intended to do in harming their younger brother, God turned it around for His glory; for if Joseph's brothers had never sold him into Egyptian slavery, he would have never became the second most powerful man in that region. The Word of the Lord was fulfilled in Joseph's life, and he used his power and influence to save the lives of the ones who tried to kill him. You see, no matter what people say or do to you, if God's hand is on you and He has purposed to bless you, then no one can take that away from you. Your responsibility is to remain under the shadow of God's wings, continue to obey His commands, and exercise His Word in your life. The only way that the curse of man can come upon you is when YOU disobey the Lord. Your obedience to Him is the key to your success. This is what I learned and experienced during the next phase of fulfilling my dream.*

*D*uring my undergraduate years, I had met and fell in love with someone at the school. I was a freshman and he was a sophomore, and we were crazy about each other. He was my best friend, and truly a breath of fresh air. While I had been used to guys hitting on me all throughout high school, I never had anyone interested in me who was as intelligent, goal-driven, and ambitious as I was. By my third year in college, we had discussed plans to marry, and that was probably the most exciting thing for me at that time. It would seem that my life was moving forward and progressing well, and the one thing that would truly make my happiness complete would be to marry him and live out the typical American dream. But just when I thought things were working well for me, the Lord made it clear that this was not the path that He wanted me to go because my priorities had shifted.

Because of my devotion to this man and the relationship, I had actually considered dropping my dreams of becoming a teacher to become a wife to him. I determined that wherever he went, I would be there to follow him because I was so deeply in love. After graduation, he had planned to apply to medical school back east; and not wanting us to be separated, I told him that as long as we were married, I would have no problem following him down there.

I don't know what it is that happened between the both of us, but it seemed like the more we discussed getting married, the more he and I grew a part. You would think that with two people in love, the very thing that solidifies their relationship would actually make them happy. But it didn't for us. It made the relationship more difficult, and before I knew it, we were breaking up because our plans no longer coincided with each other. By my senior year in college, our relationship had been completely broken. I found myself entirely devastated—emotionally and physically. The break up literally had taken its toll on me physically, and I had to visit the doctor's office a couple times because the stress of it all made me very sick.

I couldn't understand why this relationship, which had been functioning so well for so long, did not result in what I had hoped for. I couldn't see why the Lord wouldn't fix something that was so dear to me. Looking back on what happened, I see that it's because this relationship had taken the place of so much. For one, that man became my priority. I still loved the Lord, but He wasn't my focus. Neither was my pursuit of education at the forefront of my mind. I still maintained good grades in school, but I was willing to give up on my dreams in pursuit of him. That was my error. God would never put someone in my path to draw me away from His will. And that's what had happened. Even though I loved him dearly, I knew I had to let him go because it would have stifled something that God birthed in me years ago.

When the break up finally happened, I knew that I had to make immediate plans for my future. Since I would not be a wife anymore, I had to construct Plan B. With very little time to spare, I made haste to prepare myself for graduate school.

I must have spent countless months trying to research all the information for applying for graduate study. While I could have attended any institution, I was only interested in UC Davis' Credential and Master's program. I put all my efforts into completing all the necessary requirements for admission; and when I was accepted into the program, my heart was reignited with my first passion.

Everything about the program and experience was so exciting. The planning, the preparing; everything was so much fun. As a part of the course work, credential students were required to complete educational field labor in addition to their academics; and I completed my field study at a high school in Sacramento, California. I was able to work with a great group of students who really connected with me, mostly because they liked that I was so young and that I dressed cute. I really impressed my professors and my mentor teachers, and most of them reported that I was well advanced for a first-year educator. I always received great reports from them, and they had no doubt that I would make a great instructor. But just when things were going so well, I ran into my first professional challenge and obstacle.

While working with a group of tenth graders, I was placed under a teacher who was quite jealous of my progress as a new instructor. When we first met, I really thought that she had liked me. I liked her a lot, too; and her teaching style was quite impressive. She had this way of connecting with her students, and I admired the work she had done with them. Unfortunately, she did not consider how good of a teacher she was, and I was incredibly surprised when she told me at the beginning of our mentoring sessions that she had planned on leaving the school at the end of the year because she was burnt out; but the teacher was only in her early thirties! She mentioned that she was tired and always worried about her work, and she never felt happy or satisfied with things. I was so shocked to hear all this, especially since she agreed to be a mentor teacher in the first place. Unfortunately, she was not giving me anything to look forward to as a new educator, but I remained focused and continued to receive her advice.

By the time it came for me to take over her class, for that was a requirement in the credential program, it was a smooth transition for me. I spent a couple of days getting to know the kids, and for the most part, they were receptive. Because they really liked their regular teacher, they found it difficult to adjust to me; but I tried to reassure them that I was there for them, and that their regular teacher would still be around.

This class, however, was a little rambunctious and loquacious. Often times, when I tried to get my lesson completed, it wouldn't click with them. I found myself spending more instructional time telling Johnny and Sandy to sit down or stop talking than I did in actually giving them their education. While I was frustrated and angry by it all, I was not the type to cower under pressure or conflict; I had to think about how to overcome this obstacle rather quickly.

I asked my mentor teacher for some advice, but she only gave me small suggestions like separating some students or talking to them privately about their behavior, but nothing more. I took her advice into consideration, and tried it out for a couple sessions, but things still were not working. I realized that the problem was not with the students, but the fact that *I* wasn't really connecting with the lessons myself. (I had to teach the same lesson that the other instructor created. But it was hard to teach these children something when I didn't enjoy the activities myself.) I made mention of this to my mentor teacher, and I told her of my concern. She then suggested that I teach a new topic of my choice, but maintain the same learning skills. Surprisingly, that was the key I needed in order to release my creative abilities, and hopefully get this class to work with me. For the next session, I had a whole new topic that was challenging and engaging; and, well, it worked! The kids loved it, and I was really beginning to connect with them. I no longer had a problem with massive negative behavior because we were all enthused about the lesson. The change happened so rapidly that it seemed to have frustrated the mentor teacher. Apparently, she did not like that the children were connecting with me, and it really began to manifest in our working relationship. It was almost as if she wanted me to fail at this job; and every time some bit of trouble surfaced, she would refuse to help me. Allow me to share one such example.

Just when things were improving between me and the class, I had a scholar who really gave me a hard time. He was an African-American student—and I can talk about Black people because I'm Black. So for all those people who think I'm racist against my own kind, oh well. I keep it real—and I was really becoming bothered by his constant, disruptive behavior. I would often pull him to the side and share with him that it was important that he took his education seriously; and that playing around with it was truly detrimental to him, especially because he was a young Black male. Well, he didn't appreciate my correction too much, and he often ran to my mentor teacher (who was White) to express his complaints. When she pulled me to the side to talk to me about it, I was a little bothered that she pacified his actions rather than correcting them herself. When she informed me of his statements, I told her that he was really a disturbance to the class, and he was hard to get under control.

Rather than siding with me to try and work with this scholar, she left me out there to handle it myself. (Well, the way I see it, if you're not going to give me suggestions for dealing with a person, don't be mad at how I choose to reprimand him. And don't side with that negative behavior because you do a disservice to the kids in the long run. That's to all you administrators who refuse to help your teachers with disciplinary actions. Do better.) She never really gave me instructions on how to work with him, so I continued to do what I thought was best with the situation.

Consequently, the friction between the student and I escalated; and as much as I asked for assistance, my mentor would not give it to me. It was clear to me that she was more concerned with cradling that student's poor behavior instead of correcting it, even though it was negatively affecting his education and that of others. (Unfortunately, that's not how I handle things, especially with Black students. Whether it's politically correct of not, I have no tolerance for stupid, unruly, and disrespectful behavior from students, especially minority ones. These scholars, in particular, need to understand that our education is something that people died for. We were not always afforded the rights of an equal education, and we have a reason to value it more so than others. For many people, education is their ticket out of drugs, violence, prostitution, and poverty. If students choose not to care about their learning, I can't force them to do it. However, if that's the case, sit down and stop disrupting things; and don't disturb the learning of others or my instructional time. I don't have time to waste on that.) When I saw that she would provide no help to me, I stopped going to her for mentorship, and proceeded to teach and discipline the class as if I would be with them forever.

Even though I only had a few months to educate them, I did not take that time lightly or for granted. If I wanted my kids to be the best, then I had to be the best at my job. And this was not only intimidating to the teacher, but also frustrating to her because *the children responded so positively* to this change.

(I suppose my seriousness to learning may seem a bit harsh and sharp, but I don't care. People are constantly destroyed because of their lack of knowledge; and if you are a teacher who could care less about my children's learning, then step aside, and let another do the job. In fact, I believe that it's because of a teacher's cheap and slothful attitude towards education that many students, in fact the majority of students, do not appreciate learning. When students see that we care about their learning, then they will begin to value their education more. I carried this philosophy with me throughout my career, and it worked! In spite of what the critical online commentators have said about me, students who worked under me began to love and appreciate their learning. They began to see themselves beyond the scope of graduation, and began to dream of a future when others said they would never make it. My blatant seriousness towards education was so infectious that students had no choice but to value at least their ability to read and write and voice their opinions concerning important matters. My approach to student behavior and learning was unconventional and unorthodox, but it produced results [unlike what we see now in most public school classrooms]. If you are a young teacher who wants to make a change with your scholars, be ready to love hard enough to cause your babies to love learning. Trust me when I say that your students will love you more for your sincere attitude towards education rather than your slothful, mediocre one.

Having genuine concern for the students, even the roughest ones, are what will cause them to appreciate you more. Even the Black student who gave me a hard time in my first tenth grade class came to understand that I only wanted the best for him, and he later apologized for his behavior.)

As the days progressed, I noticed that the teacher's attitude towards me began to change. All of a sudden, she wasn't so open or friendly towards me. Before I knew it, she was sabotaging my work with the students, and spreading lies about me to the administrators. Not only that, but she had told my credential supervisors that I was not a good teacher, and that she wouldn't recommend that I move forward in the teaching profession. When I read her report, I was so shocked by it. I had two other mentor teachers who were blown away with my performances, and here was this teacher about to crush what I spent years working on. When my supervisor showed the report to me, I immediately knew I had to do whatever I could to combat it, so I called dad. (Don't laugh…I always call my father when people are mean to me—daddy's girl, I guess.) I told him what was happening, and he instructed me to stay in prayer about it. I did just that, and I asked God to help me because I knew this woman was telling a multitude of lies that could ultimately destroy my dreams.

After seeing that report, I mentioned to my supervisor that I wanted to have a meeting with the teacher, but that I also wanted her (my supervisor) to be there so that we could have a mediator. When my supervisor scheduled the conference, that teacher went into a frantic panic. She was so nervous about the entire thing, and I was thinking, *Why, if she was the one that had some much to say?* My mentor went so far as to disturb another class that I was instructing to see if I could inform her about the content of this scheduled meeting. I told her that it was to discuss the report she gave my supervisor, and that seemed to only upset her further.

On the day of the meeting, dad had prayed with me and told me to stay encouraged; he reminded me that it was important that I told the truth so that things could be cleared up; but to also trust that God would work this out. (Being truthful and honest are so very important. It's what has always been helpful to me when I was in my most dire situations. It's what helped me especially during my criminal case).

When I entered the library where the meeting was held, I was surprised to see that not only was my supervisor present, but that teacher's supervisor as well. The teacher mentioned that because she didn't really like confrontations, she asked her supervisor to be present with her for *moral* support. (What that teacher didn't know was that her supervisor was really impressed with my work, and had already sought to hire me for the next school year. She had no intention on supporting that mentor's negative remarks.)

When we began the meeting, my supervisor stated that the meeting was simply to get some things clarified about the evaluation she made of me, and that we were not in any way trying to be confrontational or intimidating. I added that all I wanted to do was to perfect my teaching craft; and if there was something I did wrong, then I wanted to hear it so that I can do better. But the remainder of the meeting turned out to be something I had never anticipated.

My supervisor and I had expected to hear her reiterate what she reported on my evaluation. Instead, she didn't have anything conclusive or accurate to say because there was nothing negative to report. Every time she said something to try and "attack" me, both supervisors spoke on my behalf. When the teacher did speak up, she finally admitted that it was my confidence in teaching that actually intimidated her; and I remember thinking how stupid that was considering the fact that she was also a good educator. She mentioned that she had never worked with anyone who was this young and confident, and it made her uncomfortable. I tried to ease her "nerves" by letting her know that this was not my first teaching experience. In fact, I had been a Sunday school instructor since I was twelve, and this thing just came to me naturally. In spite of what little I shared, she still did not want to work with me. All we could do at that point was move on, and place me with a teacher that wasn't intimidated by the little Black instructor from Fairfield.

I would say that for 90% of the time, I did not have to say anything to defend myself because both supervisors did it all. What's more is that her supervisor indicated that not only was she impressed with me, but she commented that perhaps the mentor teacher's frustrations with work had caused her to see me in that negative light. Needless to say, it was like God had taken this devastating situation, and completely turned it around in my favor. When the enemy tried to prevent me from continuing in the Credential Program, God came through and completely cleared all the negative lies and accusations. (God will always work with those who are willing to be truthful and honest. He will magnify Himself in your most heinous situations. No matter what the liars say, God will cause even your enemies to be at peace with you; and He will show your enemies that He is with you and for you! That's His favor.)

I left that conference feeling really good. That meeting revealed to everyone that she had some kind of animosity towards me because of her jealousy—so lame. Although I had won that small battle, I lost something in the end. Because she was so angered by the meeting, she told her supervisor that she did not want to mentor me anymore. As a result, I was forced to leave the students that I had spent so much time working with. I had built such a rapport with them that it was extremely hard to let go and say goodbye. I remember crying (yes, I'm a crybaby) because it seemed so unfair. I wasn't even sure if the students had felt the same way that I did towards them; but they later showed me that they had. They were very upset about me not working with them anymore, and they asked the mentor teacher if they could give me a goodbye party. She agreed, and those students, my first set of scholars, gave me a farewell celebration. I still have the pictures from that day.

I guess I never really understood how jealous people could be when it came to teaching. It was clear to me that the mentor teacher wanted to curse and destroy what God had already blessed. I always had this naïve understanding that all educators wanted the best for children, and no matter who the teacher was, if he or she could reach this generation, we all should be satisfied. But my father always told me that there were wicked people in the system that cared more about themselves than the kids. And while I heard what he said, nothing hit me harder than when I had seen it happen to me directly. I honestly believed that this would be my first and last struggle in the public school system, but this small battle could not compare to the issues I would soon face as I transitioned to Rodriguez High School in Fairfield, California that following year.

# My Dream Comes True
# 2006-2007 School Year, First Year at RHS

*Roll your works upon the Lord [commit and trust them wholly to Him; He will cause your thoughts to become agreeable to His will, and] so shall your plans be established and succeed. The Lord has made everything [to accommodate itself and contribute] to its own end and His own purpose—even the wicked [are fitted for their role] for the day of calamity and evil. (Proverbs 16:3-4)*

*As stated before, when God gives us a prophetic word, He intends for that word to not only be fulfilled in our lives, but the blessings to also come along with it. No matter who tries to destroy you or that word, God's protection is upon you; and He will order and direct your steps as long as your mind is stayed on Him. As the Bible states, God will even cause your thoughts to line up with His perfect will. You will find yourself walking in oneness with the Spirit of God. Your faith in Him is NECESSARY for your survival and success. It is what keeps you in right standing with the Lord. When we are in that position, then nothing by any means shall harm us and the hand of the Lord will remain on us for good.*

ometimes I think it would have been better if I stayed at that Sacramento high school. But the Lord always has a way of placing His people right where He wants them to be. I think if I had it my way, I would have gladly called that supervisor back, told her I accept their vacant position, and looked forward to working with them for the new school year. After all, I had already won her heart and the heart of those children. I knew I would always have it easy that way; but I guess the desire to want more and to work in a District that was closer to home was my longing.

My time with that mentor teacher was a learning experience for me. I learned that it was all right to be me and to do what I believed in my heart was right, even if others would not agree with me. More importantly, I learned that if I remained right before God, and kept a pure heart for my children, then no matter what, God would always be my shield.

Before graduating from the program, the staff at UC Davis held their annual job fair for their scholars. While I should have been excited about the prospects of landing a great teaching position, that day was a wreck for me. I was so nervous the entire time. I was scheduled to meet with at least five or six employers, and it seemed like my head was all over the place. For two interviews, I remember thinking that they went well, but I didn't really sense that I had nailed a teaching position with them. On others, I felt like I could have gotten the job with my eyes closed; and for some reason, it turned my off. And then the moment came for me to meet with the representative from Rodriguez High School, Amy Gillespie-Oss.

I don't remember what time I was supposed to convene with her, but I remember being late to the interview. It was embarrassing, especially because I am a stickler for time; but for some reason, that was the only interview that I was late for. Although I could have said, "Forget it," and moved on with the other employers, I stuck with it, and managed to schedule another interview with her.

To try and "butter things up," I purchased an "I'm Sorry" card for being late to the first interview. Whether or not it would help, I couldn't tell. But I wanted her to at least know that this mistake was in no way any indication of my professionalism.

I can't recall the questions she asked me, but I do remember thinking that this woman was really intimidating. It was something about her eyes that made me feel this way; and in all honesty, I was sure that this interview was a failure. In fact, I did not anticipate any calls coming from her or her supervisors for a second interview. Because I didn't think it went well, I dismissed even the thought of working at RHS, and shifted my focus on other school sites.

After we talked, I thanked Gillespie-Oss for taking the time to meet with me. She told me that if I wanted to, I could come by the school to see how it was; and I eventually made that trip. I was so impressed with the school because it was clean, and I have serious OCD issues—Obsessive CLEANLINESS Disorder. It seemed like the ideal place to be, except for the fact that I had seen no Black staff there, even though there were a lot of African-American students. The tour was good, and I was able to meet some teachers; but I still was not sure if this was the place for me.

You could imagine my surprise when days later, I was called in for a second interview. Because I had this school at the bottom of my list, I almost declined the offer. I was really interested in working at Vanden High School, which was only a few minutes from my house. But I attended that second interview, impressed both the assistant principal and the principal, and was offered a teaching position. When the door to Vanden had closed on me, I realized that I had no other choice but to attend RHS if I planned on staying in Fairfield; and so I accepted.

On the first day of school in 2006, I was very surprised to see that we had received a new principal. I had heard that they had issues with keeping a principal, but I didn't think it was that bad. Who would have thought that only a couple months after being hired by one principal that I would have to go through a meeting process with a new one? But it actually turned out to be a great change for me professionally.

This principal was a God-send, literally another angel that He sent to protect me from what I was about to face. Even others recognized that I had so much favor with her; and many were shocked to see that favor coming from a new principal to a new teacher. I can't count the many times she saved me from being hurt or damaged by parents or other teachers. It always seems that when I am about to face something that is too strong or difficult for me to handle alone, God brings someone who is a physical shield against every evil work. (To Toni Taylor, I thank you for what you taught me, and for the love and support you showed me that first year. You literally prevented me from abandoning my teaching profession at that time; and for that, I thank you.)

When I began that school year, I was the youngest teacher there. At the age of 22, I had not only succeeded in obtaining Bachelor's Degrees from a university, but I had a landed a great teaching position. At RHS, I expected to continue my success, for that was the nature of my character. And from the moment I stepped on campus, I became an instant hit.

As one of three Black educators at that school of over 100 staff members, I noticed that many of the African-American students flocked to me. (Now, I'm assuming that it was because of my ethnicity and the small number of us educators that were present that this is why so many congregated in my classroom every day...but this is just my assumption.) Seeing this, I really wanted to take advantage of an opportunity to teach Black history and Black culture to students who I knew had not been given this during their educational career. I knew I hadn't received it when I was in school, and so it was in my heart to share it with the rest of my classes (in addition to other multicultural education—I love that kind of instruction). For the first two weeks, I used some of the slave narratives in my lessons, and I also added some of the poems written by Tupac to supplement the material.

Overall, I received a lot of mixed reactions from the students regarding my lessons. On one hand, the Black students really took a hold of the teaching, and began commenting on the issues of racism in the past and the present. (This was the first time I had ever heard students talking about prejudice and racism in the school setting.) But on the other hand, I had a couple of White students who were becoming agitated with the discussion of racism, mostly because they were racist themselves. (I don't want the reader to assume that all the White students were like this. In fact, I would say that 95% of the Caucasian students that I had were supportive of multicultural education, and they appreciated the different lessons.) This was extremely new for me, but I was never the type to stop these learning moments or to stifle students' voices, even if it bothered some.

I knew that racism still existed in our society, for I had a glimpse of that while attending UC Davis; but I did not think that students in high schools also believed that it was present. It wasn't until I listened to their frustrations that I realized how profoundly they were affected by it. To some degree, I thought their talk was merely a bunch of complaints that had no substantial evidence; but I did not let that cause me to stop what they wanted to share. In a lot of our discussions, they talked about how they felt like their teachers mistreated them; how the administration at that school targeted them over White students; how they were always being suspended for stupid reasons when others had done more heinous acts and received little punishments for them. They honestly believed that they were marked because of their race; but they also felt that nothing could be done about it. As far as they were concerned, it was something that they just had to deal with. I didn't know it then, but the discussions I permitted in my class at that time were only "symptoms" of what would be discussed and addressed a year from then.

Evidently, my class sessions became too much for one scholar in particular. This student, a White student, told his mother about what I had been teaching. That mother contacted me and left me the meanest voicemail. In so many ways, she made it clear that she did not appreciate the fact that I was teaching Black history, and that I "had more than just Black students" in the class. She was basically accusing me, only after two weeks of teaching, of being a biased teacher. (If she and her boy had been patient, they would have seen that we would learn and read the literature of all races. The problem, it seemed, was that fact that as a Black teacher, I was providing lessons on Black history; and because a lot of students spoke out about racism, then it offended him. This is what I had to deal with *in 2006*.

I'm sorry. I thought we had moved on since 1954.) I didn't bother returning her phone call because it sent shock waves through my body. I never anticipated such a response from a parent, and I never imagined someone getting that upset because I taught Black history. Plus, as a new teacher, I didn't need any negative report getting to the new principal regarding my teaching. I was trying to establish a lucrative teaching career, and I needed only positive comments to be on my record for the first two years so that I could eventually receive permanent status. (I discuss this in more details later.) The whole situation set me back so much that I wanted to leave that school. I never wanted anyone to think that I was trying to hurt my kids by teaching cultural history; and if this was the nature of the students and parents at this school, then I needed to leave.

When I finally told my principal what happened, she immediately came to my rescue. Whatever she said to the parent and student, it made the world of difference for me. She had the student placed in another English class, and assured me that this was not the nature of the school. She encouraged me to keep doing what I was doing, and that she fully supported me. It was her protection that solidified my position in the school for that particular year.

Not letting that situation get to me too long, I continued my efforts in educating my children, and performing good work as a new educator. That same year, a special education teacher and I were chosen to pilot a co-teaching plan for the District. The program consisted of combining special education students with general education students in the hopes of bridging that achievement gap between both groups. And we were phenomenal! Our collaboration produced outstanding results, which were later recognized at a particular School Board Meeting that same year. All of our scholars, both special education and general education, had passed the English class with a B- average or better. All of our students, except one (who refused to come to class), had passed the California High School Exit Exam on their first try. Because of our efforts, the co-teaching program expanded not only at our school, but also at the other high schools in the District. Such accomplishments were rare in the District (as I would later find out). And to know that I, as a first-year teacher, had been a factor in creating a solid program for students of all learning backgrounds was my most gratifying moment of that year.

In addition to that success, my principal had asked me to attend a professional development conference in Arizona, all expenses paid. One teacher, who became a dear friend to me later, told me that no first-year teacher had ever been asked to attend these conferences before. And that if a principal wanted me to go, then that meant they were interested in keeping me permanently. After hearing that and seeing the success I was experiencing, I was on a professional high. I had truly won immense favor with God and with man. I was loved by my kids; loved by their parents; appreciated by my principal; and so many things were happening for me that I just could not contain it. It's true that a lot of the teachers that year did not like me or were jealous; but my success overshadowed their negativity, and I knew that nothing would stop me.

There were other moments that I recall when my principal conveyed how impressed she was with my performance. One day during the beginning of that school year, she brought the superintendent to my class, and personally introduced him to me.

She praised me and told him that I "[was] the total package" in what they needed in an educator. Just hearing her say that made me truly grateful that God had given me this job at this location. Imagine having all of this success come your way, and you're only 22 years old. It was incredible, and I knew that God's hand was on me for good. I received great reports from her; she gave me a good evaluation; and my success was seen by everyone. All of this was overwhelming and astounding, and I was so grateful to the Lord for His supernatural favor.

Even though things were going significantly well for me, on the outside of my class, there were a lot of teachers who were bothered by me. Many of them made multiple complaints to administration because they didn't like how close I had been with the students, and how well the students responded to me. They hated that whenever they spoke evil about my children, I always had a different report about the kids. I was flooded with students that other teachers did not like, did not trust, and refused to work with. These same students, while they were not perfect, did put forth an effort in my class, and received grades that exemplified that effort. One student in particular stated that because I didn't judge him based on what other teachers said about him, he found himself wanting to do the work in my class. This was the testimony that I received from a lot of students, especially the minority kids. But while I was succeeding with the scholars at the school, I was receiving fierce attacks from teachers. You would think they would be happy to know that students are at least trying now that a new teacher has come around. But the opposite happened, and it was quite hard for me to "mingle" with these educators. By the end of the year, I was not sure if I would return because the tension was so thick at times. I felt like I was reliving the memories of my experience with my mentor teacher just less than a year before. But even though I wanted to leave, my students kept me there. After all, it was about them and not me, so I decided to stay. And even though I had a deep love for them and their success, a part of me wishes I had left that school after that first year.

# I Really Hate RHS
## 2007-2008 School Year, Second Year at RHS

*"It is time for the Lord to act. They have frustrated Your law" (Psalms 119:126 AMP).*

*When we are confronted with a particular problem, we have the God-given right to provide a resolution to the situation. When that problem affects a segment of society, we must call upon the Lord to act on our behalf. If there is one law that God will not allow us to "frustrate," it is His commandment to love others. Racism and hatred are direct violations of God's law of love, and when these demonic forces come to the surface and manifest their destructive work, it is time for the Lord to act.*

*Y*ear two was a huge turning point for me in my teaching career. We had another new principal, but it was the same person who interviewed me at Davis, Amy Gillespie-Oss. To be honest, I was a lot more nervous at the start of this year than I was last year. If there was one principal that I needed to have my back during this time, it was that one from the previous year. I wasn't sure how things would pan out for me, but I knew that in spite of what I felt, God obviously had me there for a reason. I was a bit hesitant about that school year because I wasn't sure if this principal would give me the same protection that my first administrator gave. But I had to trust God.

For the most part, everything ran rather smoothly for me. I had no trouble with students. I continued teaching cultural history. Unlike the previous year, I had a better relationship with the teachers. Everything was going well for me individually. But like the first year, there was always something going on at that school that disturbed my spirit, and often made me want to leave that site.

I know it might seem like an overstatement, but every time I walked around the campus, I could always hear students (no matter their race) saying some of the most racist, insensitive, and intolerant comments I had ever heard. They seemed to say and do things with little concern as to how it would affect others; and they did it with no threat of a consequence. In addition to that, I continued to witness how so many minority students were getting in more serious trouble (multiple suspensions and expulsions) than their White counterparts. Although all groups had been guilty of breaking some school law, the minority groups seemed to receive the harshest punishments for the most minor school offense; while White students seemingly got away with a slap on the wrist for committing similar acts. That school had one assistant principal who always appeared to target the Black students, and I remember how much it bothered me. But I couldn't really say anything because they were my bosses, right? I wouldn't even know how to bring up the situation to them, so I continued to do my teaching, and tried to avoid the topic altogether.

(This is an issue that many people have. We see a problem going on in our society, and rather than having the courage to say something about it, we let it go on in hopes that one day it will disappear. I wonder what life would have been like if Dr. King, Malcolm X, Harriet Tubman, and others simply ignored the problems of their day. At some point, we have to put aside our fears, and step out in faith. If we want change in our nation, our schools, our churches, and our homes, then we must be ready to act. No one will do a better job of making a difference than you. Be that change agent.)

Whenever minority students complained to me about the discrimination in punishments, I told them that while I understood their anguish, they had to do everything in their power to not draw that negative attention. If they knew they were being targeted, then they needed to simply comply with the school's rules and regulations even more. I knew that my advice wasn't alleviating their frustrations too much, but I didn't know how else to help them avoid this trouble other than to work with them individually.

Even when I saw how my students, who were the "trouble makers" of the school, attempted to do better academically and behaviorally, I noticed that some teachers and administrators continued to harass them in spite of their accomplishments. I started to bring this discussion to my classes (as was my custom), and I asked them all (of all races) if they noticed a discrepancy in how administration dealt with the students. To my surprise, they all reported that there was a clear distinction in the way that minority and White students were treated. White students in my class noticed this, and explained that they knew they could get away with things *because* they were White; but they also indicated that if a Black student did something, they

(Blacks) would get in more trouble for committing the same offense. Initially, I assumed that this was only seen by minority students; but when my White scholars spoke on it, I knew that things were more serious than I could have ever imagined.

Now, everyone who now knows me understands that I am not the type of person who can simply watch an injustice go by and say nothing about it forever. ("Keep justice, do and use righteousness" [Isaiah 56:1.]) Unlike many people, I internalize the hurts of those closest to me, and my students were my children, no matter their race. Even though I was close to them in age, I still saw them as my babies; and if you hurt my children, I'm coming after you.

I could see how much this discrepancy in discipline affected my kids. I knew that if they were in the office all the time, then they missed out on their education. I knew that if they were always suspended, then they would miss days of pertinent instruction, which was not a guarantee that they could make up. Minority students, especially males, are already dealing with a disadvantage in the *public* educational system, and the last thing they needed was extra harassment or mistreatment from their educators. (Conduct research on the *Educational Crisis among Minority Males*. The statistics will alarm you. The same trend that is found in this particular research was also noticed in the Fairfield-Suisun Unified School District. It wasn't until this issue was brought to light by me and my heroes that the District was forced to address it. But I'm getting ahead of myself again.)

Now, I will not say for once that my kids were perfect. I had drug dealers in my class; I had drug users in my class; I had prostitutes and pimps in my class. I had students who were violent and outlandish with people. I had all kinds of kids. But there was something working between us; and I knew that if I could see the good in them, then if others gave them the chance, then they could see it also. I saw them as human beings, and not trouble makers. They were my babies; and if other teachers and administrators had given them the love, time, and patience that I did, then they would experience the same results. That's the kind of teacher I was and still am. No matter what wrong they did, I would always be there to help them achieve success and bring them out of this bondage that we call ignorance and self-destruction. I believed in them so much, and many students had never experienced that kind of devotion from a teacher. I knew everyone thought that my children connected with me because I was attractive and young, but that mess wears away. Looks and youth are vain, and after a while, one's personality will have to make the difference. My kids felt my heart and had my spirit, and they knew I was there for them. That's why they connected to me. That's why we worked well together. On top of that, I had the presence of God with me, and the anointing attracts people. (Look at the kind of people that flocked to Jesus. I learned from His experience.)

Seeing the students suffer because of racism, discrimination, and prejudice was killing me. I hated knowing that certain kids would receive harsher punishments simply because they were made a target. This is not to say that what my kids engaged themselves in should have been ignored; but to only ascribe harsher punishments, such as suspensions and expulsions, on a particular group and not others reveals a blatant act of discrimination that leads to other fallacies. In the case of Rodriguez High School and the Fairfield-Suisun School District, racism and discrimination were huge problems before and during 2008. And in case people do not know, racism is a demonic spirit that influences anyone who allows it in their hearts. It is not restricted to Whites against Blacks or Blacks against Whites. Racism and prejudice emerge among all cultures, and those who exercise such hatred will suffer the consequences of it. Racism is full of bigotry, revenge, ungodliness, and perversion. It leads to molestation, rape, incest, murder, oppression, discrimination, and slavery. It is a sin against God to exercise such things, and the only answer to this is repentance and forgiveness. This will change the ways in which society operates. However, when people refuse to change their racist attitudes towards others, then we have an obligation to get active. This is something that I had to adopt and exercise myself. It was not enough that I address this problem with my kids, but I had to let this thing be addressed to those who carried the most influence at the school: the adult educators. If people continued to remain silent about the situations that hindered the kids' progress, then it would continue for decades. At some point, enough has to be enough. And I had to do more than simply addressing this issue with my scholars.

I knew that by becoming active in voicing concerns over inequitable treatment at the school, especially with regards to race, I was jeopardizing what I had worked so hard for—a lucrative teaching career. But I also knew that unless someone did something about this racism and prejudice in the system, then it would persist for years, and my children would continue to suffer for future generations.

To be more specific, in April 2008, our school witnessed a hate crime that went poorly handled by the principal. The purpose of sharing this story is to highlight the ineffectiveness of adults who try to pacify ungodly behavior among our youth. I want the reader to be aware that it is not the act of the crime that had me mostly upset; but the role that the school administrators had in *ignoring* the severity of the crime that made the situation unjust. As I sat back and watched the situation go under the radar, I felt compelled to do something. (We must always remember that children and youth will sometimes do things out of ignorance and stupidity; but it our responsibility as educators and leaders to correct that behavior in a way that will not only deter such crimes from happening again, but also educate our youth to love as Christ loves. That's our job!). This event, as you will soon learn, became so large that it received massive media coverage; and while neither I nor my kids were recognized for our efforts in addressing this matter, it was because of our voices that a wave of social change occurred in the District.

It is important to note that as time went on, the story of the crime committed on school grounds has changed; but what I share has remained constant. Because I was so immersed in the situation, I purposely recorded the events as they happened day by day. The story told is based on eye-witness accounts and my own personal testimony of the event. Whether or not people believe the story is on them; but it is accurate, and I have provided evidence to support what I share. It is the story of what my students (the ones mentioned in the "Dedication") and I did in order to see radical change in our school. Little did we know that we would profoundly impact the entire District. I pray that as others read this story, they will feel a sense of urgency to act on behalf of those who are disenfranchised and mistreated. When God gives us a platform to make a change, we must honor Him and fulfill that purpose, regardless of the cost. This was that "Queen Esther" moment that had been given to me when I was just a young a girl. I knew that I could have easily said nothing, and carried on with life as usual; but my children were suffering and hurting educationally. And that burden was too much for me. If I perished by my actions, then that was a risk I had to take.

# April 2008: Oh, My God. Look What I've Done!

*"Our lives begin to end the day we become silent about things that matter."*
*-- Dr. Martin Luther King, Jr.*

*Separation of church and state is a lie from hell. You cannot separate the two unless you literally remove the Church (God's people) from the state. Don't be fooled into thinking that by exercising your right as a Christian in an ungodly institution such as the modern American public school that you are violating the principles of "separation of church and state."*

*As the Church, the Body of Christ, we must not be complacent in our ways, patterns, or behaviors. We have an obligation to exact God's power in every aspect of our society. We have to do this, otherwise God will require the blood to be on our hands (Ezekiel 3:18). In other words, if we neglect to warn, admonish, and compel the world to change their evil thoughts and ways, they will die in their sins, and it will be our fault. If we see the oppressed and the disenfranchised, we must come to their aid. When the Church cries aloud in the earth, then we will see the revival that God intends to bring to the world.*

*I refuse to believe that we have reached the point in society when it is too late to alter discriminatory laws and practices in institutions such as the schools. This discrimination is not limited to one's race, but even in the area of religious freedom; for what many people fail to realize is that Christianity is among the most persecuted religious sect in a supposedly "free" nation. As long as we have breath in our bodies, we have grace and mercy to carry out the Great Commission. The greatest revival is coming and is already here, and it will change the course and direction of the American system, especially in the schools. We must become active in altering the policies that destroy our children and godly educators, no matter the cost. We must "Cry aloud, and spare not" (Isaiah 58:1).*

*I* don't remember what I was teaching the day of April 7, 2008, but I will never forget that day in my life. During lunch time, there were about six African-American girls who approached me to discuss something that had happened on campus. These girls had been a part of my Black Student Union club, and they were curious to know if I had been made aware of the many things going on at the school. When they approached me, I was a little confused because they looked so distraught. One of the young ladies finally spoke up, and the story she shared literally set me off.

She asked me if I was familiar with the significance of April 4th. I told her I wasn't, so she explained that it was the anniversary of Dr. King's assassination. (I knew when she began the story that it obviously had something to do with racism and prejudice again.) She proceeded to share that there were White students in the parking lot on that morning, driving recklessly and yelling out "White power" for others to hear. In addition to that, they waved their Confederate flag around as they were in the car. When she said all this, I asked her what administration had done about it. That's when she told me that the boys had only received a Saturday school detention for the entire episode—and that punishment was simply for their dangerous driving. (I wonder what the punishment would have been had those boys been Black. Things that make you go, hmm.)

At this point, I had enough of all this mess. Too much had been going on over the last year and a half; and I was fed up with the stupidity of the administrative leaders, especially when it affected so many of my scholars. How could the office only issue out a *detention* for dangerous driving on school property, shouts of racial words around a multiethnic student body, and a display of an historically pro-slavery flag? Yet, other students were suspended for *days* for saying a cuss word around a teacher. My anger was so aroused at this point that I could not keep still. I was so frustrated with how administration allowed some students to get away with doing these racist things, but would never do anything to protect or help the other students who had to witness this behavior. I mentioned to the young ladies that this time, I was going to do something about it. No more silence. No more thinking that it might go away eventually. If no one was going to speak on it, then I would. And before I knew it, I made my way to the computer, pulled up the school's email service, and began composing a message that demanded that we (the educators) do better in educating our students in the area of racial tolerance, and changing the policies regarding discipline for blatantly racist acts, no matter what race committed them.

From:          Felecia Killings
To:            RhsGW
Date:          4/7/08 12:52PM
Subject:       Racial Tension

Dear RHS,

Some of my African American students approached me today and informed me of an incident that occurred last Friday in the student parking lot. This incident happened before school began, and it is especially disturbing to me and this group. Last Friday was the anniversary of the assassination of Dr. King. While in the student lot, a young man took his confederate flag out of his car, placed it on the antena, and proceeded to drive recklessly around with it. While doing so, he shouted out "white power" with a number of my students listening. Many of my students are shaken by this event, especially since they felt like he did not receive the proper repercussions (and to our understanding, it was a Saturday school). It seems like this issue is not being addressed properly, and not doing so makes it appear like there is little concern for my kids. To many, this is threat because of what the flag represents. The parents of these students are highly upset with what took place, and as a teacher, I am thoroughly offended because I have witnessed some of the same incidents (and sayings) among students, and they go unchecked.

* * *

I don't know what I expected to come out of the email. To be honest, I was a bit surprised that my impetuous behavior had resulted in my speaking out to the whole staff. I won't lie. I was scared by the potential backlash; but as soon as I sent it, I was flooded with responses, which were also sent to the entire staff. Most of the teachers who replied were outraged by what took place; more importantly, they were disappointed by the lack of appropriate punishment for such actions.

From:
To:
Date: Monday - April 7, 2008
Subject: Re: Racial Tension

This is horrible incidence of racism — but it is also a teachable moment. Perhaps the student in question should do a research project on the confederate flag and maybe even educate everyone during the weekly video about why the confederate flag is considered disrespectful to the African American community. I agree that some apology is in order.

*  *  *

From:
To: Felecia Killings
Date: Monday - April 7, 2008
Subject: Re: Racial Tension

Thank you for bringing this to everyone's attention. There is a group of obnoxious skin-head types on campus--and they tend to be sneaky and not get the proper punishment. I was not aware of this incident, but we cannot tolerate it. I have a feeling the flag kid is someone you had dealings with last year.

*  *  *

From:
To: Felecia Killings
Date: Monday - April 7, 2008
Subject: Re: Racial Tension

That is very disturbing! I had not heard about the incident but I am glad you called it to our attention. Hopefully we can all work together to make this campus a safe and harmonious environment for teachers and students alike. The racial tension definitely needs to be addressed.

*  *  *

From:
To:
Date:        Tuesday, April 8, 2008
Subject:     Re: Racial Tension

I think this is a major issue that we should take very seriously. One way
to address it is by advocating change in our district policy. I think all hate
related offenses should be considered at a higher level and we should adopt
a "no tolerance" policy. There have been several incidents recently inovling
racist thinking/action from all ethnic groups on campus. I think we should
send a clear message that any and all racist or hate related behavior will not
be tolered at RHS.

* * *

From:
To:          Felecia Killings
Date:        Tuesday, April 8, 2008
Subject:     Re: Racial Tension

oh...just as fyi...a student told me that one of these staff members chastened
a student for talking to you about this. The info given to me is that a student
was told that she had no right to discuss this incident with either staff or
students. It goes without saying that I wasn't there and cannot verify the
accuracy of this, except that the emails I read were written in a similar spirit.

I told my student to encourage her friend to talk to _____ and tell her
about the incident. Our students have the right to talk to any staff member at
any time about their feelings and concerns. They absolutely should not be
told otherwise.

* * *

From:
To:
Date:        Tuesday, April 8, 2008
Subject:     Re: Parking Lot Incident

Felecia,

I just want you to know that I understand your reaction and that of your students to the parking lot incident. I didn't know it had happened until I read your e-mail.

I would think that what that student or those students did was considered something akin to a hate crime and would carry with it serious consequences. It's like flaunting gang names and insignias.

It merits serious discussion by our staff because of the potential for this kind of thing to spread and cause schoolwide unrest.

I hope to speak with you more about it at a later time, and hopefully it will be addressed in a larger forum by our administration and faculty as well.

The students offended by this need to know that we all stand behind them and find it reprehensible and degrading.

* * *

From:
To:
Date:        Tuesday, April 8, 2008
Subject:     Re: Racial Tension

Well said. I think the first step is to come together and agree that it's not okay. Sounds simple enough, but sometimes I think we let things go because it's easier than addressing a difficult and often intimidating issue. As I tell my students all the time, you will never solve a problem by pretending it isn't there.

When our students feel the strontg culture in our school (as communicated by our staff and administration) that we do not condone or tolerate hate in any form, then they start to understand that, at least here in this place, it is not okay. Which, hopefully, will begin the process for them to understand that it's never okay anywhere. But, it has to start somewhere, why not here? We can't

control the values they are taught at home, but we can c ontrol the ones they
are taught at RHS.

\* \* \*

I would like to point out here that every one of these emails
came from the White teachers at the school. They testified that they
had seen similar acts, but nothing was ever done about it. You see,
racism or prejudice does not hurt just one group. It hurts us all. This
was not a Black issue, but rather a systematic problem that needed
serious attention. The administrator who brushed over the crime,
Amy Gillespie-Oss, is not to be blamed entirely, either. She only did
what those before her did. She only behaved as the officials at the
top behaved. So, is it any wonder that when I finally said something
about this issue, that one of the main suggestions from my White
colleague was that we call for a "change in our District policy"? Even
she recognized that the error lie not at RHS itself, but in an entire
organization that permits such tyrannical and degrading behavior.
What child, in 2008, should have to hear such rhetoric at a school
that "promotes" fairness and equality? What student, in 2008, should
have to witness such lazy and slothful consequences for students who
endanger (physically and emotionally) the lives of other students? I
wish I could say that if it was done by Black students, the same
punishment would have been given. But I can't begin to tell you how
many times I have heard of minority students getting suspended
because they said a curse word to a friend. I suppose if these same
Black kids yelled out "Black power" while driving recklessly in the
parking lot, then maybe they would have gotten off with a slap on

the wrist like those other students. But we know that would not have happened. Apparently, committing such acts as those described above is far less heinous than simply saying a cuss word to a friend. In fact, in this District, that gives a child a three-day suspension.

Because my email addressed the issue of unfair punishments, Gillespie-Oss sent me a personal email, which was clearly a sharp reprimand for challenging her administration's behavior.

From:
To:      Felecia Killings
Date:    Monday, April 7, 2008
Subject:   Re: Racial Tension

Felecia,
I wish you had spoken with me first before sending this email out. Like many situations this one evolved throughout the course of the day and with student talk/rumors. _____ was right there in the parking lot– she immediately stopped the students and brought them in. We discipline, advocate, and support students consistently. Please don't question our discipline to the whole staff-it undermines my position. Unfortuntely, some of what was reported to you by students and that you shared with staff isn't accurate. If you think I handeld this poorly please come by and we will discusss it. Additionally, if you have students who are worried about we can meet them and provide support.

\* \* \*

When I read her email, I was immediately remorseful. First of all, she indicated that what I had heard was not accurate and only spread by rumors on campus. Secondly, I had no intention on challenging her personally, and from the email, it was clear that she felt attacked, especially since a multitude of teachers also believed the students' punishment was light. When I read her email, I sent out another one to the staff to let them know how apologetic I was, and that my intention was simply to get us thinking about how we could change things at the school.

(When I had sent out the first email, I had no idea which administrator distributed the light punishment. I assumed it was the assistant principal that was seen in the parking lot who gave it. But I later learned that the vice principal who witnessed the act had initially issued the students suspensions pending expulsions; but it was the principal—Amy Gillespie-Oss—who overturned the suspensions, and gave the boys the Saturday school detention. Is it any wonder why she took personal offense when I sent out the first email?)

>>>Felecia Killings 4/7/2008 1:59 PM>>>
I have to apologize for publicly undermining the authority of admin. for hat was never my intention. I simply wanted to address an issue that has been so concerning the students and myself. So often I read emails from others about what has bothered them, and I thought that this was a venue for us to discuss this.

* * *

Now, I'm not the type of person to want to stir up trouble, and that's why I apologized to the staff. But I could not let go of the fact that this issue was still a problem in 2008! But as the day went on, I realized that what I did was exactly what needed to be done. We needed to not only address what the students did, but also the lack of appropriate responses to such actions. While it was clear that nothing about the punishments was satisfactory, the principal, nevertheless, addressed the staff, and told us that *their*—the administration's— actions were appropriate and according to Ed. Code and District policy.

From:
To:
Date:         Monday, April 7, 2008
Subject:      Re: Racial Tension

Dear Mustangs-
This was an unfortunate situation that RHS administration did not take lightly; however, like many other situations in high school the story has changed when it passed from student to student. _____ was in the parking lot when these students began to fly the confederate flag. She stopped them and brought them into the office. Student consequences were appropriate according to district policy, ed. code, and the Constitution.

* * *

When I saw this email, I think it only angered me even more. How in the world did the Constitution support her actions or lack thereof? Where in the Constitution does it say give students a detention for racist rhetoric and reckless driving? Oh, yeah, I remember. That must have been the part that the founders left out, but was later added by the Fairfield-Suisun Unified School District: Amendment 28— We Do What We Want. Or maybe she was referencing a student's "right to free speech." That must be it! Every student has the right to reference hate and say all manner of evil on school grounds. Well, if that's the case, why suspend children for cussing? Why get angry at them when they talk back to their teachers? Why is it okay to tolerate racial comments, but wrong to say a curse word? At what point does "free speech" have its limits? I suppose if some of my children had argued the "free speech" defense during their disciplinary meeting, then they would have gotten off with no punishment—well, maybe not because most of the troubling kids were Black as the discipline numbers in the District suggested. But I guess dropping the F-word while speaking to friends is a lot more heinous than speaking racist words that remind an entire group of lynchings and segregation. Obviously, the latter is more "precious" enough to be "protected by the Constitution." (How long must we tolerate this "upside down" way of thinking and behaving?)

As the day progressed, I continued to receive emails from staff members; not only that, but emails from outside individuals started flooding my Inbox. At that time, I didn't know how they found out about what I had done, but it was later conveyed to me that another teacher at the school had forwarded my email to other teachers in the District. In a way, I suppose my email sparked what others had been trying to do for years, and that was to get something done about the racism, discrimination, and prejudice in the District and its schools. Some people had brought the problems to the attention of previous school officials; but as usual, their comments and concerns went unheard. The following email speaks of this:

From:
To:           Felecia Killings
Date:        Monday, April 7, 2008
Subject:    Re: Racial Tension

Mrs/Ms. Killings, my name is _____ and I was formerly a Campus Monitor at RHS during my senior year of college, and witnessed some of the same activities in the parking lot and made several mentions to administration about these very issues. The problem is very real and from this e-mail, and it appears the issue is yet to be addressed. Now, as a teacher in the district, I see that it is very possible that this issue will never be addressed. They will get rid of you before addressing an issue as important as this. I am willing to stand with you if needed. Just let me know.

\* \* \*

The tone of his email suggests one of pain and disappointment. Here was another employee of the District who had witnessed similar acts as the one I described, and in his opinion, he did not feel that the issue would ever be addressed. His prophecy that the District would "get rid of [me]" before addressing this important problem was as accurate as the details provided in this story. At that time, I did not know the extent to which professional backlash and retaliation could go. I did not understand the degree to which an entire organization would seek to annihilate a person's dream and career, simply because he/she asked them for better protection and equal treatment in their schools. It says a lot about the people we have in positions of power in the public education system. Apparently, they can do whatever they want, and still protect each other without hesitation. But they only do these things because we, the teachers, allow them to do it. Last time I checked, there were more teachers at a single high school site than there were administrators in the entire District. They can't fire all of you if you all stand together for a common cause. (But, don't let me start any trouble. I'm just the little Black English teacher in Fairfield being charged with rape against a student. What do I know?)

After reading this email and the others, I knew I had started something big, and I desperately wanted to get out of that school as soon as possible. (To be honest, I don't know why my voice was the one to break through a system that had been functioning uninhibitedly for so long. I don't know why the voices of others did not thwart these types of negative school behaviors. Even looking back, I can only say that it was because God was ready to act, and the time was just right for it to happen.) What I had thought would be a simple matter addressed in our own setting soon turned out to be a community uprising with no end in sight. But just when I had thought the situation in the student parking lot had been difficult enough to handle, I soon learned that more had taken place than what was initially told to me.

As soon as the 2:50-pm bell rang on that Monday afternoon in April, one of my scholars came back to my classroom and told me that in addition to what she already shared, a life-size teddy bear was dragged by a rope from the truck that the boys drove. (Now, perhaps the reader sees no harm in that, but allow me to explain the implications of such antics. There have been countless times when minorities—not just Blacks—have been strung to a rope, and dragged from the back of a truck, only to die a devastating, embarrassing, and heinous death. This "comic relief" displayed by the boys could have been "innocent" [to say the least] had it not been combined with the waving of the flag and the shouts of racial phrases. Altogether, such actions scream a hate crime; but because the District had no policy with which to measure their actions, the boys technically committed no crime. So I guess the principal was right when she said she behaved according to "District Policy." As long as there was no policy, there could be no punishment. How fortunate for them.) When my scholar told me that, I couldn't believe how blatant those students' actions were. This time, I didn't bother bringing this to the teachers' attention. I had already been reprimanded for what I initially shared, and I definitely did not feel like reading another email from the principal if I made the staff aware of the teddy bear also. I just wanted to leave that place because I had ignited a fire, and it was too late to quench it.

When I finished speaking to that student, I rushed to the staff parking lot and headed towards my car. I didn't want to run into any administrator because I could not afford to deal with any other reprimand. As soon as I got to the lot, I called dad to tell him what happened and what I had done. When I got to his house (I was living with him at the time), I shared the rest of the story with him. I remember telling him that I couldn't even concentrate on teaching because the whole situation bothered me so much. It wasn't even what the students did that irked me, but more so the lack of proper consequences that blew my mind.

Trying to sleep that night was difficult. No matter how hard I tried to move on and forget the entire situation, it was like God continued to place the issue before me. But I didn't know what to do with it all, especially after I had stirred up so much by my first email. I was more nervous about what would happen when I returned to work on Tuesday, April 8th.

Interestingly enough, the next day was no different than that Monday. I continued to receive emails from the teachers at the school. Students were speaking about the entire situation all day. Concentrating on my lessons was out of the question. The only way I could release my stress was to vent to my kids.

In the midst of our conversations, one of my junior students told me that she informed her mother about what happened, and that she had contacted a local news station to air the story. She then told me that they wanted to talk to me to get a first-hand look at what was happening. Still not knowing what to do about it all, I agreed to speak with the news station, but nothing really came of it. Perhaps because I had not filled them in with all the details, then that's why they didn't run with it. At that point, my concern was not with media anyways—I hate them…any wonder why?—but on getting the issue addressed properly and fairly at the school. Needless to say, I was still so confused. On one hand, I was glad that I spoke out; but on the other hand, I did not like the mark I was receiving as the "renegade teacher." But later that day, during a scheduled staff meeting, I quickly learned that my efforts in trying to help this school better its race relations was appreciated by more than I could imagine.

When I entered the multi-purpose room for the staff meeting, I was so nervous and scared. I don't even remember who I sat by, but I really felt alone. Typically, during any staff meeting, the principal would allow teachers to stand up and honor another teacher for something that he or she did. So, when the meeting began, Gillespie-Oss opened the floor for this activity. One teacher in particular, a dear friend to me, stood up in front and mentioned that she wanted to recognize me for what I did in sending the first email. She said that if I had not done that then they wouldn't have known anything. What really hit home, especially against the principal, was that the teacher stated that my second email (the "apology") was "unnecessary" because I had done nothing wrong. And she wasn't the only one to stand up and say something. Two other teachers gave their applause for the work I had been doing with the Black student body, and my efforts to change the way students behaved on campus.

When that part of the session was over, I looked over at the principal. She seemed surprised that teachers acknowledged me for what I did. When she returned to the front, she even tried to back track her words that forced my apology email, but it didn't work. The staff knew she was wrong. Even she knew she was wrong. (I guess if enough people stand up for something right, then the ones issuing the wrong acts will have to back track their steps and move out the way…oops, that's me starting trouble again. Let's move on.)

Right after the meeting, Gillespie-Oss, in a quick twist of fate, came up to me to *applaud* me for what I had done. She *thanked* me, of all things, for speaking out and supporting the students. She even asked if I would be a part of the RHS Planning Team to address hatred and intolerance at the school. When she asked me that, I looked at her and told her that I would attend the meeting; but in my mind I'm thinking, *Didn't you just reprimand me for what I did, and now you want my help just because others applauded me?* (It's amazing what people will do to win over the favor of the majority… so fake!) But it didn't stop there. Later that afternoon, she sent me an email stating that she "supports and appreciates" my passion for my children and their welfare.

From:
To:           Felecia Killings
Date:         Tuesday, April 8, 2008
Subject:      Planning team

Felecia-
I just want to let you know that I support and appreciate your passion for

students and their emotional well being. I don't know if I shard with you before but the two students were cited by the police.

* * *

After reading that email, a part of me was offended. I didn't care about the students being cited by the police! All I cared about was the fact that this principal, who tried to make a fool out of me to her staff, had just asked me to be a part of her planning team! Not because she really wanted my help; but because she needed the applause and acceptance of others. (These are the kind of leaders in the Fairfield-Suisun School District.) Here I was, sitting at my desk, reading an email from the same woman who took personal offense to the fact that I spoke on administration's unwillingness to address the hate crime committed on campus; and this is the same woman who was so sharp in her disapproval of my first email that it caused me to apologize to the whole staff for sending it all together! But now she solicits my help and says she "supports and appreciates" what I've done? Be for real! At that point, I was convinced that more was wrong with this whole situation than what appeared. This only angered my spirit further. And for some reason, the fakeness of her approach towards me made me realize that she could care less about me, my children, the school, and what happened there. She cared about her own image and reputation, and if others saw that she was reaching out to the teacher that called the administration out, then she could win their approval by trying to "support" me.

By Wednesday, April 9th, I had not received any more emails from teachers or other individuals; but I continued to receive complaints from students and parents. Everyone wanted to know if the administration was going to investigate the whole situation and properly punish the students for what they did. When they asked me if I knew anything, I told them that I didn't. Some students had shared that they had talked to Gillespie-Oss about the whole thing, but she continued to deny what had taken place, particularly with the bear and noose (or rope). (Yes, dear reader, she denied, at that time, that there was any bear in the first place, even though countless students saw it.) Nothing was being done whatsoever, and so many had tried to prompt her to at least properly investigate the crime. But we couldn't even get that.

Before the April 2008 incident occurred, I had asked my father to come and speak to my Black Student Union on any given Wednesday afternoon. Of course at the time of my asking, I wanted him to simply give them spiritual words of encouragement, and so I scheduled him to attend the April 9th session. (Isn't it amazing how God arranges things to happen in order to get His perfect will performed in the earth?) Naturally, the discussion that I initially wanted him to lead was thwarted by the racist incidents of April 4th. At first, I wasn't sure if I would still have him speak, but I did. And when he came to the lunch meeting, we were both surprised to see my class filled beyond capacity with students. The blessed thing about this session was that it wasn't simply filled with Black students, but students of all races. They all came because they wanted to hear what they could do about the situation at hand. I must have had 60 or more students in a class that comfortably sat 35-40; so you can imagine how crowded it was.

When dad spoke, he opened the floor for the students to discuss what had happened on April 4th. As others spoke, my father told them that they didn't have to sit back and let nothing happen. As he stated, if the principal was not going to do anything, then they had a right to do something about it. Nothing violent. Nothing illegal. But something active.

When the session was over, my students were pumped. They looked to me to see what we could do, but I still had no answer for them. I knew that if we did make a move, then it would have to be tactful, appropriate, and hard-hitting. We needed people to know that we were truly hurt and we were in dire need of school change.

That day, I went home feeling the weight and burden of my children's hearts. I knew I could not let them down at such a time as this. If it cost me everything, then I had to be willing to risk it all so that real change could come to this school, but I was so afraid.

People think that leaders and change makers like Dr. King, Ghandi, or other prominent leaders have some kind of superhuman power that makes them invincible when executing change. People think that leaders who stand out do so without fear or nervousness of what could happen as a result of their actions. But I know all too well that there is a sense of trepidation and anxiety when decisions to make a change arise. Fear was there for me as well. And while I dare not compare myself to such great leaders, I do empathize with their fears. I was terrified of losing my job. I was nervous of the professional backlash. I was scared that my principal and other District officials would ruin my career if I continued to push this thing any further. Yet, the burden rested on me heavily to the point that I could not function effectively in my teaching role.

The day after the BSU meeting (April 10th) was tense. Just my appearing at that school made it hard for me. I knew the principal had no intentions on doing anything about the April 4th incident. I knew that there would be no change in the students' punishments. I knew nothing was getting done; and the reason I knew this was because no staff had received any follow-up to the situation. Neither were parents and other students getting responses from the principal. So, while in my classroom, I went to the computer and searched the District website for the contact information of the school board members. I intended to write to them in order to share what was happening at our school, and to solicit their help. But when I looked on the site, I noticed that there was a scheduled Board Meeting that evening at 7:00pm. So, I had a decision to make: I could simply email them our problems, or I could show up to the meeting to speak on the matter. I chose the latter.

I informed my students about the session, and mentioned that I was going to inform the Board about our problems with the administration. I told them that I could not take this situation anymore, and I wanted them to tell their parents about it in case they wanted to come. Truth be told, I never anticipated anyone showing up besides me. And believe it or not, I was prepared to speak, even if I was alone.

That afternoon, I went home and told my dad what I had planned to do. In support of my efforts, he came with me to the District office at 7:00pm. When I arrived, I was shocked to see some students and their parents there, the majority of whom were the heroes that I mentioned in my "Dedication." They came there, not only to support me, but to do their part in the effort to affect change.

We waited nearly three hours before we were allowed to speak. We all sat in the back rows of the Board room, strategizing on what we would say. We had an order of who would go up first, but not all of us knew exactly what we would utter. While a few of my babies had their speeches typed out, the majority of us simply wanted to speak from our hearts. My kids were really worried that if I spoke up, then I would jeopardize my career; so we decided that instead of me telling the story, I would simply state that I was there in support of my students and their parents; but they would do most of the talking regarding the details. (My babies loved me so much. I miss them.) We didn't know how everything would pan out; we just knew that this was our time and our moment to do what others should have done years ago. We needed the Lord to be with us, and as nervous as we all were, we knew we could not turn back.

As we were each called to the microphone for the public speaking portion, the room became silent. As each person spoke, the Board members seemed confused, yet attentive as we discussed the atrocities that occurred on our school grounds. I didn't realize the extent to which that incident wounded so many of them until I saw the tears falling down from some of their faces. It's one thing to speak to one another privately about the events, but to publicly express to our Board Members the effects of the incident was truly emotional. They could not believe that something like this had happened. Furthermore, the lack of appropriate discipline had them flabbergasted.

One by one, approximately ten of us spoke about what had happened. We shared about the many times we asked Gillespie-Oss to do something about it, but were turned down each time. We discussed how Black students were targeted by administrators, and received harsher punishments when compared to their White classmates. We brought it all to the table. And when we all finished speaking, we didn't wait for any Board Member to say anything to us. Instead, we left the board room and congregated in the foyer.

A summary of our testimonies was recorded at the meeting, and it is reproduced below. In addition, I have included two speeches from two students who spoke at the Board Meeting (with their permission). It was the power and thrust of their words that compelled the School Board to act on our behalf, and I am grateful that my scholars allowed me to share the essays in my book. (The responses are unedited, and were only meant as reference notes for the speeches. Please forgive any grammatical errors that are present.)

Student #1 Speech

When I found about the incident involving some RHS students driving around with a confederate flag and a noose around THE NECK OF A STUFFED ANIMAL I was very upset and furs rated. To me the confederate flag represents SLAVERY AND OPPERISON. Even though it may have been a joke I think they crossed the line. I also think their punishment should have been something more than just Saturday school. It should have been addressed in a different want instead of being brushed off. For example: I was suspended a day for using inappropriate language which was no threat to anyone. I accepted my punishment, but I was not given the option to attend Saturday school. Waving around a confederate flag and a noose around the neck of an animal, suggest a threat and a demonstration of future actions.
I'm not exactly sure what the school by-laws states according to this situation. I d do know that Saturday school does not seem appropriate enough for the actions of these students. I am saddened to know that I still today, live in a society and attend a school where the same rules don't apply for everyone.
Thank you for your attention and your time.

* * *

I don't know what it was about that moment, but for the first time, we really believed that God would surely cause at least these leaders to do something on our behalf. As I said goodnight to them all, I felt this sense of accomplishment come over me. More than that, I knew that now we would see God work on our behalf.

When dad and I came home, all we could do was boast of what God had done through my children. (As mentioned in my "Dedication," a leader like myself can prepare the way for a profound movement; but without the supporters and followers, that movement will never flourish.) The students and parents were so eloquent in their speeches and their pleas to obtain a full instigation into the situations occurring on campus; and the fact that each speech came one after the other seemed to hit the Board even harder, compelling them to act immediately for the sake of the safety of the students. My babies were respectful and courteous. They epitomized the non-violent approach of the Civil Rights Movement. While many folks half expected to see students retaliate through violence, my scholars demonstrated that progress could be made when people decide to let their words be their weapons. I cannot emphasize enough how perfectly things went; not because we had arranged it, but because God had orchestrated it. It takes a great deal of courage for young adults to stand for something as important as justice and inequality in a school. Even more courageous is the act of a single teacher, who is willing to risk it all to save and help her children, to take on what others refused to acknowledge. Here I was, thinking that I would be the only one at the meeting; instead, several others came, even parents that I had never met before; and this revealed the extent to which a community was ready to bring forth some righteousness in this terrible system.

When I think about it, what my students and I did (in speaking to these officials) could not have been done if anyone else tried. I know this because God didn't allow just anyone to attend that Board Meeting. Everything was divinely orchestrated. He brought the right students and parents to that session, and gave us the exact words to speak. I don't think it could have been planned any better. In addition to that, no teacher (in her right mind) would ever willingly jeopardize her career to challenge an entire organization. There was nothing special about me to suggest that I was a "renegade" or an activist. But I knew that God anointed my mouth to speak, and I knew that whatever position I was in, God could use it to perform His will in that organization. This is what happens when God's people are placed in secular jobs. We are there to affect change at any cost. We are here in the earth to expand the kingdom of God and perform His work. You never know what God's plans are for you while you are at your job, your college, or your school; so be open to the Spirit of the Lord.

That night I had a peaceful rest for the first time in days. But when I woke up on April 11th, the day after the Board Meeting, I dreaded the thought of stepping onto the campus. There was no telling of what would happen next.

When I entered my class on April 11th, the co-teacher that I worked with told me that the office had been calling my name for a while, and that only terrified me more. Even though they had summoned me, I didn't bother going to the office; I was trying to avoid them as much as possible. But after about an hour into the school day, one of the students who attended the Board Meeting with me came to see me. He told me that I needed to go to the office

**REQUEST FOR APPROVAL OF MONITORING REPORT FOR CORRECTIVE ACTION IMPLEMENTATION AT FAIRVIEW ELEMENTARY SCHOOL** (continued)

- continue corrective actions for full EPC compliance
- 2008 STAR testing
- California Department of Education review/entry to SAIT Level II status
- demonstrate consecutive two-year API gain to exit SAIT.

Dr. Debrule reported that Fairview Elementary is going to serve as a demonstration school for Educational Consultants, LLC.

** Motion was made by Mrs. Tilley, seconded by Mrs. Griffin, and carried unanimously to approve the Monitoring Report for Corrective Action Implementation at Fairview Elementary School.

**QUARTERLY REPORT ON WILLIAMS UNIFORM COMPLAINTS**

There were no staff presentations on the Quarterly Report on Williams Complaints.

**PUBLIC COMMUNICATION**

Adam McCray, Rodriguez High School student, spoke regarding an incident that happened at school last week involving two students driving around the parking lot with a Confederate flag and another in which a teddy bear was dragged by a vehicle through the parking lot. He commented that attending Saturday School does not seem an adequate punishment for such offenses.

Melanie Driver, Fairfield-Suisun Unified Teachers Association (F-SUTA) President, acknowledged the site visitations made by the Superintendent and Board members; reported on the collaborative planning session held at Suisun Valley School; and stated that F-SUTA has declared impasse. She noted that there are two bargaining sessions scheduled before the first impasse meeting on May 2 and encouraged the District to work towards a settlement.

Roman Robinson, Rodriguez High School student, spoke regarding incidents that occurred last Thursday and Friday in the Rodriguez High School parking lot involving a Confederate flag, shouts of "white power," and a teddy bear being dragged by a vehicle. He stated that he was very offended by these acts and questioned the lenient discipline the perpetrators received.

Allyson Rosemond, Rodriguez High School student, expressed concern that these incidents were held on the fortieth anniversary of Dr. Martin Luther King's death, were an expression of racism and harassment toward fellow students, and that the white males who committed these acts were only given Saturday School as punishment.

Felecia Killings, Rodriguez High School teacher, stated that she supported the students who witnessed these incidents and that she is thoroughly offended, as were many of her fellow teachers at Rodriguez High.

Fairfield-Suisun Unified
School District

Board Minutes
April 10, 2008

**PUBLIC COMMUNICATION**
(continued)

George Guynn, Jr., Suisun City resident, thanked Ms. Heumphreus for pointing out that the History book should be reviewed before being adopted as an instructional text, and encouraged all Board members to do research before voting in the future. He also commented on the incidents at Rodriguez High and immigration policies.

R. Gaines, Rodriguez High School parent, spoke regarding the recent incidents at Rodriguez High, and asked what would be done to protect all students. She stated that she feels not enough is being done about this type of conduct.

Shalamar Jamerson, Rodriguez High School student, expressed her concern that the recent incidents are being taken very lightly by school administration and that the consequences seemed very minor. She stated that these were terrorist acts, that racism does occur today, and that she does not feel safe on campus.

Sylver Wallace, Rodriguez High School student, said that she considers the recent incidents on campus hate crimes and questioned why the students involved only received Saturday School, when this is a minor punishment used for cell phone infractions. Sylver commented that incidents such as these can escalate into shootings and stabbings.

Gerardo Chavez, City of Fairfield resident, reported that he lives one block away from Rodriguez High and his daughter will attend this school in the future. He stated that this behavior should not be tolerated.

Nicholas Rogoff, Rodriguez High School student, reported that he was an eye witness to the incident at Rodriguez High last Friday, and expressed his shock and concern regarding this event.

Mrs. Griffin asked that the Board receive an update on the events at Rodriguez High.

**APPROVAL OF REVISION OF BOARD POLICY 5123, PROMOTION/ACCELERATION/ RETENTION**

Dr. Goldstone reported that a report was given at the last Board meeting regarding revisions to Board Policy 5123, and recommended the Board approve this item.

** Motion was made by Mr. Gaut, seconded by Mrs. Tilley, and carried unanimously to approve revisions to Board Policy 5123, Promotion/Acceleration/Retention.

**PRESENTATION OF FAIRFIELD-SUISUN UNIFIED TEACHERS ASSOCIATION CONTRACT OPENERS FOR THE 2008-2009 SCHOOL YEAR**

Ron Hawkins, Assistant Superintendent of Human Resources, reported that according to the California Education Code, prior to beginning negotiations between a bargaining unit and the school district, there needs to be a public disclosure of the proposals. He stated that the F-SUTA proposal for the 2008-2009 school year would be presented tonight by Rosemary Louisaint, Bargaining Chair, and Kevin McNamara, Bargaining Team member.

From the day we enter first grade we are introduced to pre-set biases of who the most influential people in history are. Every year, we learn more about figures such as Christopher Columbus, George Washington, Thomas Jefferson, Abraham Lincoln, Rosa Parks, and Martin Luther King Jr, building on our knowledge each year until we have a complete picture of who each of these people are. Often times however, we are forced to see these people through a clouded lense of white lies that inhibits our view of the truth about them. The truth is, Christopher Columbus imprisoned a whole race of people, whose culture nearly died; Thomas Jefferson, the man who said in the Constitution of the United States that "all men are created equal", actually kept slaves himself and had nine children with one of his women slaves; Abraham Lincoln didn't actually free all of the slaves at the end of the Civil War, only those from the states who rebelled actively against the United States of America. Despite these disappoints and disillusions, there has been one character who has remained true throughout the years, Martin Luther King Jr, the man who had a dream, the one who said that injustice anywhere is a threat to justice everywhere, the one who lead the famous Montgomery March and spoke at the Washington Monument. This man, the leading character in the Civil Rights Movement of the 60's, whose greatness is only shadowed by Malcolm X and Francis Douglas in the history books, became a powerful and influential figure through his advocation of civil disobedience in the face of violent retaliation. His peaceful methods lead him to be respected among not only his own race, but also by those who suppressed them and allowed him to become one of the best known characters in American history.

Throughout his work in the civil rights movement, Martin Luther King knew he was putting his life and the lives of his family in danger. On more than one occasion, his house was targeted to be bombed, one of which destroying their entire house while he spoke at a church meeting shortly after Rosa Parks sit in on the bus. He knew that his movement was powerful enough to bring great change, and with that, great anger from those who feared a progressing America. His life was finally brought to an end on April 4, 1968 in Memphis Tennessee as he stood on the balcony of his motel room which he shared with one of his two sons, planning his next march. His murder sparked massive riots all across the United States in which a total of 46 people were killed. On that fateful day, the Civil Rights movement could have been ended, curtailed by the death of its strongest leader, dragging to a halt with the fear of further deaths, however the people of the United States kept fighting for it. Unfortunately, we are still forced to fight for it today.

because Board Members were there, and they wanted to meet with me. I asked him if everything was good, and he said it definitely was. At that moment, the fears of losing my job vanished, and I left my class to go speak with them.

When I reached the conference room, my student and I sat at the table, and had another chance to share what was happening on campus. During that meeting, Gillespie-Oss and Lisa Wilson, one of the vice principals at that time, mentioned that they did not know anything about a bear—a clear lie since one of my students and her parent approached the principal about it on Monday, April 7th—and that they were deeply sorry about the whole thing. When we met with them (administration, the Superintendent, and the Director of Secondary Education), we were finally able to get the full investigation of the incident, which proved that the story my students shared with me on that Monday was true. In fact, the evidence from video surveillance showed that not only had it happened on April 4th, but on the 3rd as well. Clearly, this behavior had been going on for a while, which validated the comments of the former RHS staff member who stated that it had been occurring for years. At this time, my students and I believed it was one of the vice principals who gave the weak reprimand to the boys; and when we didn't see her in the meeting, we assumed that something punishable would happen to her. But she wasn't the one to blame. The one who did the wrong was sitting right in front of our faces, and at that time, we didn't even know it.

While talking to the Board Members, the Superintendent asked my student and me two important questions. He wanted to know why we felt the need to go public with the story, and what came to mind when we saw the Confederate flag. I mentioned to them that we (students, parents, and I) did try to get help on the inside, but we were readily denied it. To address his second question, my student spoke up.

He explained that one day while learning about Black history, he came across a picture of an elderly African-American woman. She, he had learned, had a great family who loved her dearly. Like any elder, she took pride in caring for her children and grandchildren. Although she was appreciated by those in her community, Southern Whites saw her as nothing but trash because she was Black. This elderly woman, who committed no crime worthy of such actions, was met with a fatal death. Picking up another photo, my student saw this same woman hanging from a tree, lynched by White Southern racists. My scholar then proceeded to tell the District officials: "*This* is what we are reminded of when we see the Confederate flag." Lynchings. Anger. Hatred. Bigotry. While others may see the flag as a symbol of "Southern pride," the rhetoric and antics of the boys on that day said so much more.

The eloquence of his words and his ability to draw us into his feelings hit home even further. Whether it was the first time they (administration and the Board Members, who were all White) heard a Black person sharing their feelings regarding real racism, I did not know. What I did know, however, was that this was exactly what these officials needed to hear so they could understand the magnitude of such actions on school grounds.

(I want to point out here that it is virtually impossible to change the way people behave because the root of their actions stems from their heart. We cannot make people love one another, especially when they have issues with folks because of their race. This goes for Blacks, Whites, Latinos, Asians, Polynesians, and any other ethnicity. We all are guilty of exercising race prejudice at some point. While we may not be as blunt as others, it does not mean that the evil in our hearts is invisible to God. He is always watching, and He commands us to love one another. What people choose to do in the privacy of their homes is one thing. If supremacists want to congregate so they can boast of how great they are, so be it. But there must be limits to where such dialogue can occur. Those limits must be placed in the schools, especially the public schools because they are open to the public. If administrators refuse to curtail such rhetoric or explicit actions, then the problem lies not with the students, but with the bosses.)

Now, I don't want the reader to think that I came into that school planning to be an advocate of Black rights. I came there to affect change with all students, regardless of their race. It just so happened that because I was one of a few Black teachers at that site, so many of them felt comfortable enough to talk about their problems to me; and because I could connect with all students, any problems they had soon became a burden for me. In the case of minority students, I could relate to their struggles because I experienced it before; and when I saw a need, in this case a great need, I acted on it. During that whole struggle, that entire week in April 2008, I had no choice but to trust that God would protect me. I literally walked in faith every step of the way. I never knew what to expect as each day came, and the threat of losing my job, my safety, even my life at one point constantly bombarded my mind. But God proved then that when we trust Him in all our ways, He directs our paths, and He provides coverage and protection. I won't pretend that everything I did at that time was "perfect." On the outside, I undermined my leader; I ridiculed an entire system; I brought shame and embarrassment to the leaders. But everything I did was motivated by the love I had for my children and their protection. Love should drive us to seek for the betterment of others, even at the cost of losing our own life. This is genuine love. This is real power. This is how God operates. *(Lord, I hope that my children learn at least that one thing from me.)*

By the time we finished the meeting on April 11th, the administration, my Cultural Coalition (a new group I formed that included students of all races), and the Board Members were developing activities that could be implement immediately to address the racism. (I formed the Cultural Coalition on April 9th when I saw that there were others who wanted to be a part of the change. My heroes inspired me to form this, especially because it was such a mixed group. Days after the Board Meeting, media reported that Gillespie-Oss formed the Coalition as a part of her "activism", but she didn't. Funny how she never clarified that point to the public. Moving on.) We came up with school rallies and class visitations; and at this point, we did want media attention, but only to publicize the good that had come out of this moment.

Word about the incident spread quickly throughout the city. The superintendent made immediate contact with the local NAACP chapter in Fairfield. (Why he did this, I don't know—maybe to get to them before we did.) After school, my group and I met with the *Daily Republic* to share our story. Somehow, they caught wind of it, and wanted to meet with the ones who got it moving. At that time, we really believed that things were looking up. We honestly thought the fight was over, and now we could start the healing process. But we were sadly mistaken. The fight was not over. It had only just begun. While my group and I believed a week of discussing this issue was enough, it appeared that others disagreed. The next two months would prove to be the most difficult moments for all of us, especially as more people began investing their interests in the school's affairs. We slowly began to see that this movement was going to take a turn for the worst because more and more people were becoming involved with the issues; and when there are too many hands in the cookie jar, things become contaminated very quickly.

One individual, a union representative, acknowledged his frustrations with the teachers at RHS for not acting out on the incident, and that stirred up a wave of animosity at the site. Although I appreciated his efforts to address the staff, this revealed the extent to which so many others were offended by the incidents. Before I knew it, people outside the school were criticizing the situation without knowing what had actually taken place. This, I believe, is why so many teachers began to turn on me. I can only assume that they thought I had gone mad, and told everyone about our problems. But the degree to which this story exploded was not a result of my direct action, but because others had spread it themselves. I guess one could say I became that scapegoat for others to place their blame. I didn't mind the backlash, just as long as my kids received justice and equal treatment at school. That's all that mattered to me. Below, you will read bits and pieces of the email from the union representative.

>>> _____ 4/11/08 12:12 PM>>>
Last night at the School Board meeting, students, parents and teachers from Rodriguez high told of an incident that happened on the anniversary of the death of Martin Luther King.

Not only is it appalling that such an event happened, it is even more appalling that none of this was mentioned to FSUTA as the Association represents our teachers on issues concerning safety on the campus and minority issues thru our MAC committee

The level of disgust became even more unpalatable when the final adjudication was mentioned (Saturday School and a ticket for reckless driving).

Is the staff of RHS really so unmoved about this event that staff is willing to accept such a minor punishment for such an egregious offense to those of color?

Are RHS teachers that complacent that they just turn their heads away without saying anything? Some of your teachers are of color, what do you say to them? What does the administration say to them—don't take offense that they get away with little or no punishment for offending you—take it in stride because you are a professional?

No suspensions, no community service hours, no removal of the right to park in the school parking lot, no sensitivity training, nothing but a Saturday school? Absolutely unbelievable.

Just what do we a teachers expect from our administration? When do we band together and say, "this is wrong and the administration's culture needs to change". It is time teachers expect more from the administration in teaching morals and ethics than turning their head the other way with minimal adjudication. It is time for teachers to look into their souls as to the expectation of what should be done if it was against their person and make their voices heard or you condone what happened.

Administrators/teachers are you complicit in just sweeping it under the rug? So when the teacher, parents and students of color come down to the

School Board meeting this is the first time the issue is mentioned, in front of the school board? Just what are we teaching our students and community? That this behavior is not only tolerated but not offensive to the surrounding community and that it is condoned as acceptable.

Saturday day school for punishment, wow!

Now the RHS staff has a problem. Since the administration/staff did not raise the roof on this issue, how do they justify any other form of discipline other than Saturday school for other personal offensive remarks? You cannot justify anything but Saturday school.

It is a sad day when administrators/teachers will allow things like this to go un-noticed until the injured parties must take it the school board and a part of our student community is lost to another injustice.

* * *

Although I didn't have to, I made a response to the representative in defense of the teachers. While it was true that more people should have spoken out against the situation, I knew they were too fearful of what might happen if they spoke up. Professional backlash is a fear tactic that administration and District officials use to keep their employees in check. At the same time, there were those who really had not heard of what took place because our administration said nothing to us. But trust me when I say, he made solid points in his emails that to this day, I fully support.

>>>Felecia Killings 04/11/08 8:42 PM>>>
Good Evening,
I am the teacher that attended the board meeting and the one working with the students to get this issue resolved. I don't know the ethics of responding to this email, but I feel it is important to do so.

When it was first brought to my attention about the incident, I immediately reacted according to what I felt was right by sending an email to the staff. In due time, the actual events of what took place on the part of myself and the students during the course of this week will come to light. But I want you to know that when I sent the email out to the staff, I received immediate feedback from teachers who were very concerned and supportive. They (many, not all) too wanted immediate results. I appreciate your outrage for what happened, but I do not want anyone to get the impression that there was no sympathy on all the teachers' part. For many, today was the first time that they are getting the whole story.

The students and I needed our voices to be heard in this matter and immediate action needed to take place...this is why we attended the Board Meeting. Other factors contributed to our going there, but I do not feel a liberty to discuss that. Needless to say, the community's outcry for this situation is something that we would hope would happen. This means that the community cares for the safety and security of its children, especially at school. Things are in motion now as far trying to remedy the problem; but this will take A LOT of time, dedication, love, and support from all those were directly and indirectly affected.

We (the students and I) want everyone to work together concerning this incident, for this is what Dr King strived for. We anticipate great things to come out of this.

Sincerely,
Felecia Killings

* * *

Even though I sent this reply to try and ease any tension among the teachers, there were quite a few staff members who were bothered by his email, and made it a point to express their feelings.

>>>_____ 04/13/08 11:18 AM>>>
_____, are you here? No you're not. You don't have the slightest idea of what is going on here. Until you know the facts, don't make yourself look so bad.

* * *

Even though this teacher was offended by the representative's remarks, there were others who wanted to point out the necessity for addressing the issue. The next few emails reveal a heated discussion between the teacher in the previous email, and the same individual who used to work at RHS (the one who told me that the District would get rid of me before addressing the issues).

>>>_____ 04/14/08 2:17 PM>>>
I recall events that were swept under the rug in the past _____, don't you? Let's not attack each other unless we are ready to disclose our own personal feelings. If you have ever been denied opportunity or hated for the color your skin, you would understand. I know for a fact that _____ and Killings have personal experience in this matter and _____ has openly spoken out against incidents of this nature. As someone that has put my own personal safety on the line for both teacher and administrator, I too am qualified to speak on this matter. Attitudes of this nature existed at RHS when I was there and now has cropped up again. Miss Killings and _____ are correct.

* * *

>>>_____ 04/14/08 3:19 PM>>>
You need to look over the emails and see who was attacking who. I didn't "attack" anyone. It was, are you here and do you know all the facts. The answer is no. We were judged by people who have no right to judge us until the situation is resolved. Isn't that what any of us would want? Sorry to hear that you actually _____ is right. Sad.

* * *

From:

To:
Date:         4/15*08 8:25AM
Subject:      Re: Events

Yes, I understand _____. Its' just that I've witnessed this at Armijo and
RHS, and nothing was ever done. I know how ti looks because I know some
of the kids that exhibit this type of behavior, I also see them in juvenile
hall and they have issues with people of color there too. It always leads
to a cell extraction and a isolated cell after that. Believe it or not, when I
meet with our local police forces to discuss gang activity, the majority of
our kids involved in this type of activity are located at RHS. You can seek
this information out of yourself. It is public knowledge. Although I can't by
law give you names, there are close to thirty students in all. Keep your
eyes open and be the awsome deterrent that all adults are supposed to
be. This will all pass. _____ was coming from a stand point of knowing as
a union representative of the teachers. On the other hand, the reason why
understanding _____ is so easy is because I live it everyday. My own
mother was under ownership in the State of Louisiana until 1945. I hear
my people say, "I wasn't there, you need to get over it." Here's the problem
with that, my mother was still alive. And still, under she died, wasn't allowed
a birth certificate or an education by this nation. It wasn't until after 1965
that our own federal government said it was illegal to discriminate against
blacks. Thats not too long ago. While both uncles served in ww2, they were
on a daily basis denied equal treatment under the law, even though they
dodged the same bullets and suffered equal injuries. So it is bigger than
just offending someone or hurting their feelings. Things have to change
or it will repeat itself. So it is not about revenge or soap boxing, it about
acknowledging and healing. For all of us. Good luck to you _____, you
do good things for the kids in this district, and are a great mentor. Use that
power wisely and we will all be  better for it.

* * *

A few days later, the union representative sent an apologetic email
back to the teachers for his initial comments. (In all honesty, I'm
glad he sent the first one, and I feel that this email was unnecessary.
But that's just my opinion.)

From:
To:          RhsGW
Date:        4/15/08 7:38AM
Subject:     Painful Memories

I'd like to address all the staff and teachers of RHS. It seems that I have offended a number of you and that was not my intent.

Many things cause people to reach conclusions that may be not be totally accurate upon closer review even i the initial premise was correct. Such is the position I find myself in after Thursday night's School Board meeting.

Having lived in the South during my sophomore and junior years, going to a segregated high school in a small town, one lears how educational silence on racism keeps minorities in their place.

The confederate battle flag is forever a reminder of slavery, the use of the "N" word and the reprehensible thought of the KKK and lynching.

The memories of those youthful years are indelibly embedded in my mind and are even more distasteful now than they were then as I knew and understood less at that time.

The hostility in my voice is the reflection of those past painful years of watching people instill fear in others for no other reason than the color of their skin and to keep them down.

Educational silence is what gave the power to do that. The seemingly apparent silence that RHS could not go unnoticed.

The shock that this could happen in our community brought back a flood of revolting memories that I thought I had out grown.

I apologize to all the RHS staff that did take action to deal with this in a peaceful and orderly manner reminiscent of Dr. Martin Luther King.

Sincerely,

_____

* * *

While I still believe he was in his every right to say what he wanted, I suppose that because of his position as a union leader, he could not say such harsh statements to the entire RHS staff.

Later that day (April 11th), one of my scholar's parents informed me that she had made contact with the NAACP. From what she shared with them, the president wanted to speak with me and my kids, and we were scheduled to meet them on April 13th. (The reader will recall that the superintendent had already contacted the organization. They were aware of what he shared, but more interested in hearing our story before meeting with the District's officials.)

On April 12th, I met with my Coalition group to prepare for our meeting with the NAACP the next day. The atmosphere of expectancy was always with us. We always anticipated that something big would come out of our efforts, but we didn't imagine that it would take so much of our time and energy. On this same day, the *Daily Republic* published our story. It didn't focus on what we had shared with them. Instead, it seemed to focus a lot on the good that *administration* was doing. This set us off a lot; but I always tried to reassure my scholars that every truth would be brought to the surface one day. Besides, media is too controlled; and our principal had connections with the city's newspaper, which influenced their perceptions of the current events.

It's so interesting that the ones who perpetrated the problem were also the ones receiving the praise for what I and my children accomplished. This frustrated the group. But I always told them that God knows what happened. He directed our steps, and in due time, our names and what we accomplished would be recognized. It's always discouraging when the people who do the hard work get little or no praise for what they accomplish. But when the leader who did the damage gets all the accolades, it's like a slap in the face. What's worse is that our principal never publicly acknowledged what we had done. And why would she when she felt that I had basically damaged her reputation? I tried to encourage my group to not be moved by who media applauded. They only knew so much. But I promised them that one day I would share our story with the world, and then everyone would know the truth. *(My heroes, I hope that you are pleased with this.)*

On this Saturday, April 12th, I received a very appreciative email from one of the School Board Members. He was so impressed with our approach at the Board Meeting; and he wanted to come and speak to the group to express his gratitude and favor towards us. Of course, we received him.

From:
To:           Felecia Killings
Date:        Saturday - April 12, 2008
Subject:    Re: Events

Felecia,

Thank you for addressing the Board. The straight forward approach and the well thought out and articulate presentations made by the students could not have been made better. The Board was appalled by the actions of those boys in the parking lot and the weak response of staff. As you saw, there was immediate response on Friday. This kind of behavior will not be tolerated in this district. I applaud your work with our kids at Rodriguez. Hoperfully the "stand" on Thursday evening will be the beginning of a new attitude at Rodriguez. Sometime I would love to come and meet the BSU and thank them for their MLK apporach to this matter.

\* \* \*

That same day, Gillespie-Oss sent out an email to the staff to update them on what had happened throughout the week. Mind you, the only updates that staff received came from what she shared. In their minds, she was doing a bang-up job. No staff knew why we attended the Board Meeting in the first place, and they had no idea what went on behind the scene. They did not know what was shared between us and the School Board Members. All they knew was what she told them.

At times, I wanted to tell them the truth, but I never felt led to do so. I didn't think it was the appropriate moment to inform them of the hell we went through to even get change on campus. I didn't feel comfortable trying to explain to them that the spontaneous rallies that they saw on that Friday were not birthed from their principal, but from my kids and pressure from her bosses. It was more important to me to maintain peace with administration *only* because it would benefit the students in the long run. I knew that if there was constant feuding and backbiting on our parts, then nothing would get done for my babies. They were always at the forefront of my mind. So I let many things slide, including her receiving all the praise. The only people I wanted to know the truth about it all were my kids, their parents, and the community.

By the 13th, so much had already happened, but like I said, it was just the beginning. After going to church in Antioch, Sister (who was fully supportive of me during this time) and I met with my Coalition members at the St. Stephens Baptist Church in Fairfield to discuss the events with the NAACP leaders. There were about 45 people in attendance. Basically, the NAACP wanted to know our side because they were scheduled to meet with the District the very next day. As we shared our story, the leaders wanted immediate action taken against the administration, particularly the principal. One of the leaders suggested that they start a petition to have Gillespie-Oss removed, and he asked if any of us wanted to sign it. Of course, the first one in line was Sister! (That girl had me cracking up. She hates when people attack her sisters, and she will get active.) My kids and I neglected to sign, figuring it would only lead to a series of backlash that we did not need. The NAACP also gathered witness reports; and my group and I would soon learn that this would be the first of many meetings with the organization.

On the 12th and 13th, Gillespie-Oss and I exchanged emails regarding plans to conduct class visitations the following week. I suppose I could have told her what the NAACP meeting entailed; how there was petition being made to have her removed; but there was something in me that prevented that from happening. I don't know if it was simply my mistrust of administration or what; but for some reason, I didn't feel right telling her everything. In the back of my mind, I really believed she was only doing it because of the pressure from the District officials and media attention. When people are that fake with me, why should I be real with them? No, I had one goal in mind, and that was to start programs and activities on campus that promoted racial tolerance and cultural acceptance. I knew that the second the pressure was off of her, then she would return to doing nothing for us. Plus, it bothered me that she had no heart to act on our behalf in the first place.

On April 14, 2008, the Coalition, administration, and I conducted classroom visits. The purpose of the visits were to tell about the incidents that occurred, introduce who we were as a new

# Racial incident prompts resolve at Rodriguez

BY NIKA MEGINO
DAILY REPUBLIC

FAIRFIELD — One week after a controversy sparked frustration and disbelief at Rodriguez High School, students gathered Friday to rally for change.

On the morning of April 4, 16-year-old Felicia Williams was sitting in her car in the school's parking lot when she witnessed one student driving recklessly through the parking lot, while another student stood on the car waving a Confederate flag.

It was the 40th anniversary of civil rights leader Martin Luther King Jr.'s assassination.

Williams said the students also tied a noose around a "life-sized" teddy bear and dragged it along and yelled out "White Power." The junior and her peers found the incident disturbing.

Investigations by the school found the two students indeed waved a Confederate flag, but there was no evidence the students had a bear or yelled bigoted statements that day, Principal Amy Gillespie-Oss said. District officials gave the two juniors Saturday detention because displaying a

*See Incident, Page A6*

*See Incident, Page A6*

*From Page One*

flag is protected free speech. On Friday, however, school officials determined the two students did tie a stuffed bear on a rope and drove through the parking lot on the morning of April 3, Gillespie-Oss said. Officials are withholding the names of the two juniors to protect them and their privacy.

School officials won't tolerate such an act and will investigate the incident further, the principal said.

"I have to apologize for what happened last week," Gillespie-Oss said to dozens of students who attended an impromptu rally after school Friday. "A lot of tears were shed. . . . Hatred is not OK and it is not accepted on the Rodriguez campus."

The pseudo-lynching is something different than exercising free speech, officials said. The Fairfield-Suisun School District, the school and law enforcement officers are now determining what the appropriate punishment will be.

Interim Superintendent Steve Goldstone said he first heard of the incident when students, parents and teacher Felicia Killings, adviser for the school's Black Student Union, spoke at the School Board meeting Thursday.

"You can tell the pain was real," he said of their testimonies. "It was hard sleeping after that."

Goldstone and Director of Secondary Education Roxanne Rice met with administrators, staff and students Friday to learn more about the events.

"We're trying to find a good, positive way of moving forward after a series of appalling events," he said.

As word of the event spread throughout the week, students of the Black Student Union decided to stand up and express their distress.

At the Friday rally, senior Elijah Robertson stood in front of his peers and confessed how the situation has been an emotional one.

He said hearing of it reminded him of how his grandparents experienced segregation and hatred firsthand.

"That really hit me deep. That really hurt me, because it took me back," the 18-year-old said.

"When I heard about it I was thinking of Emmett Till, Martin Luther King, Malcolm X," senior Roman Robinson added. "They wanted change.

"For every action there's a reaction," he added. "We have to make a change and that's important. It starts off with you making a change with yourself, and you can change the world."

Moving forward was the phrase of the day for the Mustangs. Students of all ethnic backgrounds participated in the rally. Some expressed sympathy, others experienced frustration with discrimination.

Junior Lisa Mattis said she was angry and couldn't believe the two students had the "ignorance" to do it.

"I'm just so tired of disrespect," said Mattis, 17. "We need to recognize racism. . . . If we don't do anything about it, then it will go on forever."

Tearing up, 15-year-old Traisa Keenton, a sophomore, shared how she experiences racism often because of her Middle Eastern descent.

Keenton told the students about how her church was shot at after the terrorist acts of Sept. 11, 2001.

"When is it all going to stop?" Keenton asked. "When is it going to end?"

Gillespie-Oss said tolerating differences isn't enough.

"We need to accept and respect one another," she said.

A group of school administrators, teachers and students will visit classes to discuss the events and discrimination in general throughout next week, Gillespie-Oss said.

*Reach Nika Megino at 427-6953 or nmegino@dailyrepublic.net.*

organization on campus, and discuss how we wanted to make change in the school. I remember when we went into one of my sophomore classes to talk to my scholars, the administrator who came with us tried to dominate the majority of the conversation because she wanted to do all she could to tell their side of the story. So, one of my students raised his hand to ask her a question. He asked, "Isn't true that if Ms. Killings had never said anything, then none of this would have ever come out?" Her response to my critical student was that although it was true that "Ms. Killings spoke about it, eventually it would have been investigated, even without her saying anything." Yeah, right. My students weren't stupid, and they didn't buy her response at all. The administrator even had the nerve to tell my kids that the office did a thorough investigation from the beginning, but found nothing. But then all of a sudden, *they* found the problem and were working on the solutions...liars.

By the time we left my room to go to another one, my Coalition members were a bit disgruntled with the class visits. They expected to be the ones to tell of the events, and to gain the students' support in bringing change. But it turned out to be an opportunity for the administration to "cover" themselves and their actions. In spite of this, I told them to go with the flow of things because we were at least getting something done. We all knew that no matter what, they would try and make themselves look good in front of others. But we had to remain focus on the ultimate goals, and that was to get cultural programs on campus to change the atmosphere of racial intolerance.

Later that day, after many class visits, Gillespie-Oss asked me to attend the District's meeting with the NAACP with her to show "solidarity" of all things. Mind you, I already knew what the NAACP wanted to say because I had just met with them the day before. I declined her offer, and told her that I wanted to stay with my kids to support them. She mentioned that she wanted me to attend so that she could show them that we were collaborating with each other, and that change was happening. Truth be told, she was nervous about the prospect of meeting with a race-conscience organization like the NAACP. Everyone knew what they accomplished since they first organized in 1909. I suppose she had a reason to be fretful, but my presence at the meeting wouldn't have changed anything. In my heart, I sensed that it was still only about her, and I could not support that selfishness. The principal had already proven to me that she was not concerned with doing the right thing in the whole situation. I had no intention of making her "look good" at the cost of stifling the movement. If I had pretended that everything was "well" to the NAACP, then they would have backed off; but I knew that more needed to be done at that school and in that District, and I was not about to give into her wants. Why should I when she obviously wasn't willing to support our needs the week prior?

By the end of the day, my group and I had spoken to over half the student body. We had planned to speak to the other half the next day. In addition to this, we submitted to administration a list of activities the students wanted to do in order to foster cultural education and acceptance. Our first major activity was scheduled for April 25, 2008—a school-wide assembly. As mentioned, our hopes were high; and we knew that as long as we had this window of opportunity, we would take full advantage of it.

On April 15th, we continued the school visits. This was another successful day for us as a group, and the student body seemed to really enjoy this move that we were making. But then things began to turn for the worst. (After careful reflection of what has happened, it's clear to me that all the things that could go wrong *did* go wrong because too many adults put their hand in the matter. I'm not talking about the parents of the students who came in support of me. I'm talking about other teachers, administrators, media agents, District officials, and the list goes on. This movement was about the kids, and it should have remained with the kids. While we were making great progress at our site, many of their accomplishments were overlooked by the increase of adult participation. I think we do a disservice to our youth when we strip them of the power to make a change in their own communities. We assume that because of their age, they are too "immature" to act rationally or intelligently. Many people don't know this, but the Civil Rights Movement would have gone nowhere had it not been for the youth—the Black Southern children in elementary, middle and high schools, and especially the colleges. They exhibited more courage and stamina than the adults in their community; yet no praise or recognition is given to them simply because they were youth. When educators begin to give young adults a chance to show forth their leadership skills, I truly believe that we will see an increase in student achievement. The longer you treat them as little boys and girls, the more they will behave in that matter. Start raising a standard of excellence for them, and celebrate them for their accomplishments. *To my heroes, you get the credit for this movement. I just showed you the way.*)

On the afternoon of April 15th, I received a phone call from one of the parents of the group. She informed me that she contacted

KCRA about the story, and they wanted to speak to me and my kids immediately. By 4:00pm, one of the Coalition members informed me that KCRA was at the school. At this point, I didn't know if it was the best to put my name and face on the news; but at the same time, it was also too late to be concerned about job security. Everyone knew I was the culprit who got this whole thing going in the first place. Even though I had the opportunity to show media who was responsible for starting the cultural activities on campus, I declined to speak. I was still so focused on my kids having the spotlight; so they shared their stories with that news station. By late that evening, our story was on Channel 3 news. The online article can be found at www.kcra.com/news/15896898/details.htlm.

I knew that my group members, other students, and their parents were pleased that attention was drawn to the atrocities of the school and District; but I was petrified. It takes a lot to face opposition on a daily basis when you know that people are set hard against you. I lost a lot of friends because of this incident, and so many teachers turned their backs on me because they felt I had brought them public scrutiny. Every day, the tension on that campus left me seemingly broken because I knew that one day, all this would come back to hurt me. I knew that the District and the administrators would soon find an opportunity to get me out because of what I had done in exposing this tyranny. I knew that the rest of my days at Rodriguez High School would be spent in heartache and difficulties. The only hope and happiness I felt at that school came from the love and support of my kids, their parents, and the community. I knew that as the story continued to spread, the attention would make me a prime target. But like Queen Esther, if I perished, then I perished.

I had to do what I had to do, and trust that God would take care of me the entire time.

On April 16th, the day after the news report, tensions escalated on campus. Everyone was frantic, not only because of media attention, but also because there was a scheduled conference with the public and the NAACP at the St. Stephen's Church regarding the matter. I informed all my classes to let their parents know about the meeting, and I encouraged them to bring their families so they could share what was on their hearts. Seeing this as another window of opportunity, I needed them to understand the importance of this community forum. But I wasn't the only one trying to rally support.

Staff members, many who were appalled by the negative publicity, began soliciting support, not for my kids, not for their parents, not for the community, but *for Gillespie-Oss and her administration.*

From:
To:                    _____ RhsGW
Date:       4/16/08 9:42AM
Subject:    Re: Tonight

Thanks for the info _____
I will be there, and I think it is very important that as many of us go as possible. Let's go support our school! Let us especially go and support _____ who has really been amazing through all of this. I have never in my 10 years teaching watched a principal act as vulnerable as _____ thorough all of this. She, along with the amazing students, inspired me during lunch last Friday.
>>>_____ 4/16/08 9:28 AM>>>
Hi,
Tonight at St. Stephen C.M.E. Church, parents along with the local chapter of NAACP are holding a meeting regarding the events that have taken place on our campus. The meeting is open to parents, students, teachers and concerned citizens. They have asked _____ to attend. I think it is

important for the teachers at RHS to attend as well, to show united support for our school, our students, and our principal. The meeting will start at 7 p.m. at St. Stephen Church, 2301 Union Avenue, Fairfield—near Sullivan. I hope to see you there.

\* \* \*

From:
To:          RHsEdGW
Date:        4/16/08 9:43A
Subject:     In Support of _____

Good Morning 'STANGS!

I wanted to let you all know that _____ is in need of our support tonight. She was invited to attend a meeting at the St. Stephen's church tonight at 7 pm (2301 Union Ave., Fairfield, 94533, here's the Google Map http://maps. google.com/maps?hl=en&q=+230+Union,+Fairfield,+CA,94533&um=1&ie=U TF-8&sa=N&tab=wl) that is being hosted by the NAACP. This is in rgards to the events 1 week ago Friday. I know that I would really appreciate support from my colleagues if I were being brought to answer tough questions regarding a situation as sticky as what has been going on over the past week, so if you have the capacity to be there and support _____, that kind of solidarity would be greatly appreciated.

I still believe that we are the best staff in F-SUSD, and _____ has been nothing but supportive and energetic at RHS, both as AP, and now Principal, so join me in showing the community how much we believe in _____, and how much we care about race relations on our campus! The community is watching. Please show up early (6:15) or so so that you may get yourself a seat. I believe that the church is under some sort of construction at the moment, so it is likely that seating will be limited.

\* \* \*

I remembered first reading this email and thinking, *Why in the world are they so bent on supporting the administration when a week ago they were appalled by what they had NOT done properly?* But then I recalled that some people will always show support for wrongdoers simply because they are friends with each other. It doesn't matter how their actions hurt others. In addition to that, many staff believed the principal had every intention on doing right by the students and the school, and that she was demonstrating this effort by the various activities that had occurred already. But they had no idea about the multitude of meetings that my group and I had with her bosses because she *wouldn't* do anything in the first place. They didn't know a lot, but only saw the effects of our actions. Remember, it wasn't until after the Superintendent and Director came to the school that we finally received a full investigation into the matter, which revealed more than what was initially reported! And that did not come until I and my group attended the Board Meeting. But I wasn't about to judge the staff on their ignorance. They weren't my concern in the first place. What was important to me at that moment were the voices of my children and this community; and their opportunity for change was about to come at that community meeting.

By the time the session opened, the church was filled to capacity and more (hundreds of people). On the right side of the church at the very front sat the school's teachers. On the opposite side sat me, my group, and countless disgruntled members from the community. (Reflecting on that moment, it did seem like it was me against the school. I made it a point not to sit with the other teachers because I needed them to know that my allegiance was not to that school or its leaders. My service was to my kids, their parents, and the community.)

The meeting was incredibly tense. There were news stations from everywhere who were ready to broadcast the discussion. The forum lasted for nearly three hours because so many people had questions for the administration and the District officials. The community went hard on them, very hard. One parent testified that she contacted the principal on April 4th and told her about the bear incident. The mother said that when she spoke to Gillespie-Oss about it, she denied there ever was a stuffed bear. When I heard that, I was so upset. All this time, the principal had been telling me and my kids that she didn't *hear* of any bear until much later, and that's why there was never any investigation. What was also surprising is that one of the boys who committed the act attended the same meeting with his girlfriend; but no one recognized them. I later learned from one of his teachers that the reason he came to the church was because he wanted to apologize to the public for what he did, but was told not to. A part of me wishes he had said something. It says a lot about a person's character when they are willing to rectify the wrong that was done to others. (While I never had the chance to speak to him, I hope that one day he knows how much I appreciate him attempting to convey his remorse.)

During a portion of the community meeting, the boy's girlfriend took the microphone, and addressed Gillespie-Oss directly. When she stood up, no one really knew who she was; but she had mentioned something that let us all know that the principal had not been honest from the beginning. (This is what the community had issues with as well. It's one thing to make a mistake and repent of it. Take responsibility for it, and show others that while you are a leader, you will make mistakes. But this principal refused to do even that. No matter what, she would not be honest about the situation; and as much as *everyone* tried to get her to do at least that, she still refused. To be honest, I would much rather have leaders who are honest about the right and wrong they do than to have ones who lie about everything just to keep face. At least they have integrity.) The girl testified at the forum that she and her boyfriend gave the bear to the Gillespie-Oss a while ago, and apparently it had "disappeared." She then questioned the principal as to its whereabouts; but the principal said nothing to these accusations and questions. It seemed like the more time that was spent on this issue, the more the lies and deceptions surfaced. It was disheartening to witness the blatant cover up. If there was no crime done on the campus, then why go through the motions of hiding things?

For many parents, this forum was also an opportunity for them to discuss the primary problem at the school. Many raised the issue of discrepancies in punishing minority students and White students. So many testified that their children were suspended for smaller, less complicated issues; and yet hate crimes on school grounds only warranted a detention. More testimonies were spoken that related to this incident, and it made the tension in the church that much thicker. It is important to note here that parents were not asking for administration to be "easier" or show more favor towards minority students; they simply wanted them to be fair. Another parent, who is a dear parent of my deceased former student, stated that if "Ms. Killings had never said anything, then parents would have never known what was happening on campus." (This is when I began to receive massive support from the community.) But in spite of their constant pressing, the community received NO response from the principal. Neither were any of their questions answered. I knew that they felt like it was a waste of time to be at the meeting because they expected answers, but the mere fact that they showed up testified of their willingness to fight for change.

Things really became heated when the same man who made the petition to have the principal removed spoke up. He informed the entire community of his intentions, and this led to an uproar from the school's staff. One teacher stated that if that principal left, then they would all leave. Someone else quickly replied, "Well, leave then!" It was a seemingly hostile moment. Those who were in support of the principal and the administration tried to calm the community down; but that was not going to happen. Some teachers stated that administration was doing everything possible to make a change at the school. But the community was not trying to hear all that. They wanted answers to their questions; and until they got that, they could care less about the principal's supporters and their comments.

Although many parents, students, and teachers spoke at the meeting, I purposed to hold my peace for that evening. For one, I did not want any attention drawn to me. I did not want the news looking at me as if it was my movement or my thing. In addition, this meeting was about the people, not about protecting the administration or highlighting my name. It was the community's opportunity to speak up about their frustrations. You can only suppress and oppress people for so long. You can only force them to keep silent for a period of time. Once that time is up, they will have the chance to speak up, and April 16th was their day.

Historically, parents had tried countless times to address these issues with all the administrators that Rodriguez had; but NOTHING was done for them. They tried to do everything according to the procedures set forth by the District, but still nothing came of it. One parent testified that the principal who was present before I arrived had ignored several complaints made by Black parents. She said that when her daughter was in high school, she received several racial slurs from classmates. When it was brought to that principal's attention, nothing happened. For many parents, their hurts rested in the fact that it was 2008, and they were still dealing with the issues that their ancestors combated. While their kids were not being told to use separate bathrooms and separate schools, they were still being treated as second-class citizens who had no rights to equal protection at their school; this was further supported by the fact that their children were readily being suspended and expelled for stupid offenses. Whether Rodriguez High and the Fairfield School District wanted to admit it or not, that was blatant racism; and the community was fed up with it. It is true that I could have stood up and "calmed" the community down, but then what? What good would it have done for them? The issue of racism and discrimination had to be addressed, no matter how difficult it was for others to hear.

When the community had seen that their answers would not be addressed, they stopped in their complaints for that evening. The president of the NAACP chapter wrapped up the meeting, and informed everyone that there would be other forums to discuss change in the city. At the conclusion of the meeting, my kids and I walked out of the church and towards our cars. I did everything I could to dodge any teacher who came to support Gillespie-Oss because I knew how angry they were. Although it may not have seemed like it, I was very stressed and nervous that evening. I was happy for the community in that their voices were heard, but I was apprehensive in going back to work the next day. Things were only getting worse.

One can imagine what it was like for me the following day. It was full of hostility and outrage. Gillespie-Oss didn't come to work because of the stress from the night before; however, we were told that she left town to celebrate her aunt's 90<sup>th</sup> birthday; but I knew that meeting overwhelmed her. It overwhelmed me.

When I turned on my computer to check my email, I noticed that one of the English teachers had sent me a message that really disturbed me. He wanted to know why I had said nothing at the meeting the night before, and that other teachers were criticizing me for it. They felt that I should have defended Gillespie-Oss against the community members, and pretty soon, other teachers started sending emails in the same light.

>>>_____ 04/17/08 11:21 AM>>>
Hey Felecia,
I have been heard other teachers ask why you did speak in support of _____. I think some of the attacks on her have gone too far. She is being turned in a scapegoat for the actions of two students.
Sincerely,

_____

\* \* \*

>>>Felecia Killings 4/17/08 11:45 AM>>>
I want to understand this email correctly:

You're saying that teachers are asking why didn't I speak in support of _____???

When you have some time, I will share with you what you want to know. But the staff is not ready or willing to hear the truth of the entire matter. It is not what it seems. A lot went on behind the scene tht I was heavily involved with. _____, trust me when I say that it is not what it seems

\* \* \*

From:
To:          Killings, Felecia
Date:        4/17/08 12:52PM
Subject:     Re: _____

Hey,

Several staff members are highly concerned about the calls to remove _____. Some of them are talking about leaving if she does not return next year. I have worked at a school that lost key administrators. The replacements were utterly incompetent and working there became intolerable. Yes, I understand that you have good reason to be upset. The first few weeks when I started working here _____ and I got into a massive disagreement, which seemed to threaten my working here. Today, we get along great. I would argue that it is in the interest of the school and students that _____ stay.

I plan to stay late to grade if you want to talk.

\* \* \*

At first, I had planned to speak with the English teacher, and respond to the other teachers' emails, but I thought, *For what?* I knew that no matter what I said to them, they had their minds made up about the matter already. Plus, the story was too long for me to go through step-by-step. They had honestly believed that their principal was innocent in the whole matter, and they had forgotten the fact that she allowed such a low punishment for the boys in the first place. They didn't know the whole truth, and I wasn't about to waste my time trying to explain it to them. Instead of questioning why I didn't defend the principal, they should have tried to listen to what the parents were saying; but they were so locked in feeling sorry for her that they saw the community as a potential enemy to the school.

Other teachers expressed their frustrations with the community forum at the St. Stephen's Church:

>>> _____ 4/17/2008 7:54 AM>>
Friends,

I left the meeting last night frustrated and worried about the future of our school. I don't know about you, but I didn't sleep very well. I fear that there are those in our community (and it was expressed last night) who will not be satisfied unless there is a change of leadership.
I feel very strongly that we must do what we need to do to support _____ and our other administrators. They are doing a fantastic job. They are supportive of staff and students. I fear what the outcome will be if racial politics forces any of them out.

* * *

Racial politics? Was she serious? This wasn't some political game where we played the race card. This was a real issue, and in spite of the concerns that the community brought up, these teachers refused to take notice. This is exactly why tensions have been around for years—because people won't listen. But it's impossible to change some folks when they have never been in another person's shoes. Still, a flood of emails began to surface as more expressed their antagonism against the parents' comments.

>>> _____ 4/17/2008 8:10 AM>>

_____,
I totally agree with you. I left the "meeting" last night after about an hour. I couldn't take any more than that. I was very frustrated about what was being said and what accusations were being made by many people who had never set foot on our campus. I feel this whole situation has been blown way out of proporotion and I am worried about the negative impact all of this is having on our administration, staff and students. This is a great school with a caring

administration and staff. I too think we as a staff should do something to help alleviate these problems I'm just not sure what that would be.

\* \* \*

The ironic thing about this teacher is that the administration dismissed him later, gave him a hard time at the site, and made it difficult for him to try to get his property off of school grounds. It's funny that when the attacks weren't directed towards him at that moment, then somehow they were a "caring administration." I'm sure he has a different opinion of them now since he became a victim of their hostile treatment.

I couldn't agree with you more! _____ is an amazing Principal, and the Assistant Principals are doing an excellent job a well. I had a bad feeling taht what happened last night, was exactly what would happen. This is why I wanted to be there, to help support _____. I don't know what we can do to help, but I agree that we need to do something. Also, why was it that, two years after his leaving, _____ name was dragged through the mud as well? I know that racial tensions are nothing n ew, but what happened to focusing on the here and now, and what happened now?

\* \* \*

In this email, the teacher was upset that another principal from two years prior had been brought up at the meeting. He failed to listen to what the parent was saying. She was attempting to show the pattern of behavior from those who were leaders over that school. But again, when we refuse to listen to the fears, hurts, and pains of others, then we speak from our ignorance and potentially escalate the problems further. Because they would not listen back then, things continued to erupt, eventually leading to the April-2008 incident.

Listening is much more powerful than ignoring. We can accomplish more that way.

Other teachers wanted to actively support the administration by voicing their concerns to the Board Members.

From:
To:         RhsGW
Date:       4/17/08 4:25PM
Subject:     Re: first steps
Hi,
Today many of us met afterschool to debrief from last night's meeting and to discuss ways to show our support of _____ and Rodriguez High School. Some of you couldn't attend the meeting, but still wanted to be kept in the loop. We decided that a good first step would be to write letters to the school board to make sure that they understand how much we support and have always been supported by _____ and the other administrators.
We have included the email addresses of the board members and superintendent, if you would also like to send a letter to express your thoughts and feelings.

\* \* \*

My thoughts at this time were mixed. What happened to listening to the real problems going on? What happened to accountability? It's as if the hate crime became secondary to saving the principal's job! These were the priorities of the staff, and it was discouraging. Any person could see the division between the school and its community, and stuck in the middle of it all were me and my children.

At this point, my heart was growing weary. I was confused and distraught by what had happened, and I wondered why God was letting it get this tense. Even though I wanted to make the tension go away, it was like God was preventing me from stepping in and stifling this uproar. I know people today think that I was out to get the principal because she upset me, but I have no desire to ruin people's lives because I don't want them messing with mine. Through it all, my heart was pure and right. My intentions were legit and reasonable. But people cannot be deceived. Whenever there is a time of peace, there usually precedes a war. And this was truly a war in the school. Teachers and students began to take sides. It was Felecia against the administration, but I never wanted that. It's just that the cry of the students, their parents, and the community was too loud to ignore. God had something that He wanted to do there, and it stirred up the demonic forces of racism and bigotry.

There were many people who actually believed that this school was not racist, and all this attention was unnecessary. Well, if people don't think that schools and Districts aren't racist, they are sadly mistaken. The effects of it are ever present. When an institution or organization produces low results for minority students; when it has a low number of minority educators; when it readily suspends and expels minority students at disproportionate numbers, then racism is present! The only way to defeat this evil is to bind the strongman and plunder his goods. The matter is so much deeper than what we see. Believers in Christ overcome this strongman through prayers and intercessions; but God also gives grace, power, and mercy to individuals to be at the forefront of this change. That's why it is ever so important that God's people remain present in the affairs of the world. If the godly are in charge, the people prosper; but when the wicked rule, there is distress. We must never become delusional in thinking that politics, education, the law, and other important social aspects are completely separate from the Church. No, we are the Church, and we must be active in the systems. Wherever we are, wherever God has us stationed, we are obligated to perform His perfect will in that domain. If we choose to hide behind the church pews and the altar's pulpit, then we are like cowards, too afraid of what's going on outside. Our conflicts are God's opportunities to affect His kingdom in the earth.

There's going to come a time when the people of God are going to demand that the school system re-establish theocracy in education. God's people are ever present, and they are tired of the degradation of the public schools. Either they will remove their children from the system and place them in private schools to a greater degree, or they will force lawmakers to alter the policies that go against God's Word. Just as one person pushed to have prayer removed from school, so another can push to bring it back. If a law is created and it damages the people, the people have a right to DEMAND change. There are more of us than people realize. But the enemy pumps fear in our minds, and we become fretful of speaking out; yet when there are more for us than against us, whom shall we fear? In case people do not understand it, our voice is our most powerful weapon. When we speak the Word of God, we will definitely attract opposition, but we also receive the favor of God. We must not keep silent about matters that affect our children, our communities, our society, our states, and our country. God is watching, and He is searching for those who will complete His will. We cannot be ignorant of this. For in the day that He visits us, He will know whether or not we have done what He required of us. You will have to give an account for what you do or don't do. We must be ready for this visitation. We must be prepared to stand up when the time comes for us to do so.

It is not a sin to be involved in the affairs of society. It becomes a sin when we only focus on that and neglect the work of God. Not all of us are called to be prophets or pastors or teachers; some of us are called to be politicians and government officials. When we stay in the perfect will of God and exercise our divine authority in the earth, God will protect us. He protected me that entire time in 2008. I had barely made the "permanent status" deadline when I sent out my first email to the staff. If this incident had occurred before March 15, 2008, I surely would have been terminated because I had less than two years under my belt. (Tenure is given to teachers who have two solid years of service in the District.) But everything happened in almost this perfect sequence. That's why I knew God was in it. Even when my colleagues turned their back on me, I had to stay focused on what God was doing and the change that was happening as a result of our efforts. It was hard. It was stressful. It made me cry a lot. But it was necessary. The grace of God made it "doable" for me. And I was going to need it more and more, especially as things intensified.

Although there were many who expressed real anger about this exposure, there were teachers who really did sympathize with my efforts. While so many of them felt I had damaged the school, others understood what I was really trying to do.

From:
To:          Felecia Killings
Date:        Wendnesday - April 16, 2008
Subject:     I applaud you for your effort

Felecia,

I know that we do not know another very well, but I wanted to commend you for your tireless effort and support for our students. After learning more and more about the events of the last few weeks, I have come to realize how this campus can benefit from the coalition you have helped to form. I felt it necesary to teach my students about the three-edged sides of truth and discuss this openly in my class of seniors. It would be a great learning and life changing experience to have a more open dialogue in my classes, so I invite your committee to speak to my classes when they have time. I would also like to volunteer in assisting or participating with this group. I have always believed in building bridges, not just by tolerance, but by understanding and acceptance of one another for our similarities and differences.

* * *

From:
To:          FeleciaK@fsusd.k12.ca.us
Date:        4/19/08 9:27AM
Subject:     Coalition

Good Morning Felecia,

Thanks, again, for taking the lead on the many issues (Diversity, Racism, Sexual Orientation, etc.) that are currently in the face of our students and staff. For what it's worth, I thnk you and the students are doing an awesome job.

Yesterday at lunch I didn't have the opportunity to fully convey my message to you...

I've been working with students on these issues for about then years with various clubs (Students for Social Justice, Gay-Straight Alliance, PeaceJam) but felt that the students' activities had never caught fire. My philosophy has been that I would create the structure and the safety for their activities/actions but that they were the ones who needed to supply the energy and creativity.

It is in that context that I have not been present during the Coalition meetings. I truly believe that the students will best accomplish their/our goals with as little input from me as necessary.

I do appreciate that you are closer to the process than I. I will accept your guidance as to whether my physical presence is an asset to the Coalition (I know that I'm welcome — that's never been in doubt).

Please keep me in mind.

Peace,

\* \* \*

Much of the staff members by April 17th were so upset at things, and really blamed me for the negative publicity and hostile community responses. It was truly hard to function at this point, but I continued to show up every day so that my kids knew that I was there for them.

Later that day, I met with the Committee for Minority Affairs, which was a segment of the teachers' union. During that meeting, other teachers had a chance to share what they knew about the situation. One teacher reported at the meeting that the boys were deliberate in their racist acts. Furthermore, it was confirmed that administration had received the teddy bear, but it could not be found anymore. The meeting was held to give the minority teachers an opportunity to speak about the issues in the District without feeling the threats of being reprimanded later. I wish I could say I was impressed with it all, but I hate when people complain in private, and do nothing openly to fix the problem.

After the meeting, I returned home, half expecting to rest from all the drama I encountered. But by 6:00 that evening, I started getting a blast of random text messages that spoke of a possible race riot that was to occur at school the next day. Many of the text messages marked me and my group as targets. I also started receiving several phone calls from parents and students who were receiving the same text messages. (I've always been open with my students and their parents, and many of them had my contact information.) They wanted to know what was going on, and if there was really going to be a race riot the next day. I told them that I had no idea, but if they didn't feel that their child was safe, then do what was in their best interests and keep them at home. One parent contacted the police and also had them call me to get a statement of the threats. There were hundreds of messages sent out, one right after the other, and whether or not the students and parents were truly scared, the next day proved to be the most profound hit to the District.

At this point, my stress level was through the roof. Now my life was being threatened, my kids were being threatened, and we were not receiving any protection or support from administration. On April 18th, as a result of the mass threat messages from the previous evening, over 2,000 students did not show up to school. While I did not have to, I decided to go because I needed to continue to make an appearance for my children's sake. A lot of my group members stayed home because they were really worried about the retaliation. That same day, news reporters were at the school to broadcast what was happening. There were so many parents who did not know what was going on; but when they saw it on the news, they were disturbed and wanted to get their children out of school. That day, the District lost a significant amount of money due to absences—approximately $60,000—and without fail, I was blamed for it. In fact, later that evening, I saw my name on the news, which made it seem like I had told students to stay home in an act of protest. The reporter had taken a picture of a student's cell phone, which said something about me and my group; and in the context of that report, made me look like I was the one stirring things up.

While at work, one of the English teachers must have sensed my hurt and frustrations. She came in my class to see how I was doing. I told her that this was too much to deal with, but that I was okay. Other teachers were completely oblivious to everything, and had no idea why their students were not in class. To address these concerns, the administration held an impromptu staff meeting after school. I thought about going, but I refused because I knew that they would not tell the truth about the entire situation. Too many of them thought it was a stupid joke or prank used to exploit the entire situation. But what they didn't know was that there was a real fear, especially amongst my kids and me. Although we knew that no one would physically harm us on *that* day, we still were concerned that people would do something once everyone returned. I couldn't stand to look at the administration again, so I opted not to appear at the meeting. I knew it would probably get me in trouble later, but at that time, I didn't care. For all I knew, they could have fired me, and I wouldn't have complained at all. I was sick of that place.

When I didn't show up to the meeting, some teachers began to question the stories that administration had shared. In their minds, if things were working so well between me and the administration, then I wouldn't have had a problem attending that meeting, or even defending them at the community forum. Almost instantly, some staff members' perceptions of things began to change. The tide of administrative approval was beginning to shift, and a couple of teachers wanted to know the truth.

Dearest Felecia,

I am giving you my personal eamil account. From this point forward, email me to this address. I have a few additional questions. I can't thank you enough for the detailed information that you gave me.

1. **What students witnessed the situation on Thursday?** I am especially interested in finding the students that witnessed the situation with the **TEDDY BEAR on Friday.** Do you know of a !\_\_\_\_\_that witnessed it. .\_\_\_\_. didn't know the last name of the student. The only name I have at this point is !_____ It would be great if I\_\_\_\_ would come and talk to me. If you have a lunch meeting with your students, I am not available. I am a department lunch. If \_\_\_\_. **comes to your room during lunch, it is REALLY important that she talk to me. I need to know the facts from students.**

2. You mentioned Pastor Killings on April 9th. **Is he related to you?** Is he the pastor of St. Stephens Church.

3. From your meetings with the **NAACP,** do they know about the meetings with Nicole and her mother on Monday about the bear. Why isn't the press leading stories on the gaps in information from the students and the administration. **It seems like the press has been very positive on the administration side of this story.**

4. I believe some students have received threats (maybe even death treats). **Do you know the names of the students?**

5. **I heard that some students have pictures from cell phones of the incident.** Is that true? I am assuming not because I believe they would have surfaced by this time if there were.

I have had a long talk with _____ and she is very upset about the events. She brought up at the meeting on Friday about a Monday meeting with a parent and student on Monday. No one commented on it. She wants to speak out but felt unable to when no one said anything after her comment at the meeting.

I have had a long talk with '_____ She has been upset since Monday, April 7th when she wrote her 2nd referral of the year. **It had to do with a student making fun of the incidents of Friday and discussed the teddy bear.** I heard about the situation at lunch from \_\_\_\_ on that day. That was the same day that the email was sent out from you. **One student,** i_____, **was really upset and almost crying in class.** \_\_\_\_ believes she witnessed it. '\_\_\_\_ is going to talk to the student to today to find out exactly what she knows.

I also went with my department (\_\_\_\_\_, \_\_\_\_\_, _____ ) to drinks after the meeting on Friday. I was VERY open and upset about not getting the whole truth. I know that **I**\_\_\_\_y\_\_\_ and \_\_\_\_are in complete support of you.

'\_\_\_\_ **was confronted today by** \_\_\_ , \_\_\_ was concerned that _____ was going to have something on the broadcast about the incident. She wanted to make sure that NOTHING was said in the broadcast about FRIDAY. \_\_\_ hadn't read her email so she didn't even know there wasn't going to be a broadcast. \_\_\_\_ felt like '\_\_\_was making her a "spy" for her about \_\_\_\_\_! broadcast.

If you know of ANY students that have facts about the situation, please send them to me ASAP.

Love always,

_____

Another thing: Do you have the information on the ed code that you refer to in your details of the facts? Do you know the number of the ed code that refers to a 3-day suspension for what had happened. If you have copies of things, I have a copy machine in my room and I can make copies.

### My reply to her:

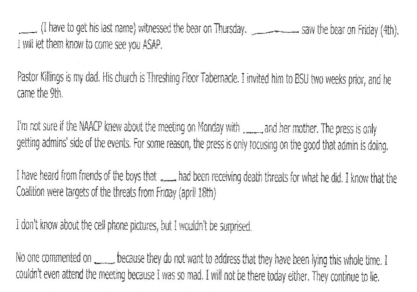

____ (I have to get his last name) witnessed the bear on Thursday. _____ saw the bear on Friday (4th). I will let them know to come see you ASAP.

Pastor Killings is my dad. His church is Threshing Floor Tabernacle. I invited him to BSU two weeks prior, and he came the 9th.

I'm not sure if the NAACP knew about the meeting on Monday with ____ and her mother. The press is only getting admins' side of the events. For some reason, the press is only focusing on the good that admin is doing.

I have heard from friends of the boys that ____ had been receiving death threats for what he did. I know that the Coalition were targets of the threats from Friday (april 18th)

I don't know about the cell phone pictures, but I wouldn't be surprised.

No one commented on ____ because they do not want to address that they have been lying this whole time. I couldn't even attend the meeting because I was so mad. I will not be there today either. They continue to lie.

When this questioning teacher asked me why I did not attend the meeting, I told her that I wasn't interested in hearing their lies anymore. In addition to that, I was emotionally drained; and having my life threatened was no help either. I lost so much in all this, and it seemed like no one was there to help or support me. In fact, the only help I received was "secret" help. Teachers would tell me that they applauded my efforts; but when push came to shove, when the time came for them to publicly voice their support for me, they wouldn't give it because they were too afraid of the backlash. I was sick of it all. I thought about quitting, and never returning to this place. But the idea of giving up on my students at such a critical time threw those notions out the door.

Although nothing happened the day of the threats, my kids and I were still very nervous and anxious on campus. The rest of that week was spent trying to defuse the threats that came on the 17th. Gillespie-Oss, after returning from her small break, sent out an email to the staff to reassure us and the students that we were safe.

From:
To:          rhsgw@fsusd.k12.ca.us
Date:        4/20/08 4.43PM
Subject:     Monday

Fellow Mustangs-
Thank you for your continued strength. I have contacted families trying to find out if anytthing is predicted/planned for tomorrow-- they haven't heard anything. Our students need to be reassured that they are safe and that this event doesn't define RHS. I will be in the staff lounge tomorrow morning at 7:45 to provide any answers and information. Additionally, we will have a faculty meeting tomorrow morning after school (not mandatory) to debrief and plan for the remainder of the year.

Let's discuss on what we do best--educating our students. Please hold on to all good things that we have done--let's continue to be one, the RHS Mustangs!

* * *

TEACHERS PLEASE READ THE FOLLOWING STATEMENT TO YOUR FIRST PERIOD CLASS ON MONDAY.

Dear Students:
Last Friday numerous rumors were spread by email, text, and myspace regarding possible violence at Rodriguez. When we heard these rumors we moved to make sure that the campus was safe. Extra police officers were on campus, district office people were here, and teachers and administrators were out keeping students safe.

Students, it is very important for you to know that we found NO evidence that any event was planned for Rodriguez. Students who were in school on Friday were safe. If you do hear of any possible problems, the responsible thing to do is to tell one of your teachers, counselors, or administrators. Please don't be a part of spreading rumors.

What happened on Friday was a perfect example of the negative consequences of rumor spreading.

Truth is, we weren't safe. Sure, we could have been safe from physical harm on campus, but we were not protected from the threats, the rumors, and the backlash that came our way. My group was ridiculed and belittled by their peers and teachers because they were the ones who spoke at the Board meeting; but somehow, this was "safe."

On April 21st, I received a note in my mailbox that read "Just Walk Away." When I first saw it, I immediately interpreted it as someone telling me to leave the school or leave the situation alone. Even though the true intent of the letter was later cleared, it came at an awkward time. When things are that bad and that hostile, it is so easy to interpret that statement in the worst possible way. A copy of the note and another teacher's response is provided below.

That same day, the school newspaper published two articles about hatred, the Confederate flag, and intolerance. Teachers were still so desperate to find out what really had happened; and even though administration had told them some things, questions still hung in the air. To address this, the principal sent out a chronological report to the staff because so many were confused by it all.

## Rodriguez High School Chronology of Events

**April 4**
7:45 am-two students were observed driving recklessly in the student parking lot and waving a confederate flag. AP _____ chased down the truck and stopped the students. Students were cited by FFPD, assigned Saturday School and placed on a strict Senior Contract.

**April 10**
7:00 pm-Ms Killings, Rodriguez High School students and parents spoke at the Board meeting.
10:00 pm-i_____ called _____ and left a message with the information shared at the Board meeting

**April 11**
7:00 am-RHS Administration, _____ and _____ met with a group of staff and RHS students concerning the incidents reported at the Board meeting. Student focus groups, now known as the RHS Coalition, were organized. In addition, counselors were made available for concerned students.
7:00 am - As a result of the bear reference made at the board meeting, administration immediately reopened the investigation. A review of the cameras—**this time beginning with April 3rd**—confirmed the incident reported at the April 10th Board meeting. The two students were given a severe disciplinary action for their involvement in the April 3rd incident.
12:30 pm- During lunch, _____, Felecia Killings, and the Coalition made a presentation in the main quad.
3:00 pm – Rodriguez students, Administration, and many staff members gathered again in the main quad.

**April 16th**
7:00 pm – Town Hall meeting facilitated by the NAACP.

**April 17th**
6:30 pm – Rumors about a possible riot began to spread via text messages and My Space. FF Police Department contacted school officials and measures were taken to ensure student and staff safety.

**April 18th**
7:00 am -
administration and the Fairfield Police Department developed a plan to ensure the safety of Rodriguez students and staff.
3:00 pm – School-wide staff meeting and debriefing.

**April 21st**
7:45 am – Staff briefing
3:00 pm – Staff meeting

Witnessing this chaos (the threats, the rumors, and the lies) had finally taken its toll on me. No staff had heard from me since April 7th, and I felt like it was time to finally say something again. By Monday of the following week, April 23rd, I broke my public silence and sent an email out to the staff. I was fed up with the blame and backlash. I needed a lot of this mess to come to order, and the best way to do that was to answer the questions that so many had in the first place. In addition to that, I was sick of the constant threats that my group and I received, and no one was doing anything about it because they all considered it a joke or childish rumors. (Even after the principal was told by other teachers that they feared for my safety at the school, the principal still did nothing for me. But I guess that was to be expected.) The email attached below is the one I sent to staff in order to address their concerns. In addition to this email, I provided a detailed Chronology Report, which filled in all the information that the principal's outline lacked.

>>> Felecia Killings 4/23/2008 1:55 PM >>>
Good afternoon,

It has come to my attention by many that portions of the staff believe that the situation at RHS is the fault of me and my Coalition group. I have received notes in my mail box telling me in bold, capital letters to "JUST WALK AWAY" with a scripture reference underneath it. The person who sent this note did not leave a name, and that anonymity is very disturbing to me. I don't know the intentions for giving that note, but with circumstances as they are, I am troubled by it. There is so much dialogue about us "getting over it" and "moving on,"which is what needs to happen; yet the issues are not completely settled, and that makes it difficult to "move on." My Coalition is not interested in festering anomosity among the student body; neither is it interested in creating more tension. But the students are hurting. I am hurting, and anonymous notes in my mail box seem aimed at intimidating me. How do we teach tolerance to our kids when a teacher receives intolerable notes and comments? My kids (and for clarification, I mean the students I work with) are willing and ready to help bring healing to this school. We would like to know that we can get the support that we need and will not receive intimidating words or notes.

Many of you have had questions about the events of each day beginning with April 4th. Attach you will find a report from me. It explains what happened on each day, giving the reasons and purposes for which I sent the first email, and why students, parents, and I went to the school board. The chronology shows how the media got involved, and particularly where the Coaliton and I are at today. Included are some emails, but names have been ommitted. They are there to simply show how the progression of events emerged as a result of them.

38    LIGHT FOR MY PATH for Teachers

## JUST WALK AWAY

*"But I tell you, Do not resist an evil person.*
*If someone strikes you on the right cheek,*
*turn to him the other also."*

MATTHEW 5:39

---

Lord, why is it that I always think it is the weak who are bullied? That is wrong! The Bible specifically tells us to turn the other cheek. It takes a strong individual to resist the temptation to retaliate while being picked on. I think of Jesus being led down the street while bullies called His name. And what did He do? He asked You to forgive them! Lord, I pray for the bullies who don't know how to socialize. I've never met a happy bully. Lord, I pray for the tormented who might dread coming to school. I pray they maintain happiness always. I pray for myself that I may be the kind of teacher who defuses these difficult situations. I desire a happy environment for learning.

**From:**
**To:**       Felecia Killings
**Date:**      4/23/08 2:08PM
**Subject:**   Re: Good afternoon

I received a note too I believe..was it on a green paper? I think it was put in everyone's boxes. I support your efforts towards healing and reconciliation. I spoke with my students in several classes about the incidents and learned that many students feel discriminated against on a daily basis. Especially regarding discipline. I told them that they are free to talk to me if they have any issues and/or feel that they are ebeing unfairly chastised. It is wrong if some students have more severe consequences than others! We also talked about the need to let people know how we feel before it all builds up and we boil over. I hope that we can all use these experiences to foster open understanding, communication, and respect among students and faculty. I think you are doing a noble and courageous thing and that you did a great job of sharing your feelings with the staff. Let me know if there is anything I can do to help.

Thank you for all your hard work

# A chronology of events as told by Felecia Killings

**April 4<sup>th</sup>**—incident in student parking lot occurred. No staff made aware of it. Witnessed by students.

**April 7<sup>th</sup>**—_____, _____, _____ and three or four other girls tell me of the incident at 12:30pm. Details of what they said were told in my email to staff:

Dear RHS,

Some of my African American students approached me today and informed me of an incident that occurred last Friday in the student parking lot. This incident happened before school began, and it is especially disturbing to me and this group. Last Friday was the anniversary of the assassination of Dr. King. While in the student lot, a young man took his confederate flag out of his car, placed it on the antena, and proceeded to drive recklessly around with it. While doing so, he shouted out "white power" with a number of my students listening. Many of my students are shaken by this event, especially since they felt like he did not receive the proper repercussions (and to our understanding, it was a Saturday school). It seems like this issue is not being addressed properly, and not doing so makes it appear like there is little concern for my kids. To many, this is threat because of what the flag represents. The parents of these students are highly upset with what took place, and as a teacher, I am thoroughly offended because I have witnessed some of the same incidents (and sayings) among students, and they go unchecked.

I received both negative and positive emails about it:

Thank you for bringing this to everyone's attention. There is a group of obnoxious skin-head types on campus-- and they tend to be sneaky and not get the proper punishment. I was not aware of the incident, but we cannot tolerate it. I have a feeling the flag kid is someone you had dealings with last year.

That is very disturbing! I had not heard about the incident but I am glad you called it to our attention. Hopefully we can all work together to make this campus a safe and harmonious environment for teachers and students alike. The racial tension definitely needs to be addressed.

2 questions. 1. Why are you writing this to the faculty. You should go directly to the administrator in charge and get his/her information about what happened, not the kids. 2. Who do you mean when you say "my kids"

This is horrible incidence of racism - but it is also a teachable moment. Perhaps the student in question could do a research project on the confederate flag and maybe even educate everyone during the weekly video about why the confederate flag is considered disrespectful to the African American community. I agree that some apology is in order.

Well said, Felecia. I totally agree!

I heard about this incident as well. I wasn't aware that it was even addressed by the administration. It is something that needs to be addressed further than just a Saturday school.

Do you know which admin handled it?

Also, can you please find a (tactful!) yet public way to address Bob Pickett's email....it's exactly his kind of "matter of fact" attitude that makes one group feel superior.

Hi,
I am saddened to hear of this incident. The under-reaction to it is worse. I don't understand why someone would ask why you'd bring it to the entire school's attention - this place is run like that - we're a team. Also, it is clear who "my" kids are... I am mystified.

which confederate flag was it? there were several, such as the "STARS AND BARS' variety that changed during the Civil War , 1861 to 1865, and stood for the civilian government of the South , or the one that has the stars shown in a southern cross pattern and was used by the military in battle from late 1862 to the end of the war in April of 1865?

Felecia,
Let me know how I can help and thank you for bringing it to the attention of the staff. Racial work is often hard for some people and they often react in a defensive way. I will gladly talk to ____ if you would like.

There are more. After sending the email, I was reprimanded        ____ on April 7:

Felecia-
I wish you had spoken with me first before sending this email out. Like many situations this one evolved throughout the course of the day and with student talk/rumors. Kristen Witt was right there in the parking lot-- she immediately stopped the students and brought them in. We discipline, advocate, and support students consistently. Please don't question our discipline to the whole staff- it undermines my position. Unfortunatley,some of what was reported to you by students and that you shared with staff isn't accurate. If you think I handeld this poorly please come by and we will discuss it. Additionally, if you have students you are worried about we can meet them and provide support.

____

She then sent an email out to the staff in reply to mine:

Dear Mustangs-
This was an unfortunate situation that RHS administration did not take lightly; however, like many other situations in high school the story has changed when it passed from student to student. Kristen Witt was in the parking lot when these students began to fly the confederate flag. She stopped them and brought them into the office. Student consequences were appropriate according to district policy, ed. code, and the Constitution.

____

Immediately after the reprimand, I sent out the following email to staff:

I have to apologize for publicly undermining the authority of admin. for that was never my intention. I simply wanted to address an issue that has been so concerning the students and myself. So often I read emails from others about what has bothered them, and I thought that this was a venue for us to discuss this.

After school, I learned that there was a bear and a noose involved.

After school, L____ and her mother had a meeting with ____. They brought up the bear. They were told that the bear was a rumor. No investigation went forth.

**April 8th**—students and staff talking about the incident; many were upset; staff was still learning about the incident. At the staff meeting, ____ recognized me for my work with the step team. ____ recognized me for informing the staff on the incident. She mentioned that the apology email was "unnecessary" but showed professionalism on my part. During staff meeting, ____ asked me to join the planning team to discuss what we could do. I agreed. (Just a note, my trust factor with admin was not high.)

**April 9th**—Pastor Killings comes to speak to the Black student Union about the incident and what they can do about it. Students mention that they want to write letters to ____. Others were still trying to get the details of the situation. I formed the Coalition on this day to address the injustice. Parents are making constant communication—they are being told there was nothing that ____ could do—it was his freedom of speech; also they are bringing up the bear—it was still being denied.

**April 10th**—I'm frustrated because the students who did the incident still have the Saturday school. My initial plan was to write the Board members; but I found out on the district website that there was a meeting at 7:00pm. I also located the students'/parents' rights handbook online. I made a copy of the rights, which has some portions of ed code in it. Students at minimum should have received a 3-day suspension for harassment. (This contradicted ＿＿'s email that the punishment was according to ed code.) I informed my students about the Board meeting and told them I would be there and to let their parents know also. During 5th period, I talked to a reported from Fox 40 news and one from the Daily Republic. I also received a phone call from a teacher that she had heard about the situation (at another school). After school, ＿＿＿＿＿ came to my class, asked to speak to me in the hallway. She wanted to know if I had been holding a meeting with adults after school hours. She asked did I bring a pastor to speak to these adults. I told her that I held no meetings after school hours. I had a pastor come, but he spoke to my kids at lunch during the BSU meeting. She asked what was the "tone of the meeting?" I told her that the kids want to do something about it. (This is the implication = that I was stirring the student body up to do something wrong and using the school facilities after hours to conduct meetings with the adults/parents.)

At 7:00pm, myself, students and their parents attended the board meeting. We waited almost 3 hours before we could speak (during the "Public Communication" section). Students included Adam McCray, Roman, Shalamar, Tamika Scott, Shalamar's mother Ramona, Nick, Ally, and another parent. ＿＿＿＿ reported to the board that ＿＿ was not doing anything, even after making a number of phone calls. This was the first time the board heard about the incident. The board wanted an immediate investigation.

**April 11th**—I thought I was going to get fired: it was the day after the board meeting. ＿＿＿＿ met with admin, ＿＿＿＿＿ and ＿＿＿＿＿ during 2nd period. He came to me in my class between 8:45 and 9:00 to tell me about his meeting. They (admin and board) wanted to meet with my students who spoke at the board. I told ＿＿＿＿ to tell them that I don't want them speaking to anyone unless I am there. At around 9:45, we met with admin and board. ＿＿ expressed that she did not know about the bear. There was (finally) a full investigation. ＿＿＿＿＿ did not stay in the meeting. The students and myself shared during the meeting how we felt about everything. ＿＿＿＿ asked two important questions:

1. Why did we feel the need to go public?
2. What came to mind when we see the Confederate flag?

I informed them (＿＿＿＿ and ＿＿) that I tried to have it handled in house. I was reprimanded for it. Also, parents have tried desperately to get ＿＿ to do something. They were denied. After the first meeting. The Coalition (still in the office) strategizes with admin to do campus-wide events that address racial hostility. Ideas include class visits, assembly, and rally. THIS is the only reason there were 2 rallies on this day— during lunch and after school. The presence of the superintendent and ＿＿enabled for the full investigation. Admin looked at the tapes, and found that the bear dragging happened also on Thursday, April 3. There were no tape footage (as far as we know) of the bear dragging on April 4th; however, ＿＿＿＿＿＿ witnessed a bear on April 4th. More police on campus because they thought there was a possible riot.

After school, we had the second rally. After the rally (about 4:00pm), some of the Coalition and I met with Daily Republic. At this same time, we hear reports that students will come in their Confederate apparel on Monday. We inform＿＿of it.

district website that there was a meeting at 7:00pm. I also located the students'/parents' rights handbook online. I made a copy of the rights, which has some portions of ed code in it. Students at minimum should have received a 3-day suspension for harassment. (This contradicted _____'s email that the punishment was according to ed code.) I informed my students about the Board meeting and told them I would be there and to let their parents know also. During $5^{th}$ period, I talked to a reported from Fox 40 news and one from the Daily Republic. I also received a phone call from a teacher that she had heard about the situation (at another school). After school, _____ came to my class, asked to speak to me in the hallway. She wanted to know if I had been holding a meeting with adults after school hours. She asked did I bring a pastor to speak to these adults. I told her that I held no meetings after school hours. I had a pastor come, but he spoke to my kids at lunch during the BSU meeting. She asked what was the "tone of the meeting?" I told her that the kids want to do something about it. (This is the implication = that I was stirring the student body up to do something wrong and using the school facilities after hours to conduct meetings with the adults/parents.)

At 7:00pm, myself, students and their parents attended the board meeting. We waited almost 3 hours before we could speak (during the "Public Communication" section). Students included Adam McCray, Roman, Shalamar, Tamika Scott, Shalamar's mother Ramona, Nick, Ally, and another parent. _____ reported to the board that ____ was not doing anything, even after making a number of phone calls. This was the first time the board heard about the incident. The board wanted an immediate investigation.

**April $11^{th}$**—I thought I was going to get fired; it was the day after the board meeting. _____ met with admin, _____ and _____ during $2^{nd}$ period. He came to me in my class between 8:45 and 9:00 to tell me about his meeting. They (admin and board) wanted to meet with my students who spoke at the board. I told _____ to tell them that I don't want them speaking to anyone unless I am there. At around 9:45, we met with admin and board. ____ expressed that she did not know about the bear. There was (finally) a full investigation. _____ did not stay in the meeting. The students and myself shared during the meeting how we felt about everything. _____ asked two important questions:

A parent informed me that '_____ (president of NAACP) wanted to meet with me and my kids.

April $12^{th}$—I met with Coalition leaders. Prepare for NAACP meeting on the $13^{th}$. Organize school events. The Daily Republic prints about the incident, but not the interviews with myself and my kids.

April $13^{th}$—Coalition and I along with parents and community leaders (about 45 total) met with NAACP. They wanted to know what happened because they were scheduled to meet with district on $14^{th}$ (Monday). The NAACP got two eyewitness accounts.

April $14^{th}$—At school. The Coalition and I make class visits to talk about the incident, who we are, and our stand against discrimination. Admin accompanies us ( '. At 11:00am, ____ meets with NAACP and district. She asked me to attend. I declined because I wanted to stay with my kids. That morning, we gave a list of school-wide

At 5:00, I met with the Committee for Minority Affairs (union reps). I will not hold any meetings with admin without my rep present. In this meeting, it was confirmed from a reliable source that ___ and his girlfriend gave ___ the bear. It was also confirmed that the boys, mostly ___, were deliberate in their racist acts. Around 6:00, I received several text messages about a possible race riot. My Coalition and myself were targets. Parents called me because they were not aware of the situation. They also wanted to know if it was ok to bring their children to school. I spoke to an officer and gave a statement on what the text messages were reading.

April 18th—Threat Day. More than 2,000 students do not show up for school. Students were in fear. We (the school) were being told to "have a happy day." I'm angry over that. Parents are trying to call the office to find out what was going on. They were watching the news. Parents are not getting any replies from the office. One parent saw the phone

off the hook. Because parents are not getting responses, they are coming to pick their children up. After school, there was a staff meeting. I did not attend because I knew that admin would not tell the whole story. At this point, I am SOO mad.

April 19th—nothing happens. Students and I are trying to cope with Friday's incident.

April 20th—nothing happens. Students and I prepare for this week.

April 21st—___ comes to me during 1st. She hopes that I will build a trust with admin again. She sends out a chronology of the events, which are lacking vital information. I construct a report on what the events truly are. A student (during 1st period) informs me that ___ gave admin the bear on Wed. April 16th. There is a staff meeting after school today.

This email sparked more conversations among the staff, but it didn't seem to defuse the situation as I hoped.

**From:**
**To:**        Felecia Killings
**Date:**      4/24/08 9:38AM
**Subject:**   In regards to recent incidents

As a history teacher I find that differing versions of the same events to be very compelling. With that said I do not want to take any sides and make any judgements. I do applaud your courage to take on the system. I do recognize that if there are serious inconsistencies in the use of suspencions and expulsions, that should be looked at and resolved. As a history teacher, my biggest and favorite unit consists of the constitution, the bill of rights, slavery, the civil war, reconstruction, the harlem renaissance, African American participation in WWI and WWII, the civil rights era, and ends with present day living standards statistics. I fullly support and try to reinforce the positives that are associated with tolerance.

With those things being said, I would like to mention two examples of intolerance that are widespread and largely ignored. African American students routinely refer to each other with the "n" word in the classroom and in the hallways, and at assemblies. I understand that there are different types of speech used, and it does not bother me if this type of word is used outside of professional areas. For example around friends or at home. My problem with the use of the "n" word is that it is an exclusionary word, and has very racist origins. Blacks are allowed to use it, but other races are strongly encouraged not to. Secondly, and this is an issue that students of all races are guilty of, is the use of the word "gay" to describe something that students do not like and find lame. I will find out when the next planning team meeting is and voice these concerns myself because it has been bothering me.

Am I sending you this email to you in private because I do not want to be a target for either positive or negative feedback. In conclusion, I hope these last few weeks will end in constructive rather than destructive decisions.

**From:**
**To:**        Killings, Felecia
**Date:**      4/23/08 2:15PM
**Subject:**   Re: Good afternoon

Hi Felecia,
I think you have more courage, strength, and integrity than many. I support you and the coalition. I am sorry to say that I don't have after school time due to obligations to my daughter. If I can help, let me know. The person who placed the note in your box acted inappropriately.

Keeping you in my prayers,

**From:**
**To:**          Killings, Felecia
**Date:**        4/24/08 10:29AM
**Subject:**     Re: Good afternoon

I will relay the message to _____ . She is staying abreast of our current situation and is very proud of you, too!


>>> Felecia Killings 4/24/2008 10:13 AM >>>
Thank you so much, _____ .Words of encouragement are so helpful during this time. Please tell _____ she has no idea how much I miss her.

>>>          04/24/08 8:30 AM >>>
Felicia, let me take this opportunity to tell you how glad I am that you are here — for everything you do — and that I hope you are happy here and stay for a long, long time.

In any organization, there is always a small group of small thinkers. Try and not let them get you down.

This whole situation can make us stronger, in the long run, but we need to keep shining a light on it.

The diversity we have at this school, while not unique, is rare, especially as when compared with high schools throughout the country. I am often amazed at how well different peoples DO get along around here.

But when problems occur, we need to deal with them. Moreover, we need to be proactive, to keep them from reoccurring.

Hang in there and keep up the good work!

PS: _____ says "Hi!"

In all the hurt and turmoil that I and my kids were dealing with, the boys and their families were also traumatized by the administration's inactions. I will say this again: It was not what the boys did on campus that brought up the strife. It was the lack of proper administrative action that resulted in this mess. Had Gillespie-Oss done what she was supposed to do, and not overturn the suspension that the other assistant principal issued, then no one would have taken issue with this matter. At least the student body would know that this kind of behavior would never be tolerated. But it seemed like the best thing for her to do was to shift blame on others for the mistakes she made. One of the boys' mother (who participated in the incident) published a "Letter to the Editor" in the

*Daily Republic* in hopes to share what she believed happened, and quite possibly to defuse this heinous situation.

I cannot imagine the hell she and her family went through, and I would never wish any harm on them. I would never tell my children or anyone to violently retaliate against those who do wrong. God is not in that. Had the information that she presented in this article been articulated to the community, especially at the church forum, perhaps the outcome could have turned out differently. People, this is what happens when there is no communication and resistance from others to listen to each other. Whether or not the boys' actions in the parking lot were done with negative racial intentions or not is something that I cannot judge. That is between them and God. But neither do I ignore what the students heard and saw on that fateful day on April 4, 2008. Her article is on the following page.

The mother was right in a lot of things: There was no substantial evidence to "prove" that their actions warranted expulsion. And why you ask? Because the District had no hate crime policy to base their actions on. And just because the police could not find evidence of what was reported does not invalidate what so many students witnessed. Clearly, this entire incident was bigger than what the boys did. It centered on an entire system and organization because it was their responsibility to provide anti-discrimination policies to protect everyone. But they had nothing! The mother was also right in stating that the school should be at fault for the incidents as well, for it was their responsibility to keep all students safe. Whether or not this mother developed animosity towards me for my participation in bringing this to the open, I would assure her that this was not an attempt to "play the race card" or "call racial discrimination at every

## LETTERS TO THE EDITOR

# Mother refutes 'racial incidents'

In reference to the highly publicized and misinterpreted incidents now known throughout the community as "racial incidents" at Rodriguez High School, I can no longer stand back and watch this travesty without voicing the truth.

I am the mother of one of the boys involved. The information I am going to provide you is what actually happened and what the Fairfield-Suisun School District hasn't told you or hasn't been truthful about.

The incidents happened April 3 and 4, and were immediately misinterpreted as some sort of hate crime. But the incidents had absolutely nothing to do with race and were not intended at anyone in particular. The boys were showing off and being irresponsible.

Unfortunately, due to the lack of proper investigation by the school administration and district and the intimidation by some who wish to claim racial discrimination at every opportunity, the incidents were labeled incorrectly.

They have become the platform for underlying racial discrimination issues at Rodriguez High that need the community's attention but have been overlooked and not addressed properly. My son, family and friends have had to suffer the consequences.

I want to set the record straight, and the following is the truth regarding the incident you may not be aware of.

■ The teddy bear was light brown, not black.

■ It was dragged by a yellow tow strap, not a noose.

■ No one involved yelled, "White Power."

■ The boys and the principal did not know it was the anniversary of Martin Luther King Jr.'s death.

■ The boys and other students dragged or ripped apart different stuffed animals during the year as a means of having fun that meant nothing racially.

■ Fairfield police conducted an investigation and found there was no evidence supporting any type of hate crime.

■ All reports in the Daily Republic indicating the boys had been expelled were false, such as reported by Interim Superintendent Steve Goldstone.

It is also very important to note there was a hearing June 11 involving a panel appointed by the district, the students involved and witnesses. The panel dropped the expulsion charges of the hate crime by the boys due to "no findings of the actions by the boys were expellable.

The evidence produced was not significant to indicate the boys acted in a racially motivated manner."

Students who testified at the hearing said the boys involved did not use any derogatory terms or act maliciously toward any race.

The misinterpretation and publicity of these incidents have had a tremendous effect on our lives. My son was suspended from school, had to graduate from an independent study program, sold his truck, received death threats, moved out of town for his safety and quit his job.

In addition to all of this, it has been a financial hardship to defend my son, his reputation and future.

I hope writing this will somehow open eyes that have been closed to the facts and help to recognize the injustice that has occurred. I find it also important to note the school district must recognize its fault in these incidents to help prevent this type of travesty from happening again.

**Brenda Zanassi**
*Fairfield*

opportunity." This was bigger than what her son did. It spoke of the injustices, not at his hands, but at the system's hands. It's easy to point the finger at everyone else, but ultimately the responsibility lies on all of us, for it was our job as adults and educators to train these children in the way that they should go. I cannot emphasize enough how powerful it would have been had that young man spoke up at the community forum. Humility and repentance (from all those who did wrong) would have settled the wave of dissention that divided this city.

Unfortunately, because of the backlash, a lot of members from the Coalition dropped their attendance. Apparently, the fire got too hot for them. Nearly everyone abandoned the Coalition except for my faithful heroes, and that is the only reason I gave them credit in this book. Anyone can stand with you when it seems like favor is all over you. But it takes a special group of people to be with you when all hell is breaking loose.

It seemed like because favor shifted towards the principal, there was no need to keep the promises made to me and my group prior to all these major events. We were promised rallies, an assembly, and cultural programs and activities on April 11th; but we only received two impromptu rallies at that time. After that, there was nothing. I think that was the turning point for me. I had been emotionally low for long enough. I had been beaten to the brim by the abusive remarks of hateful students and staff. And then, like a burst of energy erupting in my soul, I got this zest or power to get back up and fight even more. Pastor Rod Parsley once said that "anger has movement;" and sometimes when you get mad enough about a situation, you start to move. That's what happened to me. I knew that God was not done with this entire situation. He had more for us to do, and so I became active again.

I started contacting union representatives, the NAACP, and District officials to inform them of the broken promises made to us. Once again, my voice became my weapon, and there was no way I was going down without a fight. My kids and I started holding meetings with them to discuss what could be done to end that school year positively. I told them that while we were grateful for the two rallies that we had on the April 11th, it was not enough. Two rallies did not solve the problem; they bandaged it. When I told them that our promises were not fulfilled, the pressure was on once again. The Director of Secondary Education asked me one simple question: "Felecia, what do you and your group want?" I gave her the list, and she made it happen. Not only did she get active, but my union representative emailed the principal as well.

**From:**
**To:**
**Date:**       5/8/08 7:40AM
**Subject:**     Re: Follow up

Thank you for the up date.

I hope that RHS administration and staff brings this to the attention of the school board and public tonight at the School Board meeting as it shows a continuing effort to end any type of racial issue at RHS....

sincerely

>>> '\_\_\_\_\_ _____5/7/2008 2:29:25 PM >>>
A meeting was held on Monday to formulate a plan for Unity week– the week of May 27th. If you would like to meet to discuss any further plans for the future of RHS I am available.

>>> _____5/6/2008 1:06:50 PM >>>
Good Afternoon \_\_\_\_\_ ,

A lot of things have been accomplished at RHS to resolve issues that happened a few weeks back.

There are still some loose ends that need to be completed that were promised and have yet to be fulfilled.

Since STAR testing is now over, this would be a good time to finish what was started and to let the process of healing start again and finish this stage before the end of the school year.   It would be such a shame to miss this opportunity since things were promised as part of a healing process and it would be a great to finish those items now.

Questions are being asked concerning the support for a completion of this process and it should be understood that FSUTA is behind getting this accomplished before the end of the school year so it is not left hanging into the next year.   Many teachers and students at your site also agree.

If anyone thinks that this item has disappeared, they need to rethink that. There are some who would like another media event.   That would not necessarily be in RHS's best interest. It would be better if the RHS events were done on site and then reported to the School Board by the participants as an accomplishment and not a media event.

The RHS administration should take the lead on this and allow the teachers and students to have their planned events and let the process come to a full completion.

If this does not happen, then the issue will raise its ugly head again at sometime and then the question will be why the administration did not finish the process they agreed to and let the healing process finish?

An answer to making this happen would be appreciated before Thursday's School Board meeting.

Sincerely,

My babies and I got exactly what we asked for. The last week in May was scheduled to host cultural events that would foster tolerance and acceptance at the school. We called it "Unity Week." It was like a ray of sunshine lighted on us once again. We were determined to end that year on a good note.

**From:**
**To:**
**Date:**        5/9/08 1:35PM
**Subject:**     Poster Contest

Dear Department,

We will be having a Poster Contest for Unity Week. The winner will be used as the poster for the 2nd Annual Unity Week. The entries are due on Friday, May 23rd. It would be great if your students could work on it and submit some. We will announce the winner on Friday, May 30th. Here is the information for the bulletin. You can submit the entries to Felecia or I.

**RHS is sponsoring a Unity Week Poster Contest. The theme of the poster is unity. It should deliver a message of peace, kindness, compassion, or empathy for others. The poster should be saved as a graphic file such as jpg, gif, psd, or png. Deadline for the contest is Friday, May 23rd. The winner will be announced at lunch in the quad on Friday, May 30th and will be the official poster for the 2nd Annual Unity Week.**

When "Unity Week" happened, it was such a success. There were many complements on what took place; and more importantly, the students felt like they were a part of that school change. Teachers were excited again at the work being done, and sure enough the principal got all the credit for it. We had more rallies and assemblies, and the entire school was a part of the events. Members from the School Board also came; and it was a great time for students to get active again in a positive manner.

>>>          ;   , 05/30/08 4:27 PM >>>
I really appreciate everyone pulling together and making this so wonderful. We need to pick a week for fall semester and I would also like to celebrate Day of the Child (I think the international day is June 1st)-- do you all think we could weave it in?

>>> Felecia Killings 5/30/2008 2:28 PM >>>
Hello everybody:

What a great first Unity Week! It was so much fun seeing the end product coming together. We have a poster for next year! The Step team made front cover in the Daily Republic! Diversity Day was a BLAST with the combination of the assembly and the performances. I can only anticipate greater times next year. Thank you for everything.

There was much talk and anticipation of repeating the "tradition" for the following year; but as everyone knows, it did not explode to the degree that it did in 2008.

By the end of the school year, so much had happened that it seemed like there would never be an end in sight. But it did come to a close, and I and my group had much to be proud of. We boldly spoke about issues that others had tried to do also, but failed; we secured cultural activities at the school when there was so much opposition to it; and it all came because we refused to keep silent. Ultimately, the greatest victory that resulted from the entire event was the District's creation of an official Hate Crime Policy. The NAACP was truly helpful in getting this for us, for they were the pressure the District needed in order to address the concerns of the community.

From:
To:           `   .
Date:         5/10/08 10:07PM
Subject:      U S DEPARTMENT OF EDUCATION OFFICE FOR CIVIL RIGHTS INVESTIGATING
FSUSD

PRESS RELEASE

Contact:
Tri-City NAACP Branch President

U S DEPARTMENT OF EDUCATION OFFICE FOR CIVIL RIGHTS INVESTIGATING FSUSD

On May 1, 2008, Tri-City Branch of the National Association for the Advancement of Colored People
(NAACP), filed a complaint with the U.S. Department of Education (Department), Office for Civil Rights
(OCR),against Angelo Rodriguez High School (Rodriguez) in Fairfield, CA and Fairfield Suisun Unified
School District (FSUSD) for their handling of alleged hate crimes that occured at Rodriguez in April 2008.

The branch has been advised in a letter from Charles R. Love, Program Manager that OCR is
investigating, among other issues, whether African American students have been subjected to a hostile
educational environment based on their race, and whether FSUSD District failed to respond appropriately.

Tri-City NAACP has observed that the administration and teachers for FSUSD need to be trained on how
to handle hate crimes. The administration, teachers, and students would benefit from receiving
professional multicultural and racial sensitivity training. It becomes difficult to learn in an environment
where students are threatening other students with bodily harm. Approximately, 2000 students have
already skipped school because of this chain of events.

FSUSD needs a hate crime policy. In light of the Columbine, Virginia Tech and Jena Six incidents
FSUSD should have clear policies and procedures in place to keep our children safe.

Now, this fight was truly over. We knew that it was the District's policies that needed altering; and when we saw that it happened, we celebrated our accomplishments. Through much sacrifice, my babies and I took on a system that was determined to keep a generation down. Not only was the District compelled to create this form, but they also had to develop strategies that addressed the discrepancies in punishments among minority and White students.

# Fairfield-Suisun Unified School District

## NOTICE TO STUDENTS, PARENTS, GUARDIANS, AND TEACHERS: HATE MOTIVATED BEHAVIOR  (BP 5145.9(a))

The Governing Board affirms the right of every student to be protected from hate-motivated behavior. Students demonstrating hate-motivated behavior shall be subject to discipline in accordance with Board policy and administrative procedures.  It is the intent of the Board to promote harmonious relationships that enable students to gain a true understanding of the civil rights and social responsibilities of people in our society.  Behavior or statements that degrade an individual on the basis of his/her race, color, national origin, ethnicity, culture, heritage, gender, sexual orientation, physical/mental attributes, religious beliefs or practices shall not be tolerated. This policy is to be posted in every classroom.

District staff will follow all applicable California Education Code sections, U.S. Department of Education guidelines, California Penal Code sections, and district policies in reporting such instances of hate-motivated behavior as provided by law.

Any student who feels that he/she is a victim of hate-motivated behavior shall immediately contact the principal or designee.  Students demonstrating hate-motivated behavior shall be subject to discipline in accordance with Board policy and administrative procedures.  If any party involved believes that the situation has not been remedied by the principal or designee, he/she may file a complaint in accordance with district complaint procedures, which are to be prominently displayed in every classroom.

Students who are the victims of hate-motivated behavior will have the opportunity to receive counseling, guidance, and support.  The district will also provide required counseling, appropriate sensitivity training, and diversity education for students exhibiting hate-motivated behavior.

The district will provide age-appropriate curriculum/instruction to help promote understanding of and the respect for human rights.  In addition, at the beginning of the school year, students will receive and sign for a copy of the district's policy on hate-motivated behavior.

As I reflect on what we did years ago, I am amazed at all we endured and accomplished. I cannot emphasize enough how much that unique set of individuals taught me. They walked in such wisdom and etiquette. They were astounding. They possessed my heart and my spirit, and they made a change in their school when adults were too afraid to do it. I can only hope that as their leader, they learned as much from me as I did them. They will forever be remembered in my heart. And the work that they completed that year is recorded in God's book of remembrance. To my heroes: *I miss you and love you all.*

# Just When I Thought It was Over
## 2008-2009 School Year, Third Year at RHS

$C$oming back to the high school after such a tumultuous year was exceptionally hard for me. I purposed in my heart that I would do everything in my power to keep my mouth closed and restrict myself to working solely on my teaching and my students' education. I didn't want to be bothered with anyone; neither did I plan on carrying the same torch that I did that previous year. One reason for this attitude was because most of the group I had worked with the previous school year had graduated. I did not want to take the time to work and train a new set of students because that year took so much out of me. It was stressful and unnerving, and I desperately needed to relax.

During this school year, we were fortunate to acquire another African-American teacher. She is what I like to call a fireball. She was fierce. She had this presence of respect as well as authority, and it was clear that she was not one to mess with. I don't recall if she and I had been acquaintances at the beginning of the school year, but for the most part we were good colleagues. She also became a strong support for me during my 2011 criminal case. Before long, we would come to share the same frustrations with the school and its leaders.

Unfortunately my relationship with that current administration had not improved since that previous year. I still had no trust for Gillespie-Oss and her team, and I did not want to be bothered with them. People think that it's easy to be a teacher, but it's not. It's not necessarily the students that give us a hard time, although that can be a factor; but it is more so the workings and politics of the administration that really make our jobs more difficult. That's why we have a union. It's that bad.

At the beginning of the year, Wilson, the same assistant principal that was in the conference meetings with my kids and I, came to my class, basically trying to suppress any "unction" I may have had in stirring up trouble again for that new school year. Whatever her motives in visiting me were, her mere presence signified what I already knew would happen. The administration would do everything in their power to keep me "calm and quiet." I don't know what it is about me that makes people think I just fly off the handle; but I guess it's because I don't take too well to stupid people doing hurtful things to others. To some degree, I can handle personal mistreatment; but when the actions of leaders negatively affect students, I guess I do have a tendency to flip. Whatever the reason, I was hopeful that this year would not have the problems that the previous year contained.

The beginning months of that year went fairly smoothly. I had a great group of students as usual, and I enjoyed that time I had in working with them. Frequently, students and a couple of teachers had asked me why I did not have the Cultural Coalition group or the

Black Student Union like I did the year before. And I told them that it literally drained me, and I really did not want to build that again if I didn't have students working with me who were not truly serious. Although we had no official club, there were plenty of students and teachers who wanted to do something to usher in the cultural activities that we started in 2008. But again, I had no heart to lead it because I knew the outcome would be disastrous. And I was right. There's something "uncomfortable" about possessing the spirit of discernment and prophecy—you are able to see things happen in the spirit before it occurs in the natural. When you try to explain what you know to be true to others, they can't seem to understand because they don't see what you see. And before you know it, you are looked at as the crazy one.

Often times, I would find myself answering to others based on what I would see happen in the spirit. In this case, I knew that if even the discussion of cultural activities emerged once again, and there was not a group present who was like my heroes from before, then any movement would only lead to another time of stress and agony. While I wanted the school to be thriving with fantastic activities, I knew that it would mean more communication between me, the District officials, and school administration. And when you have leaders who are not open to anything remotely related to race, you will experience hell unlike any other. And this is exactly what emerged in February 2009.

By this time, news of what had happened in April 2008 spread like wild fire. It was quite exciting to know that there were others who wanted to take the same zeal from 2008, and transfer that to the new year; but none were willing to take the lead in that effort, that is until the new teacher aforementioned came along. She strongly wanted to pull from the efforts of the previous year, and create an annual Black History Month program that could essentially be a part of the school's culture. When she presented the idea to me to have a Black History Assembly, I thought the idea was fantastic. She told me that she had pitched the idea to the activities coordinator and Gillespie-Oss, but it seemed like she was having a hard time getting them to accept the notion. Whatever their excuse was at the time, it was clear that having an assembly to honor Black History Month was not welcomed.

When she told me of her difficulties, I told her that I would definitely be willing to help her get that program started; but inwardly, I was very apprehensive to get involved. In spite of my feelings, I could not let her engage in this effort alone because I remembered what it was like for me to be the only adult trying to get things going. I had to recall that the whole purpose of bringing to light the issues of racism from 2008 was to jump start cultural programs that fostered tolerance, cultural education, and acceptance. So, rather than "relaxing" for that school year, I made a promise to be there with her to make it happen.

You would think that given all the drama that occurred in 2008 that this principal would be open to doing anything to show others that we were a school where cultural celebrations were welcomed. But again, because she never wanted them in the first place, we should have never expected her to want to continue it again. When I saw how hard they worked against the new teacher for wanting this

Black History program, I told her that we needed to reconnect with the NAACP and the community because their support made things happen for me the previous year.

I immediately contacted the NAACP president and asked if there was something that could be done to help us get this program together. The teacher and I met with the representatives, and informed them of what we wanted to do. For the most part, the NAACP were bewildered as to why Gillespie-Oss had given the new teacher a hard time in the first place given the fact that cultural activities were expected to be a part of the new school culture. In efforts to help us, the representatives agreed to do their part; and because they had been in constant communication with the District's officials, they were able to secure an assembly for the teacher and I to host.

One of the reasons why we really wanted this program was because we knew that if we were able to get this ball rolling for the Black students, then the other ethnic groups would want and demand the same thing. It would have spoken loudly for the school, the principal, and the District had there been openness to cultural diversity. If the school held monthly programs that celebrated each ethnic group and their contributions to society, it would have erased the negative publicity that loomed over the school. But since there was so much rejection to this effort, it made it incredibly difficult to spread this positive feat.

In spite of the constant conflict between Gillespie-Oss, her activities coordinator, and us, we were given the opportunity to host the assembly. Although the event was permitted, there were several stipulations that led to other problems. For one, the principal would not allow it to be a school-wide event. Students were permitted to come *only* if certain teachers wanted to attend. In addition, we were not afforded the opportunity to announce the assembly to the entire school over the daily announcements; and thus, only about half of the student body was made aware of it. Furthermore, there were a number of teachers who did not care to have the Black assembly at all, and therefore restricted their students, including their African-American students, from attending. Many of the kids approached me and the new teacher, and begged that we get them out of class so they could come. I told them that the only way to do this was if they got their parents to complain; and so they did.

Another slap in the face to this program was the increase of police force awaiting the students as they came through the doors. At no other school-wide assembly or rally had there ever been extra police (since I had been there); but somehow, the principal felt it was "necessary" to have it at the Black assembly. Perhaps Gillespie-Oss was unfamiliar with the concept of racial profiling, but when I say that the minority students were deeply hurt and offended by this act, it is not an understatement. The worst part of that day was having a lot of the kids ask me why they had to see all those policemen at their celebration event; but on any other occasion, there was no extra force. I wish I could say that Gillespie-Oss wanted to "prevent" any possible "riot" that may have emerged from this Black assembly; but if that's the case, provide more protection at *all* the events. In addition to this, Gillespie-Oss told us that we could not chant the phrase, "I'm Black and I'm Proud" at the event. And all I kept thinking was how much I wanted to punch that woman in her face for all the hell she was putting us through. So, just to make her mad, we said the phrase anyways, and kept it moving. In addition to this, we were told not to invite members from the NAACP to the event; but we did so anyways.

In spite of all these unnecessary setbacks, the assembly was fantastic! It was so orderly, and many folks, including the teachers who attended, said it was the best assembly they had ever been to. Other teachers informed me that they were upset that they had not been told about the assembly in the first place, and had wondered why it was not a school-wide event. I told them that we weren't allowed to have it that way even though we pushed for it. In spite of the hell we went through to get that assembly going, it was absolutely wonderful. The students put on performances from step dancing to musical selections to poetry reading. We also had the mayor of Vallejo (in 2009) in attendance, and he brought forth an encouraging speech to the children, which taught them to value who they were and where they came from. Even though it was a celebration of Black history, the new teacher did not hesitate to speak to all the students of all races about the importance of loving their history, and celebrating the accomplishments of their community. It was such a successful event, and I'm pretty sure Gillespie-Oss received the credit for "continuing" the cultural programs on campus—which is probably why she received "Principal of the Year" award the following year. But she had nothing to do with the success. Again, it was the grace and intellect of the students that made it happen. The new teacher and I simply gave them the opportunity to shine; and they made it happen.

Even though her efforts proved to be outstanding, the new teacher was unfortunately a "probationary" instructor, meaning she did not hold permanent status. Throughout the year, she received much hardship from the administration; and whenever she needed help or support for her lessons and student behavior issues, she could not get it. By the end of the school year, she had a number of students who refused to do their work, and were on the verge of failing—even seniors—and the administration tried to pressure her to pass the kids with a D-. But because she wouldn't, it made her a target for termination. And by the end of the year, her position in the District was eliminated. I guess you could say that what I first saw at the beginning of the school year had actually come to pass; and it broke my heart that another minority teacher was fired because of her efforts to change the school's climate. In this District, your job will always be secure if you do not allow yourself to challenge the status quo. In my case, my position was secured because I had permanent status, and my personnel file was clean. But that did not mean that the District could not seek to get to me out by other means; all they had to do was build a solid case against me, even if they were based on lies. Although I made it through that year without having to deal with the administration with regards to my teaching profession, every move that I made in order to change the nature of the school and the District only added fuel to the fire. And the District was slowly but surely devising a plan to get rid of me, even if their attacks violated my rights as a human being and educator.

# Professional Backlash:
# The Beginning of the End in the FSUSD
# 2009-2010 School Year

I slowly but surely began to see what could happen to a person's career when they did ANYTHING to challenge the status quo in an organization. I knew that every time I spoke up, I was inviting the District and/or the administrators to do something against me. My strength to fight against the strong hand of racism in the school was weakening. I began to lose weight rapidly, and stress became a norm for me. I was physically and emotionally distraught because I had carried the weight of so much. I had never taken so many days off of work, but this would be the year that my children hardly saw me because I hated coming to work. Although I trusted God to keep me sane and whole in that environment, the atmosphere was too hostile for me. For many nights, I would come home crying from all the strain, and I even began to lose my zeal for teaching. I loved my kids. I loved their families; but I was losing the love and passion that I had when I first began teaching. In my heart, I knew that this would be the end of my teaching career in the public schools because

I was at the point of having a nervous breakdown. Even though I had permanent status in the District, it was clear to me that they would continue to harass me until I reached the breaking point. And even though some may wonder why I didn't simply leave, the answer is because I was so attached to my children; I didn't know how to cut the "umbilical cord." I felt that if I left them, then I was abandoning them; and so many needed my help and support.

Sometimes I wish that I hadn't cared so much, but I knew that caring was my way of reaching them when others could not. Although this brought a great deal of success with groups of students in the past, by 2009-2010, caring too much became an instrument for my demise. It made me vulnerable to a lot of abuse from students who did not know me. You see, for the first three years, I had worked with the same group of scholars who were with me from my beginning. You could say that we grew together and became a family of sort. My kids and their families became my extended family; and we would all (including their parents) often socialize outside of school. I was their go-to teacher; and because of this relationship, it seemed as though this was how I would always be with all students and families that came my way. But this was not the case for the 2009-2010 school year. In fact, the students that I acquired this year were the worst group of kids that I had ever worked with. And my assumption that they would be open and receptive to me as my other babies were in previous years was terribly wrong. I hate to say it, but it was because of them that my position in the District was demolished. The very people that I spent my life trying to help and work with were the very ones who tore me down. And this was all the ammunition that the District needed in order to launch their efforts to destroy not only my job, but more importantly my teaching career.

# The Notice of Unprofessional Conduct
## 2009-2010 School Year

*O*ver the course of this last year, I have learned how professionally and personally dangerous it could be to work in a District like the Fairfield-Suisun Unified School District. It was very clear to me that if I intended to stay in the District as a teacher, then I would always endure the wrath of corrupt leaders. You see, when you have been made a leader in a movement to bring positive change to a failing system, you are guaranteed to meet opposition from the top. In this District, they do not want to hear you tell them about the wrong they do; and they especially do not want these words coming from young minority professionals. Their politics, greed, and corruptions are so protected by individuals that to try and make them do right is to commit professional suicide. If they want to, they will destroy your reputation and good name by any means necessary; and will care less if others are threatening you. This was the situation for me. Not only did I have administrators doing things behind my back, but I also had to deal with the lies and deception from the District's officials. When I needed professional support and protection from my bosses against students who were harassing and threatening me, I could get nothing. And I knew that even if I had tried to leave the school, their lies could easily follow me to the next job. It was a terrible and frightening situation for me, especially because I was so young. Teaching was all I knew, and if this was taken away from me, I feared that I would never make it.

This next section of the book illustrates what I have already written in the previous paragraph. The only reason I have made this public is to show the people what happens behind the scenes in a public school district. Everything is done in secret so as to not draw any negative attention to the messy politics that go on. And I hope that the public will not only take notice of what is done, but also demand that change be made.

The reason for including these documents in this book is to show the reader the extent to which your leaders, your District officials, and your school administrators will go to remove a teacher who challenges the status quo. Is it any wonder that people who work in the school system like this are silent when it comes to matters of importance? Who wants to endure backlash such as this? Who deserves such treatment when it is clear that a teacher has a genuine heart for the students? The reason that the public school system is failing is not only because your leaders have removed God from the institution, but because you have corrupt, godless leaders in these positions that have no regard for the success and welfare of your children!

This portion of the book describes the District's retaliatory actions against me for the stand I took in 2008. For a teacher to receive what is called a Notice of Unprofessional Conduct is to lay the groundwork necessary for immediate removal and character defamation. I must note that even as audacious as this District was in their lies, it is extremely hard to prove that they engaged in anything retaliatory towards me. Although common sense would show otherwise, unless a District *explicitly* says "We are discriminating against you because of what you've done," then you are faced with the challenge of defending your rights, your character, and your career. And this is a battle often lost.

To give the reader some background as to why the District issued this Notice to me, I want to share what had been occurring during this school year. The reader is already aware that the new group of students that I had were very difficult to work with; and they essentially became the tool used to carry out this attack against my career. The context of the Notice of Unprofessional Conduct deals with a discipline issue that I had with a group of 10th graders during the 2009-2010 school year. Because I had not received any support or backing from the administration, I found myself dealing with the students to the best of my ability. When I had run out of all options for dealing with the kids, I wrote a personal letter to each of them, which explained my frustrations and disappointments with them. In the letter, I addressed a group of minority students, and told them that their behavior was indicative of the negative stereotypes associated with us; and that rather than acting in such ways, they needed take their education seriously. Essentially, it was my discussion of these negative stereotypes that "warranted" the District's move to issue the Notice. To be blunt, the District charged me with discriminating against Black students because I told them to "get it together." (Now, isn't that the pot calling the kettle black…a racist District accusing a Black teacher of being racist towards her own community, especially after seeing what I did to that institution the last couple of years.) Needless to say, the months following the Notice were extremely stressful and demeaning as the District strove to assassinate my character more and more. This Notice also led to a negative and falsified evaluation from one of my administrators, Lisa Wilson, which further damaged my personnel file. I suppose they thought that by crushing my character and adding more stress to my life that I would simply "comply" with the lies, sit back, and do what they wanted; or maybe I would become too stressed and leave the District. But I didn't. I came back at them with a fierce attack, which they did not anticipate. And the more I fought back to restore my good name, the more they crushed me professionally. Pretty soon, I was dealing with my administrators using some of my kids to spy on my classes. These same students would go back with their stories, all in efforts to get me out. In essence, this Notice was the driving force that led to my arrest on November 9, 2010, for every student that I had knew that my career was on the line because the administration was using them to get at me.

In what seemed like a sick turn of events, the babies that I loved so dearly were starting to despise me because I would not tolerate a slack hand to education. And when youth are required to do something that they do not want to do, they will seek a way to get rid of you. And they did this to me. Without getting ahead of myself, I want to share the following documents with you so that you can understand the kind of strain I was in. Perhaps then you will see why November 9th, 2010 was not as "random" as you had thought.

# FAIRFIELD-SUISUN UNIFIED SCHOOL DISTRICT

2490 Hilborn Road • Fairfield, CA 94534 • Telephone (707) 399-5147
FAX (707) 399-5139 • www.fsusd.k12.ca.us

January 15, 2010

**RECEIVED**
JAN 20

BY:...........................

**Governing Board**

Charles B. Wood
President

Pat Shamansky
Vice President

Dave Gaut
Clerk

Susan Heumphreus

Gary Laski

Kathy Marianno

Helen Tilley

**Superintendent**

Jacki Cottingim-Dias, Ph.D.

**VIA PERSONAL SERVICE**

Felecia Killings
1577 Meadowlark Drive
Fairfield, CA 94533

Re: Notice of Unprofessional Conduct and Unsatisfactory Performance

Dear Ms. Killings:

In accordance with the provisions of Education Code §44938 *et seq.*, this letter constitutes a Notice of Unprofessional Conduct and Unsatisfactory Performance with respect to your conduct as a permanent certificated employee of the Fairfield-Suisun Unified School District ("the District"). This letter also constitutes notice of your violations of District policies and procedures and provisions of the collective bargaining agreement between the District and Fairfield-Suisun Unified Teachers Association ("CBA").

This letter is not a dismissal notice; however, it may be necessary to recommend dismissal or suspension in the future based on the conduct set forth herein and if your conduct or performance does not improve. In the event that dismissal or suspension proceedings are filed against you, this notice is not intended to preclude causes or instances other than those set forth below.

The specific instances for this notice are as follows:

1.    District Board Policy 0100, "Philosophy of Education," sets forth the District's philosophy and beliefs regarding the educational process. Board Policy 0100 provides, in relevant part:

The education process will promote the conditions to meet the needs of all students according to their individual characteristics, interests, and abilities.
The district further believes:
1.    That Education is the Key to Success in Life ...
5.    That Students and Staff Must be Challenged to Meet the Highest Educational and Behavioral Standards and that Staff Must Meet Clear Performance Criteria ...
7.    In Positive Communication Among Students, Staff, Parents, and the Community ...

*"Our Mission is to Provide a Quality Educational System that Assures Opportunities*
*for Every Student to Learn and Meet the Challenges of the Future"*

Felecia Killings
January 15, 2010
Page 2

11.    That All Students Deserve Equal Access to a Quality Education ...
The Governing Board further believes that all students can succeed regardless of their race, background or ability. School staff shall embody this philosophy in all district programs and activities. (Attached hereto as Exhibit A is a true and correct copy of Board Policy 0100.)

2.    District Board Policy 4119.21, "Code of Ethics," sets forth the fundamental expectations the District has of its certificated employees. Board Policy 4119.21 provides:

> The Governing Board expects district employees to maintain the highest ethical standards, to follow district policies and regulations, and to abide by state and national laws. Employee conduct should enhance the integrity of the district and the goals of the educational program. (Attached hereto as Exhibit B is a true and correct copy of Board Policy 4119.21.)

3.    District Board Policy 5145.3, "Nondiscrimination/Harassment," sets forth the District's prohibitions against discrimination and harassment of students. Board Policy 5145.3 provides that, "The Board prohibits intimidation or harassment of any student by any employee, student or other person in the district." (Attached hereto as Exhibit C is a true and correct copy of Board Policy 5145.3.)

4.    Article 19.1 of the CBA sets forth the workday of certificated employees who are members of F-SUTA. Specifically, Article 19.1.a of the CBA provides,

> The on-site workday for members of this unit shall commence no more than one-half (1/2) hour before the start of the students' instructional day. The length of the workday for full-time members of this unit, including at least a thirty (30) minute duty-free lunch break, shall be seven and one-quarter (7 ¼) hours per day. (Attached hereto as Exhibit D is a true and correct copy of Article 19.1 of the CBA.)

5.    Article 23.1 of the CBA provides for sick leave of certificated employees and Article 23.4 provides for personal necessity leave. Article 23.4 defines "personal necessity" as "circumstances that are serious in nature to the employee and that the employee cannot reasonably be expects to disregard, that necessitates immediate attention that cannot be taken care of after work hours or on weekends." Article 23.4.d further provides that, "Abuse of the above guidelines will result in a letter of reprimand in the discipline process and loss of pay." (Attached hereto as Exhibit E are true and correct copies of Articles 23.1 and 23.4 of the CBA.)

6.    Pursuant to Education Code §44660 *et seq.*, and in alignment with the California Standards for the Teaching Profession developed by the Department of Education and Commission on Teacher Credentialing, the District has adopted a uniform system for the evaluation and assessment of the performance of its certificated employees. The evaluation of District certificated employees is based on the following six standards:

Felecia Killings
January 15, 2010
Page 3

- Engaging and Supporting All Students in Learning;
- Creating and Maintaining Effective Environments for Student Learning;
- Understanding and Organizing Subject Matter for Student Learning;
- Planning Instruction and Designing Learning Experiences for All Students;
- Assessing Student Learning; and
- Developing as a Professional Educator.

7.     Your Certificated Personnel Evaluation Form, dated April 20, 2008, includes the following comments from your evaluator.

**Standard 2: Creating and Maintaining an Effective Environment for Student Learning**
Miss. Killings allows students from other classes to "sit in" her class without authorization from other teachers. Consequently, students have unverified absences from other classes.
Recommendation:    Obtain written authorization (pass) from students' teachers if students want to attend your class. Inform office/attendance of students' whereabouts. (Attached hereto as Exhibit F is a true and correct copy of your Certificated Personnel Evaluation Form, dated April 20, 2008.)

8.     On Friday, October 16, 2009, you distributed to your second period class a letter from you in which you wrote the following.

Letter to 2nd period students:
... You have proven to your classmates and your teacher that you cannot be trusted with the liberties and freedoms that we could have had in this class. ... I gave a good report to the substitute, indicating that my classes have received nothing but good reviews; and instead, you revealed a side of you to a guest that I had asked to take over my class. *It is clear that you do not respect me; therefore I have no respect for many of you.* This, unfortunately, is difficult to earn back, *and now our class has been reduced to menial, laborious work* – simply because it is my job to provide the curriculum, and your job to complete it.

... Whatever the case, education is powerful, and many of you take it for granted. *For my Latino and African-American young men: do you understand that statistics show that you are more likely to end up in jail than going to and graduating from college! Do you know that the stereotypes set out for you are meant to be used against you! Do you understand that many people died, were decapitated, hanged, raped, and bombed just so that you could have the same rights as other American citizens – especially in the areas of education???*

Felecia Killings
January 15, 2010
Page 4

... Many of you have expressed that my reactions are unfair. *But is it fair to me that I have to deal with such a class?* ... Whatever the case, this class has received new procedures and routines, which will stay with us. How long? I don't know. [Emphasis added.] (Attached hereto as Exhibit G is a true and correct copy of your October 16, 2009 letter to your second period class.)

9.      To your October 16, 2009 letter, you attached a sheet in which you wrote the following.

Class Rules and Procedures
(This is your new routine for every class session.)
1.      Enter class quietly.
2.      Be seated by the second bell.
3.      Pull out your materials: class work packet, writing utensil, Holt Anthology 4th Edition.
4.      Refer to your "Holt Anthology Workbook Packet" for the Session's instructions.
5.      Work independently and quietly.
6.      All work must be completed by the end of the class session.
7.      If you finish early, move on to the next Session's assignments.
8.      When the final bell rings, you are to clean you area: make the desks perfectly straight; pick up all bits of trash.
9.      Be seated until two minutes have passed after the bell. Students will be released upon my say-so.
10.     Students will not be released until work is collected and class is spotless. (Exhibit G.)

10.     You further wrote on the attachment to your October 16th letter that there are certain consequences for not following your rules and procedures or completing work by the last bell including: a warning, removal from class, parent conferences, and/or administrative/parent/teacher/student conferences. (Exhibit G.)

11.     Your October 16, 2009 letter is unacceptable, unprofessional, degrading to your students and the District community, and violates District's policies.

12.     The method of instruction which you describe in your October 16th letter is also unsatisfactory and contrary to the standards of good instructional techniques expected of all teachers at the District. The method is also contrary to the California Standards for the Teaching Profession including "Engaging and Supporting All Students in Learning," "Creating and Maintaining an Effective Environment for Student Learning," "Understanding and Organizing Subject Matter for Student Learning," and "Planning Instruction and Designing Learning Experiences for All Students."

Felecia Killings
January 15, 2010
Page 5

13.    Your October 16, 2009 letter was brought to the attention of Amy Gillespie-Oss, Principal at Rodriguez High School, on October 16th by a campus monitor who reported to Ms. Gillespie-Oss' secretary, Robin Pitts, that a student approached the monitor asking to see their counselor because the student was upset by your letter. After reviewing your letter, Ms. Gillespie-Oss, along with Lisa Wilson, went to your classroom to discuss the letter with you.

14.    At approximately 10:15 a.m. on October 16th, Ms. Gillespie-Oss asked to meet with you in the hallway, while Ms. Wilson covered your class, to discuss the letter. When asked if you had only given the letter to your second period class, you nodded yes to Ms. Gillespie-Oss. Ms. Gillespie-Oss then asked if you had time during lunch to further talk about the letter because a parent had emailed about the letter and that there could potentially be more reaction from others to this matter. Ms. Gillespie-Oss also informed you that letters such as the one you sent should be discussed and approved prior to being distributed; that the tone of the letter could upset students and parents and that she wanted to meet with you to get your perspective and to develop a response. You informed Ms. Gillespie-Oss that you were thinking about "leaving" and that "parents should talk to [you]." While Ms. Gillespie-Oss agreed with you that parents are first referred to a teacher, she explained that she still needed to discuss the situation with you. You then nodded your head yes that you could meet with Ms. Gillespie-Oss during lunch, said "Whatever," and walked back into your class.

15.    Upon returning to her office, at approximately 10:25 a.m., Ms. Gillespie-Oss opened an email from you to her and Ms. Wilson in which you wrote, "Someone needs to take over these classes I am leaving. The students and their parents win." Ms. Gillespie-Oss and Ms. Wilson then went looking for you and ultimately discovered that your car was gone from the school parking lot. Ms. Gillespie-Oss next checked the staff sign-out log and noticed that you failed to sign out before you left the school without notice or approval. Your unauthorized departure prior to the end of your workday and failure to sign the staff sign-out log violates District policies and procedures and the CBA.

16.    On October 16, 2009 at approximately 3:55 p.m., Robert Martinez, Director of Human Resources, left a telephone message on your home telephone informing you that based upon your departure from the school that day you have been placed on paid administrative leave pending a review of the circumstances behind your departure. Mr. Martinez further instructed you not go to the school on the following Monday morning, October 19, 2009, and that the Human Resources Department would contact you on Monday for further information and direction.

17.    On Monday, October 19, 2009, the District received another complaint from a parent of one of your students regarding your October 16th letter. The parent was upset about your letter and said that writing such a letter to young adults is unacceptable. The parent further explained that your comments about Latino and African-American young men is disturbing and "heart wrenching." The parent requested that her student be transferred to another classroom.

Felecia Killings
January 15, 2010
Page 6

You are directed to do the following:

    1. Follow District directives and execute your job responsibilities in a complete, satisfactory and professional manner;

    2. Treat all District employees, students and staff in a professional and respectful manner;

    3. Adhere to District and state policies and standards for the teaching profession;

    4. Adhere to all District Board Policy including but not limited to Policy Nos. 4119.21, "Code of Ethics," and 5145.3, "Nondiscrimination/Harassment;"

    5. Do not make derogatory, inappropriate, and/or harassing comments to District students, employees and staff orally or in writing;

    6. Prior to distributing any communications to your students or parents, not including instructional materials, you are provide a copy to your site principal for review and approval;

    7. Adhere to all District and CBA policies and provisions regarding attendance and leaving the school site prior to the end of your contract workday;

    8. Attend a behavior management course and provide the District written documentation evidencing completing of this course; and

    9. Utilize effective instructional methodology in your classroom.

You must strictly comply with the above directives. The District will monitor your compliance with regards to your unprofessional conduct over the next forty-five (45) days and will do the same with regards to your unsatisfactory performance over the next ninety (90) days. You should meet with your supervisor, Amy Gillespie-Oss, and others as directed by your supervisor who will provide you help in complying with the above directives and in ways to improve your performance.

If you continue to demonstrate the type of unprofessional conduct and/or unsatisfactory performance described in this notice, you will be subject to further disciplinary action up to and including dismissal from employment at the District. Please be aware that the incidents of this notice do not preclude the District from pursuing suspension and/or dismissal in accordance with the Education Code.

Attached is a copy of Education Code §44938 *et seq.*

A copy of this notice will be placed in your personnel file. You are entitled to submit your own comments to this notice, within ten (10) days of service on you, which will be entered into your personnel file. If you choose to do so, please send your response to me.

Now, I realize that the content of the Notice can seem a little confusing, and that's exactly how I felt when I sat in front of the Assistant Superintendent of Human Resources, Ron Hawkins, as he threw this piece of trash before me. To summarize it briefly, the Notice argued that I do not believe that all students, especially Black students, can learn; that I don't treat employees and students in a fair manner; and that I harass and intimidate the students. THIS IS COMING FROM THE DISTRICT'S OFFICIAL!--the very same people who allowed White students to yell out racial comments were now saying that I intimidated and harassed students by asking them to take their education seriously, and to stop disappointing me.

To back track a little, the letter that I wrote to my disrespectful and harassing class was issued in October 2009. A student from the class, who was White, by the way, was so upset by the letter. After receiving the letter from the student and reading the content of it, Gillespie-Oss and Wilson came to my class session, and pulled me out from my kids to tell me that my letter was inappropriate and upsetting to the kids. She, the principal, then told me that a letter like that should not be given to the kids without approval from her; and I immediately replied, "What difference does it make if I say it to them directly or write it?" She then proceeded to tell me that I needed to meet with her later that day to discuss the letter and what was to happen as a result of that. And I thought, after all this time of trying to get your help and support to address the issues with these students for months, you want to reprimand me for correcting them and challenging them to do right? By this time, I was so upset of having two administrators pulling me out my class as if I was in trouble for being the adult; yet they refused to do anything to these kids for their actions. Because of that stress, I walked back in my classroom, gathered my belongings, and left the school grounds; but not before telling another assistant principal that I needed to leave because I was about to break down.

A few days after I left the school, I was scheduled to meet with Hawkins, Gillespie-Oss, and my union representative to discuss my reasons for leaving. I told them that I was tired of all the lack of support, and the constant protection they gave to these students who harassed me. Hawkins appeared quite sympathetic to my concerns, and even assured me that I would begin to receive immediate support from the administrators. After the meeting, I agreed to return to work; and from then on, I truly believed that this drama was over. But it wasn't. This same Hawkins who showed so much sympathy for me back in October 2009 had decided to take disciplinary actions against me some three months later. And in January 2010, he placed this Notice in my file, which violated my rights as teacher. Because of this, my union got involved, and this erupted into a frenzy of legal actions between both parties. The following document reveals the union's response to the Notice. The reader will see the various violations that the District made with regards to my profession. And even though they are made very plain, the District still moved forward with their actions. This is what I had to deal with in addition to working with the same harassing and threatening students on a daily basis. And this was only the beginning.

Violation of Article 5 – The District is discriminating and retaliating against Felecia Killings for participation in protected activities that have embarrassed the District over the way they have handled past issues of a racist nature at Rodriguez. Specifically, this is retaliation for Ms. Killings encouraging the school community to respond to the actions of a group of students who dragged a teddy bear behind a truck with a clearly racist intent meant to intimidate African American students and teachers.

Violation of Article 10 – The District is not allowed by the contract to use evaluations in disciplinary procedures. Sections 6 and 7, of the Notice of Unprofessional Conduct and Unsatisfactory Performance explicitly reference this. As Ms. Killings was rated as "Meeting or Exceeding Standards" in her Standard 2 of the evaluation referenced in the letter, and appended to the Notice, this cannot be the basis for the charge of unsatisfactory performance. In addition, you have quoted from the evaluation very selectively and omitted the opening statement in this section:
"Miss Killings has established respectful relationships with her students and has created a positive learning environment"

Violation of Article 12, Article 12.2,
The District has acknowledged in the Notice Section 14 that Ms. Gillespie-Oss failed to follow the provisions of this section by referring a complaining parent to meet with Ms. Killings prior to taking any further action, including any disciplinary action against Ms. Killings. In addition, by failing to take action on any parent complaint within 25 days, the District has waived the right to take any disciplinary action. Lastly, while the District failed to correctly follow the procedure in Article 12, Ms. Killings was within her rights in exercising her option of not returning to the classroom for the remainder of the day on October 16, 2009 as permitted by Article 12.2c

Violation of Article 13 – The District has not followed the guidelines and time lines of the steps for progressive discipline.

Specifically, the District did not make Ms. Killings or other faculty aware of the rules and regulations it is now attempting to discipline her for. In addition, the District is attempting to skip the steps of progressive discipline as outlined in Article 13 although Ms Killings is not accused of committing any of the enumerated offenses which permit that. Lastly, there is the matter of veracity of the charges themselves, which we will address below.

Answers to specific allegations:

1. While the contract is provided to teachers almost every time it is signed, the item you refer to, "District Policy 0100" has never been provided to the staff in any format and any other District policies are never provided to staff.

Item number 5 is listed, as this district does not challenge students to meet the highest behavioral standards. All one has to do is evaluate the standing District policies on dress code and discipline for classroom misbehavior behavior to understand that the level of standards applied is not approaching the highest level..

5. In planning for a sub, the teacher told the sub that the students behaved properly. Evidently, that was not the case for this class, as they abused the sub. The class showed little respect for the teachers request that they behave and therefore ruined the trust and respect the teacher had for the class before this incident. No hard to understand.

6. The teachers explains exactly how acting out prevents the learning of the other students in class and prevent the teacher from being able to teach the curriculum and explains to them that the law does not allow this. This teacher goes to the extreme to explain the relationship between student and teacher should be one of learning and enjoyment in order to provide and enriching atmosphere.

7. The teacher explains that education is a privilege and right that was hard earned by people who sacrificed their lives to make it happen.

8. The teacher empowers the students to learn and explains that they cannot take it for granted. As a minority teacher, who knows the value of an education, she directs her comments directly to the group that is causing the problems. She provides them with the history of what is the actual truth of their situation, emphatically. Every sentence used expresses the past happenings, truths, and the struggle of the past that allows students of minority to be treated as equals and then challenges them to do the right thing and be rewarded for their behavior instead of receiving negative consequences.

   The students have reacted to her pleas, but feel that her reaction is unfair. However, is it fair for the students to treat their teacher with disrespect and cause her to go to these lengths? Is it right for the students to not come forward and set things straight after seeing who did the wrong things?

   Miss Killings explains exactly why she has taken the action she has and none of it is beyond the scope of the Ed. Code responsibilities and expectations of a teacher. She even explains to her other students that they have been cheated out of an education because of these other students who have made the classroom an unbearable disrespectful place to be and none of them are willing to make it change.

9. The Class Rules and Procedures. Classroom rules and procedures can change with the demeanor of the students in the classroom. Each class has it own demeanor and this class needed to be taught a lesson. When the demeanor changes, the rules can change.

10. There is nothing out of the ordinary with the consequences and it is within the rights of a teacher to suspend a student according to Ed. Code 48910.

11. After reviewing the letter, and showing it to other female teachers (any name and indication of site redacted) in the high school setting, they agreed that this does happen and the administration usually does nothing about it except to tell the teacher to handle it and call parents. Unfortunately, for the 1%'ers, this does little to solve the problem. It was also interesting to note that the female teachers also agreed with the ethnicity of the individuals who caused the problems in their situations.

anarchy and see what the teacher can do about it. This is most effective when you have a group of students who have little desire to be educated and just want to do what they want to do, when they want to do it, and expect the teacher to let them proceed without any recourse.

The attitude of "talk to the hand" and total "you cannot touch me" is especially directed toward women teacher, who according to the current student sub set are only there to be used and not respected. Where do they get such values? Just listen to the lyrics of the songs that they listen to and their peer group.

This attitude with substitutes is even more pervasive and the disrespect reserved for subs is openly expressed by behavior that is worse than with their assigned teacher. That is one reason many subs do not return to sites, they do not need to be disrespected by the students and administration.

But when the students of minority turn on one of their own minority teachers, this is the highest show of total disrespect for education and total disrespect for a minority women and a demeaning of her position in the educational community.

It is evident that this school district and this site in particular does not seem to understand that, nor do they seem to understand the underlying current of the 1%'er minority student values that become pervasive as the "fence sitters" see what they can get away with and mimic the behavior. The site administrators and District administrators need to be educated on beliefs of the 1%'ers to understand how the life style feeds into the lack of respect for education and women, and women of color in particular.

This attitude is pervasive within the minority community among certain age groups and peer groups. The attitude is allowed by the community society under the flag of freedom to associate and freedom of speech. What it is generated is the debasing of the human values and respect for educational authority of teachers and women teachers in specific, minority women teachers in particular.

It also is evident that the administration does not understand the place of minority educators. As part of the educational community, it is their job to educate minority students in proper manors and call the students on their improper behavior. And when they do that, this administration calls them "unprofessional". But let a white teacher do that, it becomes racism.

It seems that our site administrators have either forgotten or have never been educated in what is expected by law of our students.

## 1. Student Responsibilities E.C. 48908

All pupils shall comply with the regulations, pursue the required course of study, and submit to the authority of the teachers of the schools.

For me, it wasn't enough that the union had their words with the District. I also wanted to express my own feelings about the Notice; and I immediately went to work on composing my rebuttal. I guess those pompous officials expected me to back down and do what they wanted; but I don't get down like that without a fight. For one, I already had distaste for them, and I was not concerned with pleasing them. At the same time, I felt the need to defend my character in the event that something would come up later. I needed evidence to support that there was discrimination, retaliation, harassment, and threatening tactics being used against me while in this District. And even if no one in that organization would listen and support me, I knew that one day this story was going to come out; and I needed to be prepared for it. Furthermore, I needed to show that I did everything in my power to protect myself; and in spite of it, I was still a victim in that institution, a victim to not only the officials and administration, but more devastatingly, to my students.

The next document is a detailed description of my rebuttal to the Notice, and my direct accusations of discriminatory actions at the hands of Hawkins and Gillespie-Oss. (The dates on the rebuttal are typos, as they should read October 2009 and January 2010.)

To: Ron Hawkins, Assistant Superintendent, Human Resources
Re: Rebuttal to the Notice of Unprofessional Conduct and Unsatisfactory Performance

The nature of this letter will serve as a rebuttal to the allegations presented against me, Felecia Killings, E nglish teacher at Rodriguez High School.

On January 15, 2009, I received this Notice of Unprofessional Conduct, which stipulated that my actions, which occurred in October 16, 2008, warranted this Notice. I begin this rebuttal by explaining the nature of what had been occurring inside and outside of my class, which ultimately led to my leaving the school and writing the letter to my students.

Since August 2009, at the beginning of the school year, I have struggled with a section of 10th graders. These students, situated in my 2nd period class, had displayed countless times how disrespectful they were to their teacher and their fellow classmates. (This same sentiment is felt by a large number of teachers at Rodriguez High School. Refer to Exhibit A, B, and C.) This is not to say that I have never dealt with a difficult class before, but never had I been in a room so full of students who not only disregarded their education (as evident by their actions), but could care less about the lesson, instruction, and education provided to their fellow classmates. In a class of about 26 students, I had approximately nine students who constantly disrupted the class. Examples of this include excessive talking during the lesson, repeatedly disturbing the lesson by getting out of their seats when they wanted to, and detracting the neighbors' attention by their loud side conversations, cussing and engaging in inappropriate conversations. These students consistently exercised defiant behavior by refusing to abide by the rules of the class (i.e. no talking when I'm giving instructions, not disrupting other students, talking during tests, etc.) As I do with all the students I work with, I handled these difficulties by issuing warnings to the students. My policy has always been to give students a chance to correct their behavior. At times, I have been guilty of providing too many warnings and chances to the students. My discipline procedure extends itself when students do not respond positively or correctly to the warnings, and as such, they would receive stricter consequences for repeated offenses. In the case of my 2nd period class, I found myself repeatedly warning the students to cease from their disruptive and defiant behavior. When I had exhausted my warnings (simply because I am tired of repeating myself), my procedure was to then ask them to take their work, and complete it in another English teacher's room. (This is a procedure that we English teachers developed in order to help each other out. The reader will notice Exhibit D, which indicates the "Pyramid To Success For All." This was established in 2008-2009 in order to reduce the number of suspensions for students. According to this pyramid, teachers have to move through various steps before actually getting administrative action for a student's disruptive behavior. At times, going through these steps prolongs the effect of correcting the students' negative behavior.) Because of the pressure from administration to keep the disruptive students in our classes, I, like the countless number of teachers, have had to develop strategies to help each other when facing disruptive and disrespectful students (refer to Exhibit C and E for a discussion of strategies that I and other teachers have had to employ because of the negative behavior among 10th graders).

Knowing that I had this disciplinary avenue to use for this 2nd period class (sending them to other teachers to complete the work), I sometimes utilized it; however, that did not seem to curb some students' behavior, and I began issuing referrals. This is not typical of my disciplinary actions, as anyone in the administrative office (including the clerks and those who handle the referrals) would state; students who receive referrals from me are very few and far between. Why? Because I strongly believe that I have to work with the students in order to build a rapport that will deter them from acting so outlandishly. But when students (like those in my 2nd period class) refuse to be an active participant in building a class atmosphere that is conducive to the learning and teaching, then that is where I must become stricter with them. According to policies issued by the Board (refer to Exhibit F), every staff member "shall be alert and immediately responsive to student conduct which may interfere with another student's ability to participate in or benefit from school services, activities or privileges." And that's what I have stood by ever since I became a teacher. I have seen in that 2nd period class a significant number of students who did not care about their education, and their actions were constantly affecting that of their peers. I had an obligation to protect the "privileges" of my students by making sure that at least they were receiving that which they came to my class for: their education. But that was constantly being thwarted by the negative behavior exhibited by these students. Apparently the measures that I had taken thus far (the warnings, the placement in other teachers' rooms, and referrals) were not enough. And for a couple of the students (particularly the ones that were ringleaders in it all), I had to eventually ask administration to arrange to have them removed from my class I knew that even before something of this magnitude could be accomplished, I would have to meet with the parents of the students in order to explain the negative behavior. I eventually met with some parents, and talked to them about their children's behavior. And like many of the parents at the school, there was the tendency to believe that their child did nothing wrong. (This is a similar circumstance that other teachers have identified with the parents of their 10 th graders. Refer to Exhibit C.) This, of course, only adds to my frustration because it means that not only am I not getting the quick, immediate response from administration, but I am also not receiving adequate support from parents who believe their child's statements over their teacher's. (When teachers have to deal with parents like that and administration who does not come to the aid of their teachers immediately, then what is a teacher supposed to do? How is a teacher supposed to feel?) Eventually, I had to let the parents know that if the child's behavior did not adjust, I would request administration to remove him from my class, and place him with another teacher because I did not want the child's negative behavior to continue in my class.

While I have briefly discussed my initial meetings with parents, I feel that it is also necessary to provide more examples of the kind of class that I was dealing with. Sometime in September 2009, I was doing a unit that examined and celebrated the Chinese American culture. We were studying the works of Amy Tan, and I thought it would be a good idea to show the students the film version of *The Joy Luck Club*. We had been studying this culture for about two weeks, and during those class sessions, it seemed that the students were very interested in the topic. When I showed the film to the students, the same nine kids (who always disturb the class) began making racist jokes about the Chinese women in the film. (They were making fun of the way the women spoke Chinese and broken English, and laughing loudly about it.) As I heard them laughing, I told them to stop because it was offensive and, as I now know, in violation of Board policy. But they didn't. They continued with their jokes, again by making fun of the way the Chinese women spoke in broken English, and they did it in such a way so that all the students heard what they were mimicking. Again, I warned them to stop because I do not allow that kind of jokes in my class. Even after this warning, they still continued until I had no other recourse but to shut the film off. I did not want any of my students of Asian descent to feel that I would allow these students to behave in that way, especially knowing that if we were watching a film about African Americans, and other students were making fun of them, I would have been especially livid because I am an African American woman. I felt just as humiliated and embarrassed about their jokes and remarks as I would have had I been Chinese. (Refer to Exhibit G and H. The reader will notice a discussion of my frustrations with staff, a tactic we teachers use in order to solicit help and support from other teachers.) And I was not going to let the students get away with that. After turning off the film, I told them to just sit in their seats quietly until the bell rang because I was too angry to do anything with them. EVEN STILL, the students continued to act like nothing was wrong and chose to act nonchalantly. The nine disruptive students who made the class very difficult did not care that they had, again, ruined a creative opportunity for learning. Not expressing any remorse only added to my frustrations and disappointment.

Realizing that students (and even adults) often make fun of other cultures because of their ignora nce, I issued this 2nd period class with a special assignment (refer to Exhibit I). I still wanted them to learn about Chinese culture, but I could see that doing more creative activities, like watching films about it, was not possible. Instead, I had them complete a research report in which they would examine the history and culture of Chinese Americans so that they could understand the various things that they went through since their first arrival in this country. I told them that they needed to show their parents the research report requirements, and bring the letter signed and dated for the next class session. Although the students were livid with the assignment, it did not matter to me because they needed to understand why it is NOT ok to make fun of others. In addition to writing this report, the students were also required to do an oral presentation to the class, indicating what they had learned and demonstrating how their own culture relates to the Chinese American experience.It was one of the best strategic tactics that I have employed as an educator. In speaking with other teachers at that time, they expressed to me that they have had the same problems with their students, and they find that giving them lectures on respecting others' cultures has not produced effective results. When I explained my situation to these same teachers (refer to Exhibit H emails), they reported that they never thought to do anything like that, and wanted to try and employ this same kind of technique. (Keep in mind, this intense assignment would not have come had the students adhered to my warnings.)

The end result of this strategy was phenomenal. The students were amazed at the treatment of Chinese Americans in the past and present. For my African American students (who were agents of the racist jokes), they were shocked that Asian Americans were called "niggers" just like Blacks; they were completely surprised that Chinese Americans had received the same kind of racist hate crimes that African Americans faced (and continue to face), such as race killings and discriminatory laws. And for them, this was an eye opener. It forced them to consider how we are more alike than we think. And this realization would not have come had I not dealt a firm hand with these students. After this project, I had a number of students, particularly the disruptive ones, ask me if they could do the same kind of research, but for another ethnic group. Of course they received a resounding yes. It seemed that only when I was firm with this group, then and only then was I getting the results that were necessary. But even that was not enough!

Whenever I was absent from work (even after the September incident), I received letters from my substitutes indicating that the 2nd period class was very rude to them. On one occasion, the students were being required to take the district benchmark assessment. While the sub was trying to get the class together, the same nine students who caused trouble for me was causing trouble for the sub. There was constant talking and disruptions (during the test). Students were eating in the class, even after being told to stop; they were chewing gum and rubbing it in my carpet; and what's worse is that they lied to the sub and told him that I allow this kind of behavior. When I returned to work the next day, I was LIVID as I read the sub's report. For sure I had thought that 2nd period had learned its lesson on respect, but they AGAIN did not care about anyone but themselves. Realizing that I had a constant battle on my hand with this class, I could no longer try and be that creative, excited teacher with them because their behavior prevented that. Neither had they ever shown any remorse for their rebellious ways, even when it affected the other classmates and their teacher. What's worse is that they refused to show any kind of respect to the substitutes, which I find completely unacceptable. (The reader will have to imagine that this kind of difficult behavior continued on a regular basis. Every time I had this class, I struggled with their disruptions and disrespect on multiple levels.)

My last resort was to do essentially what had taken place on October 16, 2009. In trying to think about how to bring this class together and working harmoniously, I reflected on how my other difficult classes were in times past. Whenever I faced a class that constantly disrupted me and was disrespectful, I told them that since they could not act right when I was trying to do the creative teaching that I love, then they would have to resort to doing menial book work. This tactic worked my first year, my second year, and my third year (refer to Exhibit J). And I wanted it to work again for my fourth year. So I told this 2nd period class that since they can't seem to act right and respectful when I'm trying to do things creatively, then I will not waste my energy and stress level on forcing them to respond to me. Instead, they will have to deal with a strict, more directed form of teaching, using the HOLT Anthology lessons and activities as opposed to reading the great novels and literature that I had planned for them (refer to Exhibit K). That is when I issued the letter (as presented in the Notice) to the students and the new class procedures. Were the students upset? Of course they were! And I was upset because their behavior had become just too much. Now, in my mind, I had no intentions on maintaining this procedure for too long because *I* was going to get bored. But they didn't need to know that. Instead, I wanted to wait out and see how long they would tolerate this kind of regiment, and whether or not they felt it was worth it to act right and return to a more creative learning environment. And in fact, they wanted that better environment immediately. This strict regiment lasted exactly ONE class session because the students HATED it, and they did not want to spend the rest of their school year like this. It was boring, non-interactive, and dry. But I wanted to show them that they have a choice with how things operate in the class. (These results were further exemplified throughout the course of the following weeks and months, which I will explain later.) After this strict, boring session, that's when the turn of events occurred; this led me to leaving the school.

After that second period class left, one of the students gave the letter to Amy Gillespie (as she told me). As such, she and Lisa Wilson came to my 4th period class to confront me. When they approached, it was completely inappropriate and uncalled for. Amy had never come to my class to ask to speak to me about anything, and had another administrator come with her. To my kids, it appeared as if "Ms. Killings is in a lot of trouble," because of how they came. I felt intimidated in front of my students, and that is not something that I needed to deal with at that time, especially because I was dealing with these difficult students. When I stepped into the hallway with Amy, she showed me the letter I wrote to the students, and she explained that "normally letters like this don't go out with prior approval." My thoughts were: *since when? I have been giving letters to my students since year one, and I am aware that other teachers routinely do the same without first obtaining her approval.* She then told me that parents had called the office to complain about the letter, and that she wanted me to come in her office at lunch to discuss strategies on how to handle it. I then asked her why weren't the parents being directed to come and speak to me if they have issues, and her reply was "normally I do that;" but I guess in my case, she didn't see fit. (Refer to Exhibit L. The reader will notice that administration did not inform the complaining parents to contact me until November 11, 2009.) I told her that I was about ready to leave because this was very upsetting. I felt that neither Amy nor the District was providing support or empathy for a teacher who was doing her best to handle a class of extremely difficult, disrespectful students, and I had just been confronted IN FRONT OF MY OTHER CLASS by TWO administrators who were clearly there to demonstrate that they were going to deal with the problem of the letter. I knew I had no support from Amy because of our history at the site (refer to Exhibit for a detailed report of the incident in 2008, which led to a negative history between Amy and me), and I knew that the lunch meeting would result in me breaking down emotionally. Knowing this, I immediately left the conversation in the hallway, and went back into the classroom. I sat at my desk and was about to explode in tears; and rather than letting my kids see me this way, I sent an email to Lisa and Amy indicating that I was leaving and they needed to get someone in the class. I packed some of my belongings and headed to the office to look for them to tell them in person. When I didn't see either one, I went to Angie Alvonitis's office, and told her in person that I was leaving (and she could see that I was emotionally upset). Angie asked if I had someone in the class at that moment, and I said no. I don't know what steps she did next, but I did not wait around to see. I left the office, went to my car, and went home because I had had enough.

The following day (October 17) I received a voicemail from the district telling me that I had been placed on administrative leave, and not to return to work until told so. When I finally received a phone call from Ron Hawkins on that following Monday, he wanted to meet so that he could identify what went wrong. He asked me in that conversation if I had planned to return to work, or was I resigning. I said that I did plan to come back, and based on that, he needed to schedule a meeting. I told him that I would not meet without having a union representative, which Ron agreed to. The meeting, due to my union representative's availability, was scheduled for October 23. During that meeting, I explained the reasons for why I left. From that meeting, Ron appeared sympathetic to my frustrations, and informed me about the legal implications for leaving students alone in a class. I understood that it was wrong to leave before students had an immediate coverage, but by informing the administration that I was leaving, I obviously exercised some professionalism by letting them know I was not staying. By the end of the meeting, Ron indicated that he did not intend to take corrective measures, but rather he just wanted to get me back in the classroom as soon as possible. We all (including my union representative) left that meeting under the notion that nothing else would be done as far as any future corrective measures, and that I was welcomed back to work the following Monday. In fact, Ron's last few words to me were, "We'll see you Monday?" That meeting left me believing that future corrective measures were not to be taken because I had explained the nature of my departure. One area that the Notice weighs heavily on is the letter that I had given to the students, which expressed my deepest disappointments towards them. During this October meeting, there was minimal discussion about the letter. Neither was there a single word spoken about how I discriminated against the Black and Latino students. All that Ron said was that a parent was worried that there was a teacher at the school who had simply "given up" on the kids. But again, there was nothing spoken of in that meeting that indicated that I would be receiving further corrective measures as a result of my leaving or my "discriminating" letter. After I left that meeting, I returned to work the following Monday. When I returned to the classroom, I received letters from my substitutes indicating that my classes, ALL my classes, had been well behaved. In fact, one substitute indicated that my 2nd period class had been "great"! I was so grateful that the kids had finally learned that I would not tolerate their negative behavior that I wanted to reward them for doing well in my absence. I told my 2nd period class that because the sub had left a good report, I saw no need to continue with the strict regimen that I left them with before my leaving. I reinstated our creative atmosphere, including doing all the activities that we could in order to make our learning fun and interactive, and the students were grateful. This is not to say that the kids were perfect afterwards; but the discipline for their negative behavior diminished dramatically. When the students started being disruptive again, all I had to do was ask them once to stop, and they did. The kids finally got that when we do things the right way, we have an atmosphere that is truly enjoyable. They did not want the tension just as much as I did not want it, and I suddenly saw a huge change in behavior. My students began to take their education seriously, and they participated thoroughly in the lessons. Some of the students who did absolutely no work during the "difficult times" were suddenly completing their work for me. And I praised them for it. Ever since that time in October, 2nd period has become my most interactive class. And this has been the nature of the class for the past three months.

This brings me to January 15, 2010, and the purpose of this rebuttal. On January 11, I received an email from Ron Hawkins's secretary asking if I was available to meet on the 15th concerning what had happened in October 2009. I responded to her by asking why we needed to meet, especially since the issue was resolved three months prior. Her response was he just needs to meet with you. So I agreed to meet (refer to Exhibit N).

When my union representative and I met with Ron Hawkins on January 15, I was completely shocked and appalled by the nature of the meeting because it came as a surprise. Ron Hawkins had indicated that although he said that no corrective measures were going to be taken in October, he was obligated (by whom, I don't know) to write this Notice of Unprofessional Conduct and place it in my personnel file. As I read through some of the Notice, I noticed a great deal of information that was false. When I asked whose interpretation of the matter this was, Ron indicated that it was his. Based on that information, I questioned him on several factors, of which, many of my questions were answered with: "You can write a rebuttal." I told him that I intend to write a rebuttal, but I that I would also like to engage in this conversation (to hear what he had to say).

With all that has been said already, I contend sharply in this official rebuttal that this reprimand is based on false pretenses, which have been fabricated by Ron Hawkins and his interpretation of the matters of October. The following list is some of the information that I verbally discussed with Ron during that January 15th meeting. I had several questions for him, which the reader will notice below:

Why are you taking "corrective measures" regarding this situation 91 days after the incident? If in the last meeting we had (in October) you indicated that you were not going to take corrective measures, why are you doing it now? (A question that I raise now: Is it the district's policy to mislead their workers into thinking that issues are resolved, only to officially reprimand them months after the incident, especially when there has been no follow up with the worker in question?)
Ron, you indicated that Amy says there have been no problems since October. If that's the case, then why am I now being reprimanded when clearly there are no issues being presented to her? Have you done an update interview with the parents and students since October? If so, you would have found that the class has changed dramatically, and we are now working well together. (The reader will recall that for the past two months, the 2nd period students have curved their behavior in such a way that allows for the creative learning environment that we all enjoy. We do interactive things now that we could not do before. In fact, 2nd period is my liveliest 10th grade session, and also the one with the highest number of As and Bs in the class when compared to my other 10th grade sections. This would not have been possible had I not dealt a strong hand with them as I had done in years past.) [Ron Hawkins's answer to this question was "no."].
This Notice indicates that I was harassing the students. How was I harassing the students? (Ron Hawkins's reply: "it depends on how others receive something, that's what makes it harassment.")
The complaint made by the parent about my comment on Black and Latino males sounds like the complaint I received from a parent that I spoke to. Have you done an update with that parent since then to see how they and their child feel now? If so, you would have found out that after I met with that parent, her last words to me were "You have my full support, Ms. Killings."
When you did your investigation into the situation, did you interview all the students and their parents? (There should have been a thorough analysis of the class to get a better understanding of the nature of the class. You would have heard testimonies from a good number of students that the 2nd

This brings me to January 15, 2010, and the purpose of this rebuttal. On January 11, I received an email from Ron Hawkins's secretary asking if I was available to meet on the 15th concerning what had happened in October 2009. I responded to her by asking why we needed to meet, especially since the issue was resolved three months prior. Her response was he just needs to meet with you. So I agreed to meet (refer to Exhibit N).

When my union representative and I met with Ron Hawkins on January 15, I was completely shocked and appalled by the nature of the meeting because it came as a surprise. Ron Hawkins had indicated that although he said that no corrective measures were going to be taken in October, he was obligated (by whom, I don't know) to write this Notice of Unprofessional Conduct and place it in my personnel file. As I read through some of the Notice, I noticed a great deal of information that was false. When I asked whose interpretation of the matter this was, Ron indicated that it was his. Based on that information, I questioned him on several factors, of which, many of my questions were answered with: "You can write a rebuttal." I told him that I intend to write a rebuttal, but I that I would also like to engage in this conversation (to hear what he had to say).

With all that has been said already, I contend sharply in this official rebuttal that this reprimand is based on false pretenses, which have been fabricated by Ron Hawkins and his interpretation of the matters of October. The following list is some of the information that I verbally discussed with Ron during that January 15th meeting. I had several questions for him, which the reader will notice below:

Why are you taking "corrective measures" regarding this situation 91 days after the incident? If in the last meeting we had (in October) you indicated that you were not going to take corrective measures, why are you doing it now? (A question that I raise now: Is it the district's policy to mislead their workers into thinking that issues are resolved, only to officially reprimand them months after the incident, especially when there has been no follow up with the worker in question?)

Ron, you indicated that Amy says there have been no problems since October. If that's the case, then why am I now being reprimanded when clearly there are no issues being presented to her? Have you done an update interview with the parents and students since October? If so, you would have found that the class has changed dramatically, and we are now working well together. (The reader will recall that for the past two months, the 2nd period students have curved their behavior in such a way that allows for the creative learning environment that we all enjoy. We do interactive things now that we could not do before. In fact, 2nd period is my liveliest 10th grade session, and also the one with the highest number of As and Bs in the class when compared to my other 10th grade sections. This would not have been possible had I not dealt a strong hand with them as I had done in years past.) [Ron Hawkins's answer to this question was "no."]

This Notice indicates that I was harassing the students. How was I harassing the students? (Ron Hawkins's reply: "it depends on how others receive something, that's what makes it harassment.")

The complaint made by the parent about my comment on Black and Latino males sounds like the complaint I received from a parent that I spoke to. Have you done an update with that parent since then to see how they and their child feel now? If so, you would have found out that after I met with that parent, her last words to me were "You have my full support, Ms. Killings."

When you did your investigation into the situation, did you interview all the students and their parents? (There should have been a thorough analysis of the class to get a better understanding of the nature of the class. You would have heard testimonies from a good number of students that the 2nd right hands. They all indicated to me that I had their full support, and that they wanted to keep their child with me because they had faith in my ability to teach their children. As far as communicating with the students, I have always been known as the teacher that students come to when they have a problem. In the case of this 2nd period class, it has taken more time to have this kind of rapport because of the nature of the class since the school year began. But the relationship is building, and we are coming to enjoy each other more and more. With regard to communicating with the staff, I am unaware of any complaint from a staff member indicating that I have said or written something to them that was not positive. If anything, I have been a victim of negative communications, especially after the April 2008 incident (with the teddy bear). During that year, I received a letter in my mail box saying "Just Walk Away." Not knowing how to interpret that matter, I presented my concern to Amy, in which case, she did nothing to address the issue with her staff members (refer to Exhibit O). Another teacher at that time had told Amy that I was receiving intimidating comments from staff and students, and Amy did nothing about it. As far as communicating with the community, the community knows my name because of my fight for justice within this school district. Ever since 2008, I have been in constant communication with members in the community who also want change in the school, changes that include a push towards cultural acceptance, tolerance, and education in this district. I have worked collaboratively with numerous parents and community organizations, including, but not limited to the NAACP (with President Cynthia Phillips), local church organizations, and a film production group called "Not In Our Town" for the sole purpose of bringing a sense of community in our schools (refer to Exhibit P and Q).

How do I show that I don't support the belief that "all students deserve equal access to a quality education;" and how is it that I don't believe that "all students can succeed regardless of their race" etc.? As an African American woman, I understand clearly that all students have the right to a quality education. My experience convinces me of this, not only because of my race, but because I have an extensive study into the history and culture of African Americans as evidenced by the Bachelor's Degree that I hold in that discipline. I have seen first-hand how students are treated differently at Rodriguez High School because of their race. Black students were constantly being suspended for offenses that other races were getting a " slap on the wrist" for. This fact is proven by the countless number of minority parents who had expressed (to administrators and district officials) their concerns of the unequal disciplinary treatment that their children had received at Rodriguez High School. For example, at the town hall meeting that was held at the St. Stephen's Church in Fairfield in 2008 (regarding the teddy bear incident), a number of parents complained that their children were being mistreated, and nothing was being done about it. Their issue was, how can two White students get away with what they did with a simply Saturday school, and yet the minority children were being suspended for "disruptive behavior." The behavior of those two boys disrupted the entire school and community, and yet their punishment was a Saturday school. This issue of unfair and unequal treatment had caused such an uproar in the school and the community that now the district has tried to create measures to reduce the alarming number of suspensions and expulsions of minority children, a number that is significantly ill proportioned when compared to the number of minorities within the district. In 2008, I demonstrated what it truly means to fight for the rights and education of my students, especially the ones that I see who are being targeted because of their race. This issue was not solely identified as a Black problem, but members of all ethnic groups felt the same racial hostility that resides at Rodriguez High, and there was a cry from the students and some staff members, and especially the community, for a dramatic change. I want my students to not only succeed because I know they can; I want them to prosper because society (based on stereotypes and negative statistics) tells them that they can't prosper! I want them to take their challenges that they face as a result of their race, and combat them. They are equal to anyone, and capable of all things, but they cannot allow society to diminish this opportunity simply because of their race. Neither should they tolerate it when organizations and leaders

The Notice then transitions to a discussion about the "Class Rules and Procedures" that I implemented as a result of the students' behavior, stating that they are "unsatisfactory and contrary to the standards of good instructional techniques." As stated prior, the approach I took with my students was something that I have employed since 2006 in order to show my students that when they behave in an unruly manner, it prevents me from doing creative teaching; and when I cannot do that kind of teaching, our only result is to move to a more directive form of instruction (refer to Exhibit J). Also, I had mentioned that had there been a follow-up or update concerning this class, one would have known that this procedure lasted ONE session because the students did not want that kind of instruction, and as such, they changed their behavior. What is also important to note is that I have spoken with other English teachers who have stated that they also have had to move to the strict book work simply because they cannot do what they would like in their classes due to disruptive student behavior (refer Exhibit R). They have not been counseled or disciplined regarding this. This is a strategy that some teachers have had to employ because classes become too difficult to handle, and yet teachers are required to provide an education for them. I question why this is unsatisfactory when the instructions I gave to the students called on them to complete the book work that the District has given to the teachers, the Holt Anthology. The lessons that the students would have completed came strictly from the text book that the District provides, and yet when I issue it out to the students, I receive the Notice of Unsatisfactory Performance. It should also be noted that while the class dynamics have changed dramatically for the good, I still maintain the same routine/procedure as I did when I first told them about it in October.

The Notice then transitions to a discussion of the events that took place on October 16, 2009, which Ron Hawkins has interpreted as unethical and unprofessional behavior. My objection to this portion is that Ron Hawkins included in the Notice that Amy had said that I should not send out letters without approval. I first mentioned my frustrations to Ron Hawkins concerning her statement in the October meeting. When I confronted Amy on this matter in the October meeting, she denied having said this to me. Her response was, "You may have interpreted it like that," but she did not tell me that I could not send letters without her approval.

The Notice also includes one of the parent's complaints about my comments towards Black and Latino males. My questions are: did Ron Hawkins or any other administrator ever inform the parent of the need to speak with me about the situation? This was a violation of my contractual rights under the agreement between FSUTA and FSUSD.

I further stipulate that the directives that have been listed for me to follow are unnecessary.

I have always followed District policies and responsibilities as evident by evaluation and observations; and in the areas that I did wrong in, I rectified them.
I have always shown respect to staff, students and other employees. What evidence is there that would indicate otherwise? None of the supposed evidence presented supports this conclusion.
I have not violated any standards from the teaching profession as evident by my evaluations and observations. Each year, I have pushed to perfect my professionalism, and there is proof of that.
I have not violated any District policy related to discrimination and harassment. As a young, African American woman who experience discrimination on three levels (as a woman, because of my race, and my age), I understand all too well the dynamics at work in society, and the struggles that minorities encounter in the workplace and on the school grounds. My efforts as a teacher in this District have been to empower my students , especially my minority students, with an education that will carry them to their next level. And I have done just that. This was not an interpretation that Ron Hawkins came to in October, and to determine that this is the case three months afterwards is unreasonable.

The Notice then transitions to a discussion about the "Class Rules and Procedures" that I implemented as a result of the students' behavior, stating that they are "unsatisfactory and contrary to the standards of good instructional techniques." As stated prior, the approach I took with my students was something that I have employed since 2006 in order to show my students that when they behave in an unruly manner, it prevents me from doing creative teaching; and when I cannot do that kind of teaching, our only result is to move to a more directive form of instruction (refer to Exhibit J). Also, I had mentioned that had there been a follow-up or update concerning this class, one would have known that this procedure lasted ONE session because the students did not want that kind of instruction, and as such, they changed their behavior. What is also important to note is that I have spoken with other English teachers who have stated that they also have had to move to the strict book work simply because they cannot do what they would like in their classes due to disruptive student behavior (refer Exhibit R). They have not been counseled or disciplined regarding this. This is a strategy that some teachers have had to employ because classes become too difficult to handle, and yet teachers are required to provide an education for them. I question why this is unsatisfactory when the instructions I gave to the students called on them to complete the book work that the District has given to the teachers, the Holt Anthology. The lessons that the students would have completed came strictly from the text book that the District provides, and yet when I issue it out to the students, I receive the Notice of Unsatisfactory Performance. It should also be noted that while the class dynamics have changed dramatically for the good, I still maintain the same routine/procedure as I did when I first told them about it in October.

The Notice then transitions to a discussion of the events that took place on October 16, 2009, which Ron Hawkins has interpreted as unethical and unprofessional behavior. My objection to this portion is that Ron Hawkins included in the Notice that Amy had said that I should not send out letters without approval. I first mentioned my frustrations to Ron Hawkins concerning her statement in the October meeting. When I confronted Amy on this matter in the October meeting, she denied having said this to me. Her response was, "You may have interpreted it like that," but she did not tell me that I could not send letters without her approval.

The Notice also includes one of the parent's complaints about my comments towards Black and Latino males. My questions are: did Ron Hawkins or any other administrator ever inform the parent of the need to speak with me about the situation? This was a violation of my contractual rights under the agreement between FSUTA and FSUSD.

I further stipulate that the directives that have been listed for me to follow are unnecessary.

I have always followed District policies and responsibilities as evident by evaluation and observations; and in the areas that I did wrong in, I rectified them.
I have always shown respect to staff, students and other employees. What evidence is there that would indicate otherwise? None of the supposed evidence presented supports this conclusion.
I have not violated any standards from the teaching profession as evident by my evaluations and observations. Each year, I have pushed to perfect my professionalism, and there is proof of that.
I have not violated any District policy related to discrimination and harassment. As a young, African American woman who experience discrimination on three levels (as a woman, because of my race, and my age), I understand all too well the dynamics at work in society, and the struggles that minorities encounter in the workplace and on the school grounds. My efforts as a teacher in this District have been to empower my students , especially my minority students, with an education that will carry them to their next level. And I have done just that. This was not an interpretation that Ron Hawkins came to in October, and to determine that this is the case three months afterwards is unreasonable.

I have not made derogatory or harassing comments to staff members or students. Again, the letter does not say that Black and Latino males cannot succeed; that would go against the very nature of my philosophical beliefs. And as a Black woman, I would sound foolish to make such a comment. I simply "kept it real" with my scholars—by telling them about the stereotypes—because this is how I reach them. The statistics are a real factor; the stereotypes are a real phenomenon; and conveying this to a group of students who act foolishly and disrespectfully to their teachers was what I knew I needed to do in order to capture their attention and their hearts. History speaks for itself, and it's important that all students, especially the minority students, know what's real. This is how they know that we really care. And my scholars get that, especially now. They understand that I will not tolerate negative behavior such as making racist jokes and mocking different cultures, or disrespecting each other and their teachers; they see that my heart is strong for them, and that I will not let them fail themselves or each other. I am an educator, and my responsibility is to push my kids to another level academically, socially, emotionally and spiritually. I, along with the parents of my kids, am trying to build strong youth who will not succumb to the trials and tribulations that the world has set against them. And I will continue to push for excellence from my scholars because I see more in them than they can see for themselves at this point. In my approach with students, I am fully adhering to school district policies.

Another issue I have with the Notice centers on a comment that Ron Hawkins made during the January meeting. It was made clear in this meeting that Ron Hawkins had contacted Amy Gillespie to see if there were any problems since October, and as he reported, she has said no. With that said, I question why he now feels it necessary to place me on this 45-day notice when I have demonstrated over the last 91 days that things are working well? I also see that in the Notice, I am being directed to meet with Amy Gillespie in order that she may "help me comply with the above directives." I respectfully request that my compliance be supervised by a different administrator as I do not feel Ms. Gillespie is sufficiently supportive.

Ultimately, I argue that this Notice of Unprofessional Conduct and Unsatisfactory Performance is based on false pretenses, and in no way do I agree with the actions set against me. In February of 2009, I filed a formal complaint against Amy Gillespie with the NAACP stating that she has created a hostile working environment for me, and I was not the only minority teacher to make this same complaint. Amy knew that I had done this because days after her meeting with the NAACP, she called me into her office and told me that if she was creating a hostile working environment, then I should tell her. Consequently, I believe the issuance of the Notice of Unprofessional Conduct to be retaliatory.

Furthermore, I contend that such actions placed against me (as stated in this Notice) are extremely harsh considering the fact that I have never been reprimanded before; neither do my formal observations and evaluations indicate anything worthy of reprimanding. I feel that this is a clear attack and form of retaliation against me because of the stance I took in 2008 by exposing to the School Board the racist acts being committed at Rodriguez High School under Amy's leadership. I also feel that this is a similar act of discrimination against me as an African American employee, which is extremely frustrating, especially considering the low number of Black teachers at a school that is over 20% African American. This is a deliberate attempt on the District's part to damage my character. This Notice is unjust and a clear sign of the District's response to the teacher who brought the racist issues in the school to the surface. It is my belief that this is a clear form of harassment and intimidation in order to push me out of a District and a school. It is also an attack on the part of my principal for exposing her actions (or lack thereof) in regards to not reprimanding students for their racist comments and actions. Furthermore, I stand by the decisions that I made in trying to work with my students of the 2nd period class because I knew that in the end, the results would speak for themselves, and they have. My professionalism and my ability to work collaboratively with students, parents, staff, and community members are immeasurable, and my four years of service to this District and to Rodriguez High School have demonstrated my unyielding efforts to educate my kids and push them to their next level.

I further contend that the allegations that I have discriminated and harassed my Black and Latino students are not only unsupported and ludicrous, but a clear defamation of my character as an educator.

And I find it quite ironic and suspicious that I received this Notice weeks after asking Ron Hawkins for an informative letter that I needed in order to complete the qualifications necessary for obtaining my administrative credential (refer to Exhibit S). These actions convince me that there is an attempt to damage my reputation and character, and place false information in my personnel file in order to hinder any future mobility within the educational system.

Now, in case you didn't read the whole rebuttal (as you can tell, I am VERY detailed), I basically explained the reasons for the letter to the students. I also indicated that had the District and administrators conducted a follow up to the parent's complaints, they would have found out that things were addressed and resolved. Furthermore, they would have learned that this class, because I would not give in to their unruly behavior, actually became the class that I enjoyed the most for the latter half of the year. But because Hawkins refused to remove the Notice from my file, my union representative recommended the case be moved to Arbitration. However, the extent to the professional attacks did not cease. One of the assistant principals, Wilson, chimed in by submitting a negative evaluation of me, which also received an extensive rebuttal.

For those who do not understand the process for evaluating a teacher and why such actions are taken very seriously by a union, here is how it goes. After a teacher receives permanent status in the District, he or she will be observed and evaluated by a school administrator every other year. In my case, 2009-2010 was the school year for my next evaluation. The final evaluation is conducted close to the end of the year, and in order to complete that, the administrator will observe the teacher at least twice during the school year. Based on those observations, the teacher and administrator engage in post observation meetings to discuss ways to improve and enhance one's teaching. Ever since my first year in the District, I had always received positive, constructive evaluations. In most cases, I fell between the "Progressing Towards the Standards" to "Meeting or Exceeding the Standards." This is what I received in year one and two. (Year three had no evaluation.) So you can understand my frustrations when by year four, I had received a negative evaluation, an evaluation that came *after* the Notice of Unprofessional Conduct. What makes this part of the case so unbelievable is how blatant of an attack against my professional character it was. It's important to reiterate that in order to complete the evaluation truthfully and honestly, the evaluator must use the previous observations as a frame of reference.

As the reader will notice, for both the 2009-2010 observations, they were incredibly impressive and positive. It wasn't until after the District issued the Notice of Unprofessional Conduct that suddenly my performance as a teacher did not meet the standards of a good educator. How ironic. To be more thorough, having such a record in one's personnel file can be permanently damaging to one's future endeavors. For example, let's say that I wanted to leave FSUSD because I could no longer handle the stress. I would have had to submit my letter of resignation and applied for another teaching position in another district. If other employers were to call the District to inquire about my professional performance, the first thing that they would reveal to them is this Notice of Unprofessional Conduct. It would not matter that what the District placed in it were based on lies; it wouldn't even matter that my union had highlighted all the violations that were made. All the employer would hear is "Ms. Killings is not a good teacher, and we have proof to show you." So, even if I left that District, I would not be able to obtain another position without having to deal with this mess. In a way, I was stuck. And my only option was to stay and fight, even if it proved detrimental to my health and safety. After all, I needed a job, and teaching was my life.

Fairfield-Suisun Unified School District

Pt observation

"Our Mission is to Provide a Quality Educational System that Assures Opportunities for Every Student to Learn and Meet the Challenges of the Future"

## Certificated Personnel Observation Form

*(Reference: Collective Bargaining Agreement, Article 10)*

Employee: **Felecia Killings**          Evaluator: _____ Lisa Wilson _____

Grade/Subject Area(s): ___9-12/ English___     Position: _____ Assistant Principal _____

School Year: __2009-10__ Site/Location: ___Rodriguez HS___     Date: __9/25/09__
*Standard Selected by the Evaluator: __5__          *Standard Selected by the Unit Member: __2__

Status: ___Temporary ___Probationary-Zero ___First-Year Probationary ___Second-Year Probationary ✓Permanent

---

### Directions for Use:

1) During the first twenty (20) days of the unit member's work year, the administrator will convene an individual or School Site Staff meeting in order to discuss the evaluation process and standards, and distribute the *most recent version of the* California Standards for the Teaching Profession: A Description of Professional Practice for California Teachers to all certificated teachers. The standards and elements of the California Standards for the Teaching Profession will be discussed in relationship to the FSUSD Observation and Evaluation Rubric. Examples of evidence-based evaluations will be provided. Staff will discuss the process and an opportunity to ask questions will be provided. *(Reference: Article 10.3, Section b)*

2) The authorized components of data to validate the CSTP include not only formal observations, but may also include observations of less than thirty minutes, classroom walkthroughs, lesson plans as designed by the classroom teacher, observation of report cards and progress reports, and records of professional development activities as provided by the teacher. *(Reference: Article 10.3, Section e)*

3) The attached FSUSD Observation and Evaluation Rubric will be used to provide meaningful feedback and to serve as a source for discussion. Evidence based comments will be provided. Following each formal observation, the unit member will receive written feedback no less than three (3) workdays prior to the post observation conference. A post observation conference will be held no later than ten (10) workdays following the formal observation. *(Reference: Article 10.3, Section f)*

4) *Permanent*, Probationary and Temporary unit members will be observed using this form at least *two* times throughout the course of the school year. *(Reference: Article 10.3, Section d)*

---

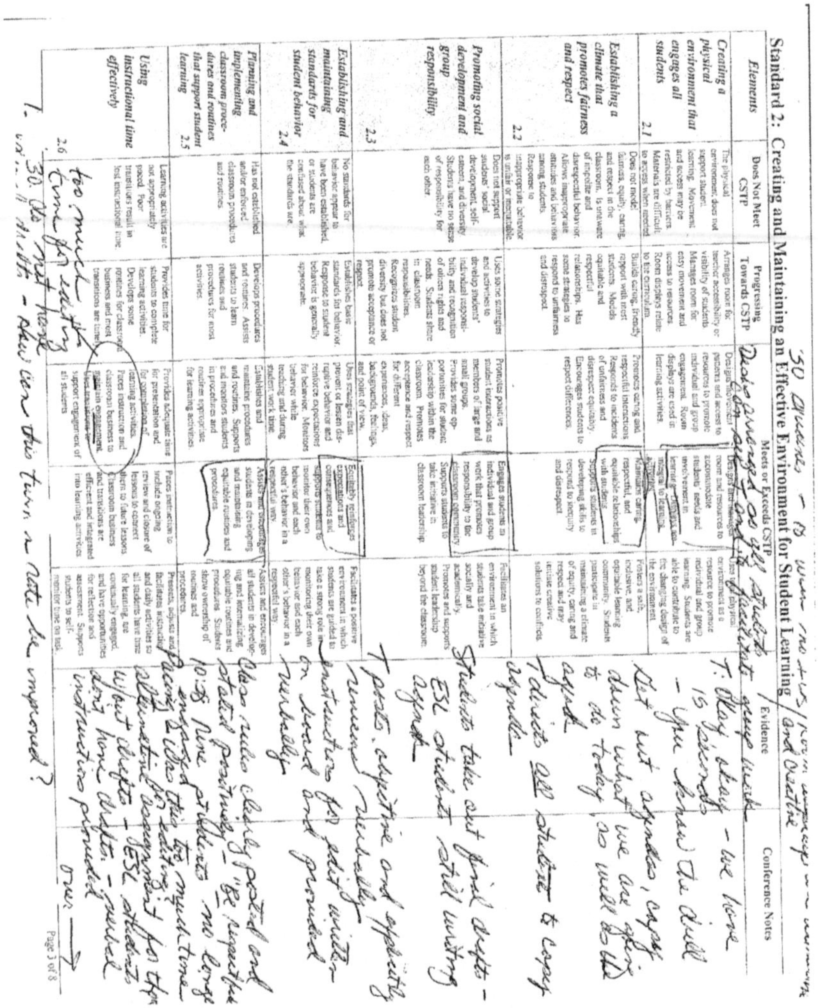

30 students – 13 with no ... / Room ... and Creative

**Standard 2: Creating and Maintaining an Effective Environment for Student Learning**

| Elements | Does Not Meet CSTP | Progressing Towards CSTP | Meets or Exceeds CSTP | | Evidence | Conference Notes |
|---|---|---|---|---|---|---|
| *Creating a physical environment that engages all students* 2.1 | The physical environment does not support student learning. Movement and access may be restricted by barriers. Materials are difficult to access when needed. | Arranges room for teacher accessibility or visibility of students. Manages room for easy movement and access to resources. Room displays relate to the curriculum. | Designs movement patterns and access to resources to promote individual and group engagement. Room displays are used in learning activities. | Designs and manages room and resources to accommodate students' needs and involvement in learning. Displays are integral to learning activities. | Uses total physical environment as a resource to promote individual and group learning. Students are able to contribute to the changing design of the environment. | Desks arranged so all students can see T and to facilitate group work. T: Okay, okay – we have 15 seconds – You know the drill. Get out agendas, copy down what we are going to do today, as well as the agenda. T directs all students to copy agenda. |
| *Establishing a climate that promotes fairness and respect* 2.2 | Does not model fairness, equity, caring, and respect in the classroom. Is unaware of impolite and disrespectful behavior. Allows inappropriate attitudes and behaviors among students. Response to inappropriate behavior is unfair or inequitable. | Builds caring, friendly rapport with most students. Models equitable and respectful relationships. Has some strategies to respond to unfairness and disrespect. | Promotes caring and respectful interactions. Responds to incidents of unfairness and disrespect equitably. Encourages students to respect differences. | Maintains caring, respectful, and equitable relationships with students. Supports students in developing skills to respond to inequity and disrespect. | Fosters a safe, inclusive, and equitable learning community. Students participate in maintaining a climate of equity, caring and respect and may initiate creative solutions to conflicts. | |
| *Promoting social development and group responsibility* 2.3 | Does not support students' social development, self-esteem, and diversity. Students have no sense of responsibility for each other. | Uses some strategies and activities to develop students' individual responsibility and recognition of others rights and needs. Students share in classroom responsibilities. Recognizes student diversity but does not promote acceptance or respect. | Promotes positive student interactions as members of large and small groups. Provides some opportunities for student leadership within the classroom. Promotes acceptance and respect for different experiences, ideas, backgrounds, feelings, and point of view. | Engages students in individual and group work that promotes responsibility to the classroom community. Supports students to take initiative in classroom leadership. | Facilitates an environment in which students take initiative socially and academically. Promotes and supports student leadership beyond the classroom. | Students take out final drafts – ESL students still writing agenda. T posts objective and explicitly reviews verbally |
| *Establishing and maintaining standards for student behavior* 2.4 | No standards for behavior appear to have been established, or students are confused about what the standards are. | Establishes basic standards for behavior. Response to student behavior is generally appropriate. | Uses strategies that prevent or lessen disruptive behavior and reinforce expectations for behavior. Monitors behavior while teaching and during student work time. | Equitably reinforces expectations and consequences and supports students to monitor their own behavior and each other's behavior in a respectful way. | Facilitates a positive environment in which students are guided to take a strong role in monitoring their own behavior and each other's behavior in a respectful way. | instructions for edit written on board and provided verbally |
| *Planning and implementing classroom procedures and routines that support student learning* 2.5 | Has not established and/or enforced classroom procedures and routines. | Develops procedures and routines. Assists students to learn routines and procedures for most activities. | Establishes and maintains procedures and routines. Supports and monitors students in procedures and routines appropriate for learning activities. | Assists and encourages students in developing and maintaining equitable routines and procedures. | Assists and encourages all students in developing and internalizing equitable routines and procedures. Students show ownership of routines and procedures. | Class rules clearly posted and stated positively – "Be respectful" 10:38 Nine students no longer engaged |
| *Using instructional time effectively* 2.6 | Learning activities are not appropriately paced. Poor transitions result in lost instructional time. | Provides time for students to complete learning activities. Develops some routines for classroom business and most transitions are timely. | Provides adequate time for presentation and for completion of learning activities. Paces instruction and classroom business to maintain engagement. Uses transitions to support engagement of all students. | Paces instruction to include ongoing review and closure of lessons to connect them to future lessons. Classroom business and transitions are efficient and integrated into learning activities. | Presents, adjusts and facilitates instruction and daily activities so all students have time for learning, are continually engaged, and have opportunities for reflection and assessment. Supports students to self-monitor time on task. | too much time for editing. Pacing & Was this too much time for editing? alternative assignment for those w/out drafts – ESL students don't have drafts – verbal instructions provided. over → |

Page 3 of 8

1. 30. Do not have ... drafts – How can this turn in rate be improved?

While it may be a little unclear as to what the observation states, the reader will notice that the evaluator is impressed with my teaching because she readily marks me as meeting or exceeding the standards for teaching.

Standard 5: Assessing Student Learning

| Elements | Does Not Meet CSTP | Progressing Towards CSTP | Meets or Exceeds CSTP | Evidence | Conference Notes |
|---|---|---|---|---|---|
| Establishing and communicating learning goals for all students  5.1 | Does not use adopted curriculum materials to establish learning goals for students that reflect the key subject matter concepts, skills, and applications. Students are unaware of learning goals. | Inconsistently uses adopted material to establish student learning goals for students. Some concept, skills, and applications reflect the key subject matter concepts, skills, and applications. Some students are aware of learning goals. | Establishes clear and appropriate goals based on student content standards. Uses subject matter standards from district, state, and other sources to guide establishment of learning goals for all students that reflect the key subject matter concepts, skills, and applications. Clearly communicates learning goals to student and families. | Integrates learning goals into all learning activities. Establishes, reviews and revises learning goals with students and families on an ongoing basis. | *Objective posted and referred to by T.* / *Students have good chance of success by means of simple rubrics on board.* / *Students actively and peer reviewed.* / *does every this happen?* |
| Collecting and using multiple sources of information to assess student learning  5.2 | The teacher uses no consistent source of information to assess student learning and/or uses assessment strategies that are not appropriate. | The teacher uses limited sources of information to assess student learning and uses one or more assessment strategies to monitor student progress. | Uses a variety of assessment tools. Collects, selects, and reflects upon evidence to guide short-term and long-term planning and support student learning. | Embeds a wide range of ongoing assessments in instruction. Uses assessment activities to provide consistent guidance for planning and instruction. | *often self and peer evaluation* / *students write a reflection* / *on how peer editing helps their writing* |
| Involving and guiding all students in assessing their own learning  5.3 | The teacher does not encourage students to reflect on or assess their own work. | Provides feedback to students with feedback on work in progress, as well as completed tasks. Some students involved in assessing their own work. | Provides guidelines for assessment to students. Assists students in reflecting on and assessing their own work. | Engages all students in ongoing self and peer assessment and in monitoring their progress and goals over time. | *Students are to take the essays home for proof reading and mark* |
| Using the results of assessment to guide instruction  5.4 | Information about student learning is inappropriately or not used by the teacher to plan, guide, or adjust instruction. | Uses information from some assessments to drive instruction. Checks for understanding with a few students while teaching and addresses confusion. | Uses formal and informal assessments to plan lessons. Regularly checks for understanding from a wide variety of students to identify student needs and modify instruction. Includes assessments as a regular part of instruction to plan and revise lessons. Identifies students understanding during the lesson and uses a variety of methods and adjust teaching to meet student needs. | Uses a wide range of assessments to guide planning and make adjustment to teaching. Enables broad-based checking for understanding in instruction, and is able to modify and redesign lessons as needed. | *How does this happen?* |
| Communicating with students, families, and other audiences about student progress  5.5 | The teacher provides some information about student learning to students, families, and support personnel, but the information is incomplete, unclear, or not timely. | Provides students with information about their current progress as they engage in learning activities. Families and support personnel are contacted as mandated. | Provides students with timely information about their current progress and how to improve their work. Establishes regular communication with families and support personnel. Engages students, families, and support personnel in regular discussions regarding student progress and improvement plans. Ongoing information is collected from a variety of sources and shared with students, families and support personnel. | Involves students, families, community personnel as partners in the assessment process. Provides comprehensive information about students' progress and improvement plans to students. | *How and how often is progress communicated to students and families?* / *Grades online?* |

*I will the early and peer access with* / *the way you try to tip with their own instruction.*

*Composite ~ score →*

This first observation occurred at the beginning of the school year. It was an exceptional observation, and Wilson was very impressed by my performance. The next document is a replica of the second observation that was conducted *after* I walked off the job; and even though my style of teaching had remained constant for the last few years, the second observation report was not as strong, but still okay.

| Standard 2: Creating and Maintaining an Effective Environment for Student Learning |
| --- |

| Elements | Does Not Meet CSTP | Progressing Towards CSTP | Meets or Exceeds CSTP |
| --- | --- | --- | --- |
| **Creating a physical environment that engages all students** 2.1 | The physical environment does not support student learning. Movement and access may be restricted by barriers to access where needed. Materials are difficult to access. | Arranges room for teacher accessibility or visibility of students. Manages some easy movement and access to resources. Room displays relate to the curriculum or to learning activities. | Designs movement, patterns and access to resources to promote individual and group involvement in learning. Displays are integral to learning. | Designs and manages room and resources to accommodate students' needs and involvement in learning. Students are able to contribute to the design of the environment. |
| **Establishing a climate that promotes fairness and respect** 2.2 | Does not create a fairness, equity, caring and respect in the classroom. Is unaware of people and their relationships. Allows inappropriate attitudes and behaviors among students. Supports or condones inappropriate behavior or is unfair or inequitable. | Uses some strategies and activities to develop students' individual responsibility and recognition of needs. Students share in classroom responsibilities. Yet different experiences, ideas, backgrounds, feelings and points of view diversity had does not promote acceptance or respect. | Promotes caring, respectful, interactions respectful and models equitable and consistent respect. Responds to incidents and supports students' developing capacity to respond to equity and respect differences. | Maintains caring, respectful, inclusive, and equitable relationships. Fosters a safe, inclusive, and constructive learning community. Supports all students to participate in developing a climate of equity, caring and respect. Promotes and models creative solutions to conflicts. |
| **Promoting social development and group responsibility** 2.3 | Does not support development, self-esteem, and diversity. Students have no sense of responsibility for each other. | Provides some opportunities for leadership within the classroom. Promotes social development and responsibility. | Promotes positive student interactions as members of large and small groups. Provides some opportunities for student leadership. Supports students to take initiative and respect differences. | Facilitates engages positive student and group work that promotes students take initiative responsibility to the classroom community. Supports students in student leadership beyond the classroom. |
| **Establishing and maintaining standards for student behavior** 2.4 | No standards for behavior appear to have been established. Behavior is generally not appropriate. | Develops procedures and routines. Assists students to learn procedures and routines for most activities. | Provides consistent expectations and support for positive behavior while teaching and sharing responsibility for learning work time. | Equitably reinforces expectations and consequences and support students to monitor their own behavior and each other's behavior in a respectful way. | Facilitates a positive environment in which students are guided to support individuals in monitoring their own behavior and each other's behavior in a respectful way. |
| **Planning and implementing classroom procedures and routines that support student learning** 2.5 | Learning activities are not appropriately paced. Poor transitions result in lost instructional time. | Establishes procedures to maintain an orderly classroom and routines and monitors transitions and routine support learning activities. | Provides adequate structures for procedures and routines so that students know what to do. Paces instruction so that classroom business is maintained and transitions are timely. | Assists and encourages students in developing and maintaining procedures and routines. Uses transitions to support engagement of all students. | Assists and encourages all students in developing and maintaining procedures. Students develop ownership of transitions. |
| **Using instructional time effectively** 2.6 | | | Provides adequate time for review and climate of to include engages lessons to connect them to future or daily activities so work students have for learning, are continually engaged, and have opportunities for reflection and integrated assessment. Supports | Students are guided to engage in self-reflection and integrated self-assessment of their own learning. |

Page 3 of 8

## Standard 5: Assessing Student Learning

| Elements | Does Not Meet CSTP | Progressing Towards CSTP | Meets or Exceeds CSTP | Evidence | Conference Notes |
|---|---|---|---|---|---|
| **Establishing and communicating learning goals for all students** 5.1 | Does not use adopted curriculum materials to establish learning goals for students that reflect the key subject matter concepts, skills, and applications. Students are unaware of learning goals. | Inconsistently uses adopted material to establish learning goals for students that reflect the key subject matter concepts, skills, and applications. Some students are aware of learning goals. | Uses subject matter standards from district, state, and other sources to guide establishment of learning goals for all students that reflect the key subject matter concepts, skills, and applications frequently communicated to students and families. | *(handwritten)* Co student work or project, T calls student for grade conference | *(handwritten)* |
| **Collecting and using multiple sources of information to assess student learning** 5.2 | The teacher uses no consistent source of information to assess student learning and/or uses assessment strategies that are not appropriate. | The teacher uses limited sources of information to assess student learning and uses one or more assessment strategies to monitor student progress. | The teacher uses a variety of assessment strategies to collect information about student learning and multiple assessment strategies to monitor student progress and inform instruction. | *(handwritten)* Rubric for newspaper? — especially writing piece? | |
| **Involving and guiding all students in assessing their own learning** 5.3 | The teacher does not encourage students to reflect on or assess their own work. | Provides students with feedback on work in progress, as well as completed tasks. Some student involvement in assessing their own work. | Presents guidelines for assessment to students. Assists students in reflecting on and assessing their own work. *(handwritten)* How does this happen? | Integrates student self-assessment and reflection into the teaching, planning, assessment through some peer assessment of work? | *(handwritten)* Students have opportunity to ask T clarifying Qs regarding grade or project / T calls individual students up for grade conferences. |
| **Using the results of assessment to guide instruction** 5.4 | Information about student learning is inappropriately or not used by the teacher to plan, guide, or adjust instruction. | Uses information from some assessments to plan learning activities. Checks for understanding with a few students while teaching and addresses confusions. | Uses formal and informal assessments to plan lessons. Regularly checks for understanding from a wide variety of students to identify student needs and modify instruction. | Includes assessments as a regular part of instruction to plan and revise lessons. Identifies student understanding during lesson using a variety of methods and adjusts teaching to meet student needs. | |
| **Communicating with students, families, and other audiences about student progress** 5.5 | The teacher provides some information about student learning to students, families, and support personnel, but the information is incomplete, unclear, or not timely. | Provides students with information about their current progress as they engage in learning activities. Families and support personnel are contacted as mandated. | Provides students with timely information about their current progress and how to improve their work. Establishes regular communication with families and support personnel. | Engages students, families, and support personnel in regular discussions regarding student progress and improvements plans. Ongoing information is collected from a variety of sources and shared with students, families and support personnel. | *(handwritten)* Grades still not posted online. Jan 15 (email Debbie) |

*(handwritten beneath table)* * New assessment

The reader will notice that suddenly, after three years and two months of teaching, I somehow drop from doing an exceptional job to "not meeting" or barely "progressing" towards the standards. By the time I have this observation conducted, I have been humiliated in front of my students, dealt with an incredibly unruly class, received not one ounce of administrative support, and still had to do everything I could and not lose my mind.

Now there are times that teachers have a bad day, and times when things do not seem to be going right, but this certainly was not the case with my students. As my next rebuttal will indicate, on this observation day, my students were using this time to work on a project that was due within the upcoming week. During these types of "work days," my students were allotted the entire class session to complete any necessary work with other classmates on their projects. I created this activity when I learned that too many of my kids were not completing my projects at home; and to make sure that they were using some time to get it done, I had specific days set aside to do the work in class. So, when Wilson came to observe, she noticed that students were talking while working; and this in her eyes was not indicative of good teaching.

Based on these observations, the administrator came to the final evaluation, which the reader will notice occurred after the District issued the Notice. Recall that it is a requirement that the administrator use the observation notes to conduct the final evaluation; and based on what I had already received, my evaluation should have been positive.

## Fairfield-Suisun Unified School District

*"Our Mission is to Provide a Quality Educational System that Assures Opportunities for Every Student to Learn and Meet the Challenges of the Future"*

*✻ completed evaluation of 15-page rebuttal*

## Certificated Personnel Evaluation Form
*(Reference: Collective Bargaining Agreement, Article 10)*

Copy 1 – Personnel File
Copy 2 – Evaluator
Copy 3 – Employee

Employee: ___Felecia Killings___    Evaluator: ___Lisa Wilson___

Grade/Subject Area(s): ___9-12/English___    Position: ___Assistant Principal___

School Year: ___2009-2010___ Site/Location: ___Rodriguez High School___    Date: ___March 26, 2010___
*Standard Selected by the Evaluator: ___·5___    *Standard Selected by the Unit Member: ___2___

Status: ___Temporary ___Probationary-Zero ___First-Year Probationary ___Second-Year Probationary __XX_ Permanent

---

**Directions for Use:**

1) During the first twenty (20) days of the unit member's work year, the administrator will convene an individual or School Site Staff meeting in order to discuss the evaluation process and standards, and distribute the *most recent version of the California Standards for the Teaching Profession: A Description of Professional Practice for California Teachers* to all certificated teachers. The standards and elements of the California Standards for the Teaching Profession will be discussed in relationship to the FSUSD Observation and Evaluation Rubric. Examples of evidence-based evaluations will be provided. Staff will discuss the process and an opportunity to ask questions will be provided. *(Reference: Article 10.3, Section b)*

2) The authorized components of data to validate the CSTP include not only formal observations, but may also include observations of less than thirty minutes, classroom walkthroughs, lesson plans as designed by the classroom teacher, observation of report cards and progress reports, and records of professional development activities as provided by the teacher. *(Reference: Article 10.3, Section e)*

3) The attached FSUSD Evaluation Rubric will be used to provide meaningful feedback and to serve as a source for discussion for the evaluation. Evidence based comments will be provided. In completing the final report, the evaluator will consider the overall performance in each of the selected standards when determining an evaluation rating. *[Reference: Article 10.3, Sections (a.1, c, & d thru g)]*

4) All unit members will receive a final evaluation report in writing, and an employee/evaluator conference will be held at least thirty (30) workdays prior to their last workday in the school year in which the evaluation took place. *[Reference: Article 10.4, Sections (a or b)]*

---

\* Applies to Permanent Unit Members ONLY

## Standard 2: Creating and Maintaining an Effective Environment for Student Learning

| Elements | Does Not Meet CSTP | Progressing Towards CSTP | Meets or Exceeds CSTP | Evidence-Based Rationale for Rating |
|---|---|---|---|---|
| **Creating a physical environment that engages all students** 2.1 | The physical environment does not support student learning. Movement and access may be restricted by barriers. Materials are difficult to access or not needed to access student learning. | **Arranges room for visibility and accessibility to students.** Manages room for easy movement and access to resources. Room display relate positively to student learning activities. | **Designs movement, access to resources and room arrangement to accommodate students' needs and involvement in learning. Displays are integral to learning.** | **Designs and manages environment to promote individual and group work. Uses total physical environment as a resource to promote individual and group learning. Students are able to contribute to the changing design of the environment. |
| **Establishing a climate that promotes fairness and respect** 2.2 | Does not model fairness, equity, caring, and respect in the classroom. Is unaware of impolite and disrespectful behavior among students. Allows inappropriate attitudes and behaviors and disrespect. | **Models respectful interactions. Models support with most students.** Manages fairly and respectfully. Encourages students to respect differences. | **Promotes caring and respectful interactions. Reinforces relationships with students. Supports students in developing ability to respect to inequity and disrespect.** | **Fosters a safe, inclusive, and equitable community. Students participate in maintaining respect and may initiate creative solutions to conflicts. |
| **Promoting social development and responsibility** 2.3 | Does not support students' social development, self-esteem, and diversity of others rights and needs. Students share responsibility for each other. | **Uses some strategies and activities to develop students' individual responsibility and appreciation of diversity.** Students have opportunities for student leadership within the classroom. Recognizes student experiences, ideas, backgrounds, feelings, and point of view. | **Engages students in individual and group work that promotes responsibility to the classroom community. Supports students to take initiative in classroom leadership, beyond the classroom.** | **Facilitates an environment in which students take initiative socially and academically. Promotes and supports student to develop classroom leadership. |
| **Establishing and maintaining standards for student behavior** 2.4 | No standards for behavior have been established, or standards are unclear about what the standards are. | **Establishes basic standards for behavior. Response to student behavior is generally appropriate.** Monitors behavior while teaching and during student work time. | **Uses strategies that prevent or lessen disruptive behavior and reinforce expectations. Monitors student behavior and each other's behavior in a respectful way.** | **Facilitates a positive environment in which students are guided to take a strong role in monitoring their own behavior and each other's behavior, and intervening in respectful ways. |
| **Planning and implementing classroom procedures and routines that support student learning** 2.5 | Has not established and/or implemented classroom procedures and routines. | **Develops procedures and routines. Assists students in maintaining routines and procedures for the next activities.** | **Establishes and maintains procedures and routines. Supports students in procedures and routines for learning activities.** | **Assists and encourages students in developing equitable routines and procedures. |
| **Using instructional time effectively** 2.6 | Learning activities are not appropriately paced. Poor transitions result in lost instructional time. | **Provides time for completion of learning activities. Develops some classroom business and transitions are timely.** | **Provides adequate time to include ongoing review and closure of learning activities. Uses transitions into learning activities.** | **Paces instruction to facilitate instruction and daily activities for learning, and continuously engaged for reflection and self-assessment. Supports students to self-monitor time on task. |

**Rating (Check One):**

☐ Does Not Meet CSTP
☐ Meets or Exceeds CSTP
☒ XXX Progressing Towards CSTP

## Standard 5: Assessing Student Learning

| Elements | Does Not Meet CSTP | Progressing Towards CSTP | Meets or Exceeds CSTP | Evidence-Based Rationale for Rating |
|---|---|---|---|---|
| **Establishing and communicating learning goals for all students** 5.1 | Does not use adopted curriculum materials to establish learning goals for students that reflect the key subject matter concepts, skills, and applications. Students are unaware of learning goals. | Inconsistently uses adopted material to establish learning goals for students that reflect the key subject matter concepts, skills, and applications. Some students are aware of learning goals. | Uses subject matter standards from district, state, and other sources to guide establishment of learning goals for all students that reflect the key subject matter concepts, skills, and applications. Clearly communicates learning goals to students and families. | Establishes clear and appropriate goals based on content standards, with consideration of students' learning needs. Involves students and families in developing individual goals to support learning. | During the announced first formal observation, Ms. Killings established clear and appropriate goals based on content standards and students' learning needs. Guidelines for assessment were presented to students, and students were provided with scoring rubrics. Students engaged in self and peer assessment of written work against criteria (rubric) and completed a reflection of how peer review will improve their own writing. Students then took papers home for parental review and assessment.

During the second formal observation, as groups were working on projects, Ms. Killings called individual students forward for grade conferences. |
| **Collecting and using multiple sources of information to assess student learning** 5.2 | The teacher uses no consistent source of information to assess student learning and/or uses assessment strategies that are not appropriate. | The teacher uses limited sources of information to assess student learning and use or more assessment strategies to monitor student progress. | The teacher uses a variety of sources to collect information about student learning and multiple assessment strategies to monitor student progress and inform instruction. | Embeds a wide range of ongoing assessments in instructional activities to provide consistent guidance for planning and instruction. | From February 24–March 17, 2010, posted objective for English 11 was "students will recognize media's projection of racial and ethnic stereotypes." Students were to meet this objective by watching and taking notes on a series of films including, but not limited to, Stand and Deliver, Breakfast at Tiffany's and Bruce Almighty. |
| **Involving and guiding all students in assessing their own learning** 5.3 | The teacher does not encourage students to reflect on or assess their own work. | Provides students with feedback on work in progress, as well as completed tasks. Some student involvement in assessing their own work. | Presents guidelines for assessment to students. Assists students in reflecting on and assessing their own work. | Integrates student self-assessment and reflection into the learning activities. Students engage in some peer assessment of work against criteria. | The posting of grades online was discussed during post-observation conferences on both October 1 and December 14, 2009, at which time Ms. Killings set a goal of having grades posted online by January 15, 2010. As of March 26, 2010, grades still not posted online. |
| **Using the results of assessment to guide instruction** 5.4 | Information about student learning is inappropriately or not used by the teacher to plan, guide, or adjust instruction. | Uses information from some assessments to plan learning activities. Checks for understanding with a few lessons while teaching and addresses confusions. | Uses formal and informal assessments to plan lessons. Regularly checks for understanding from a wide variety of student needs and modify instruction. | Includes assessments as a regular part of instruction to plan and revise lessons. Identifies student understanding during the lesson using a variety of methods to identify and adjust teaching to meet student needs. | Uses a wide range of assessments to guide planning and make adjustments in teaching. Embeds broad-based checking for understanding and is able to modify and redesign lessons as needed. | Recommendations: Use adopted curriculum materials and establish clear and appropriate goals based on student content standards, with consideration of students' learning needs. Reduce reliance on video and develop lessons to include more ELA standards to prepare students to successfully complete department and district benchmark assessments, CAHSEE, and STAR. Post grades online to improve school-to-home communication.

**Rating (Check One):**

☐ Does Not Meet CSTP

XXX Progressing Towards CSTP

☐ Meets or Exceeds CSTP |
| **Communicating with students, families, and other audiences about student progress** 5.5 | The teacher provides some information about student learning to students, families, and support personnel, but the information is incomplete, unclear, or not timely. | Provides students with timely information about their progress as they engage in learning activities. Families and support personnel are contacted as mandated. | Provides students with timely information about their current progress and how to improve their work. Establishes regular communication with families and support personnel. | Involves students, families, and support personnel as partners in the assessment process. Provides comprehensive information about students' progress and improvement plans to students, families, and support personnel. | |

Although it may be hard to read, this evaluation basically stated that my teaching performance was mostly at "Progressing towards the Standards." And you can imagine my surprise when I saw this evaluation in detail, especially when the observations had readily indicated that I was meeting or exceeding them. For the most part, I couldn't believe the stuff she had wrote concerning my teaching, especially when my observations were far better than what she indicated here. What the reader ought to know is that observations are not placed in a teacher's file, only the evaluations. From this report, it would only substantiate the negative and ludicrous accusations that were present in the Notice; and if a potential employer from another District wanted to view my personnel file, all they had to see was what the administration and District presented.

Well, I guess they must have thought I had my stupid face on or something, and assumed I wouldn't fight back on this thing either. Rarely will a teacher do anything to defend him or herself against their bosses. And this is essentially why the District and administrators feel so comfortable doing the heinous things they do to their challenging employees. In a system so blinded by its own wickedness and corruption, there ought to be a balance of power in which everyone is held accountable for how everyone is treated. In other words, teachers ought to be able to evaluate administrators to discuss whether or not they are doing what's expected of them. In addition, students ought to be able to evaluate teachers and administrators so we are held accountable to their expectations. But I guess that's sharing too much power; and well, we just can't have that now can we?

After reading the evaluation, I immediately made contact with my union representative, and we went to work on formulating another grievance report against that administrator with hopes of removing it from my file. And just as I did before, I constructed my rebuttal to the evaluation.

RE: Evaluation Conducted by Lisa Wilson

Issue: The following evaluation does not accurately attest of my qualities as a permanent teacher at Rodriguez High School. I contend that based on the past experience regarding a situation in which I walked off the job, and the subsequent Notice of Unprofessional Conduct issued by FSUSD, that this negative evaluation is another form of retaliation in order to further damage my personnel file. I contend that the following evaluator did not address any specific issues (especially in reference to the negative reports) regarding the nature of my teaching to me directly, and has therefore including information that is ill-supported based on personal biases. The evaluator did not specifically identify my standings under the categories of "Does Not Meet CSTP," "Progressing Towards CSTP," and "Meets or Exceeds CSTP" on the first copy of the evaluation, thereby making it difficult to initially form a rebuttal. When brought to her attention by Stephanie Cobb, my union representative, evaluator response was "There is no requirement that boxes be highlighted or underlined." After this was brought up to the site principal, Amy Gillespie, Wilson was instructed to underline my standings in specific categories of the standards. After looking over the evaluation in detail, and comparing it to past observation reports, I have found several discrepancies and contradictions, which lead me to believe that this is another form of retaliatory actions issued by Rodriguez' administration. In speaking with two other Black educators who have also had Lisa Wilson as an evaluator, it appears indicative of her character to use any miniscule matter as the basis for belittling one's teaching abilities. This is readily reflected in the low ratings found on the final evaluations. I strongly contend that this evaluation was completed with ill-intentions in mind, and has been created in order to denigrate my character as a minority educator in this District and at this site.

Meeting date: April 22, 2010

Context: The context of this evaluation is important to address in this rebuttal. I contend that what has happened earlier in the school year have been used by Lisa Wilson as the basis of this evaluation. The negative reports stated therein were never addressed to me directly in any observation or discipline meeting, which leads me to question the validity of her responses and subsequent low ratings.

On September 25, 2009, Lisa Wilson conducted her first formal observation of one of my classes. The evaluator and I agreed that as a permanent teacher, I would be evaluated on Standards 2 (Creating and Maintaining an Effective Environment for Student Learning), Standard 5 (Assessing Student Learning), and Standard 6 (Developing as Profession Educator). After her first formal observation, I was given her report, in which case, the observation was superb. While holding our post-observation meeting, Wilson reported that she was very impressed with what she saw. In fact, for every category that she used to assess my performance, she marked me as "Meets or Exceeds CSTP." Of my four years at this school site, this was by far my best observation. (Reader will refer to Attachment A for a copy of 1st observation.)

In the middle of October 2009, because of strenuous circumstances regarding a very unruly, disrespectful, and often harassing class, I walked off the job because I felt that the administration was ill-supportive of my needs as a teacher. In addition, because of the constant meetings that I was asked to attend to address how "wrong" I was, I became frustrated that this administration was siding with the harassing students rather than supporting a struggling teacher.

In one instance, Lisa Wilson, whom I had never expected to be involved with this situation because she never dealt with discipline issues regarding my students, was one of two administrators who came to my class during one of my teaching sessions to address what students were saying about me to them. (While Lisa did not speak to me directly about any issues, it was clear that she was included in a discussion about what was happening with me by the site principal. In recognizing the persistent problems that I was having with this disrespectful class since the beginning of the school year, neither Lisa nor the other administrator offered their support or suggestions for how to work with these students before their unexpected visit. And as such, I was left to fend for myself.) The nature of their visit was intimidating, humiliating, and embarrassing. I felt myself losing authoritative influence with my students because every time students did something wrong, I would react with a consequence. When the students did not like the consequence, they ran and told administration. Rather than administration offering a supportive hand to me, they came to my class and addressed me, leaving my students to believe that I was in trouble for some of my actions as a teacher. Because of these factors (the non-support plus misbehaved students), I walked off the job, but not without first informing an administrator to get coverage for my class.

After returning to work at the latter part of October, Lisa Wilson conducted her second formal observation on December 7, 2009. Unlike the first observation, this one was not scheduled. On the day that she observed, my students were having a "Work Day." Four years ago, I began implementing "Work Days" that allowed my students to complete any aspect of a project that was due. I developed this strategy because I noticed that a lot of my kids were not turning in their projects at a timely manner. When I asked them what I could do to help, they reported that if they had some time in class to complete it, then they would be finished with them in time. This is, essentially, what Lisa Wilson observed on December 7th. There was no set lesson. The only thing posted on the agenda was that it was a "Work Day," and students were required to complete any aspect of the project, and were to follow the instructions that were listed on their Instruction Sheet. (Students were required to create a newspaper project that addressed the history of the Salem Witch Trials.) While Lisa Wilson was in the class, the students were talking amongst each other about various things, including but not limited to the discussion of the project. While students were working, I went to every student to make sure that I provided as much assistance as possible to them. The students understood that by the end of the class period, they were to produce some work to show me. The students also understood that it was important not to waste my class time doing nothing; if they did, the consequence was that I would not take their projects if they came in late. (Again, this is a strategy that I have used for years, only because it works. I have a higher turn it rate because of my methodology.)

After Lisa Wilson left my class, one of my students approached me to ask why she was there. I told her that she was here to observe me. My student then stated that she overheard Lisa Wilson speaking to another administration about her intentions to visit my class, especially after my walking off in October. From that conversation, my student inferred that there was something negative about what was said and how it was said. My student was concerned for me, and that is why she spoke to me that day.

When I had received a copy of the 2nd observation report, it was significantly more negative than the 1st one, and portions of the observation were not completed. Lisa Wilson reported that instead of meeting or exceeding the standards, that I had not met an aspect of the standards, and that I was only progressing towards them in other areas. This was clearly surprising considering the nature of the lesson, and the fact that it was designed to specifically allow for students to work on their projects. She reported that "students are confused about what the standards are," and that I "establish basic standards for behavior." While students did ask questions regarding clarity on the project and instructions, none were confused about the standards. They understood the purpose and learning objectives for the project, but had questions on how to complete particular assignments. As far as having "basic standards for behavior," the students were talking during the session, an aspect of student behavior that I have observed is not favorable with this evaluator. When she first observed me, my class was completely silent. No student spoke unless they had one or two questions. Lisa Wilson obviously identifies this type of classroom behavior as "respectful" or "good;" however, simply because students talk during class does not mean that they are not completing their work. My students are very aware that good, respectful behavior is necessary and required in my classes. Because of the standards that I set at the beginning of the year, I have very little to no disciplinary issues with my students (except that unruly class), especially among my juniors (whom she observed in December). Lisa Wilson reported that "off-task conversations" caused her to place me in the "Does Not Meet CSTP" category; however, she did not report that there were "on task" conversations as well (on the evaluation). Students completed their work, and did so at the set deadline. If there are any doubts, please see the classroom and the walls outside my classroom door. The projects are posted.

**Rebuttal to evaluation:** On March 29, 2010, I received my evaluation report. Upon reading it, I found several discrepancies and inaccuracies. In addition, the evaluation, according to my union representative, was not complete, as Lisa Wilson was supposed to highlight or underline where I fell in regards to meeting, progressing, or not meeting the standards. Lisa Wilson argued that she did complete the evaluation, and made it clear that she did not need to highlight or underline any areas in the necessary columns. After discussing this issue with Amy Gillespie and Dr. Sheila McCabe, Lisa Wilson was instructed to underline the areas in the columns. This rebuttal addresses the evaluator's comments as well as the areas that she underlined, pinpointing each category that contains contradictions or discrepancies. My overall stipulation is that based on previous observations and discussions, my evaluation should indicate that I meet and/or exceed the standards, not simply progressing.

## Discrepancy #1--Standard 2.1--Creating a physical environment that engages all students.

On September 25, 2009, evaluator reported in the first observation report that I "Meet or Exceed CSTP." The box that she highlighted states that I "design and manage room and resources to accommodate students' needs and involvement in learning." Evaluator did not underline the portion that reads,

"Displays are integral to learning activities." On December 7, 2009, evaluator reported in the second observation report that I "Meet or Exceed CSTP." The box that she highlighted states that I "design movement patterns and access to resources to promote individual and group engagement." Evaluator made no mention of my displays in either observation. On the evaluation, Wilson reports that I am "progressing towards CSTP." She indicates that my "displays are creative and attractive but are not used in learning activities." Based on these ratings, I raise the following questions and concerns:

- On what grounds does evaluator argue in the evaluation that the displays "are not used in learning activities"?

- If both observations report that I am meeting or exceeding the CSTPs, then on what grounds does Wilson state that I am only progressing in the evaluation?

- If there were any negative portions of the lesson that Wilson witness during the observation, she neither addressed nor voiced her concerns to me during post-observation meeting. If such was the case, then on what grounds does this evaluation stand?

- Since there was no discussion of my displays at any observation meeting, on what grounds does Wilson state that my displays do not relate to the learning activities in the evaluation?

- What aspect of the displays does the evaluator not see as being a part of the learning activities?

- If my displays do not relate or are not used in the learning activities, then what types of displays are conducive to learning activities? Why was this not conveyed to me at the beginning of the school year? Why was this not conveyed to other staff members via staff meetings or department meetings? Why are other teachers' displays acceptable tools for learning activities, but my student work, unit displays, and literary designs are not considered "useful" in learning activities?

- The displays in my class include student work, literary pieces, and thematic pictures that relate to the units the students learn. The designs have not changed since the beginning of the year, that is, except the student work, which changes once students turn in projects. My classroom designs have always been creative, innovative, and educationally stimulating. The colorful displays allow for a soothing atmosphere, which helps students and the teacher feel comfortable, and help us to enjoy the surroundings.

- My class displays are used in learning activities. They contain samples of student work that I use for my classes to give them a visual aid of an intended project. Parents who come to visit the class are impressed with the displays, especially when other classrooms have little to none.

- In addition to these displays, I also have the ELA standards posted on my wall. These standards are also used in the learning activities as they provide the learning requirements for the students; they also serve as guidelines for the teacher.

- I have also created a poster with the class procedures, which is placed largely on the wall. The discipline policies, hate crime policy, non-negotiables, and the RHS Way are also posted, which serve as reminders of proper student behavior. These displays are always conducive to their learning, especially behavioral learning.

- Any viewer will also notice the thematic displays, all of which highlight the units that both my 10th and 11th grade classes complete.

- Consult any teacher, student or parent and they will report that my displays are incredible and relate to the classroom learning environment. No administrator ever indicated the type of displays that teachers should post on walls, except that of student work. To be evaluated and judged as not having displays that are "used in learning activities," yet seeing the classroom itself, is a contradiction to the facts.

- I contend that this discrepancy is a form of administrative "nit-picking" and discrimination, and there is not validity to the evaluator's statement in the final evaluation.

### Discrepancy #2—Standard 2.2—Establishing a climate that promotes fairness and respect

On September 25, 2010, the evaluator reported in the first observation that I "meet or exceed CSTP." The evaluator highlighted/underlined that I "maintain caring, respectful, and equitable relationships with students." On December 7, 2010, evaluator reported the second observation that I "meet or exceed CSTP." The evaluator underlined that I "promote caring and respectful interactions" and "responds to incidents of unfairness and disrespect equitably." On the evaluation report, Wilson indicates that I "do not meet CSTP" and am "progressing towards CSTP" in the area of fairness. She underlines that I "respond to inappropriate behavior" unfairly or inequitably; but that I "build caring, friendly rapport with most students." Based on these ratings, I raise the following questions and concerns:

- Evaluator never discussed in any observation meeting the notion that I did not treat students equitably. On what grounds does evaluator make this judgment in the evaluation? And if the issue was so pervasive, why was I not made aware of this in any observation meetings?

- The evaluator's underlined statements are a contradiction. How can a teacher have a caring, friendly rapport with students, but also respond to them (most of them) unfairly or inequitably? Students are not favorable to teachers that they feel mistreat them. Students do not like those kinds of teachers; therefore, it is impossible to have a "friendly" rapport with them while treating them "inequitably." Simply ask my scholars.

- My observation: the evaluator has been made aware of the Notice of Unprofessional Conduct that was issued to me in January. The evaluator is basing her judgments in this evaluation on false pretenses mentioned in the Notice. The evaluator neither solicited my side of any story; she never asked me the nature of the disrespectful, harassing class that I had; and she never provided support to me as her teacher in order to address the problems of the students (i.e. behavioral strategies, behavioral training, etc.)

- The evaluator is basing her judgments on hearsay and false speculations.

- If I am not made aware of the issue of "inequitable" treatment, then I should not be reprimanded or judged as behaving inequitably. Unlike the evaluation, my observation reports are not placed in my personnel file, and as such, one would argue that I treat students poorly.

- Because observations are not included in the file, it would be impossible for outsiders to see the discrepancies between the observations and evaluations.

- Evaluator does not consider or report that while my unruly, harassing class posed serious problems for me before my departure in October, I have not had a single issue with the class since then.

- Evaluator does not consider or report that four of my five sections were exceptionally good, and that I had never had a single complaint from students or parents regarding "inequitable" treatment from them.

- Evaluator can only judge based on the issues that I had with my $2^{nd}$ period class, of which she (evaluator) had never discussed the issues with me at any time during the period in which this class was difficult (August-October).

- Evaluator argues that "At times, [my] response to inappropriate behavior is unfair or inequitable. When students misbehaved for a substitute teacher, [I] responded by punishing the entire class with seatwork and refused to teach." My stipulation with this statement centers on several facts:

  - First, not once did Lisa Wilson address the "inequitable" treatment that she alleges I displayed with my students. Neither does Wilson indicate that neither she nor any other administrator had provided support or strategies to address the issues in my class. According to the teacher contract, the purpose of evaluations and observations is to help the teacher. This element of the evaluation should have first been discussed when we had observation meetings. Then I would have had the opportunity to correct the "inequitable" behavior.

  - Second, Lisa Wilson asserts that my refusal "to teach" my class serves as evidence for not meeting the standards. Lisa Wilson has never once discussed this "refusal" with me as her teacher. If she had, she would have learned that this tactic (of providing "seat work") was not a refusal to teach, but rather a sign of my frustrations with the unruly, harassing class. Had Lisa Wilson discussed the nature of my actions in the first place, she would have learned that this tactic lasted ONE class session because the students did not like the kind of atmosphere that was created. In fact, after ONE class session of implementing "seat work," the students understood that if our class was to be enjoyable, it would require their full cooperation and good behavior. The students hated the tension, and wanted to change immediately.

- Third, if by "seat work," the evaluator is referring to my students having to complete activities in the Holt Anthology, then yes, they had to do it because their behavior would not allow for more creative, innovative, hands-on lessons. From this statement, I could argue that the evaluator does not value the curriculum that the District has obligated the teachers to use.

- Fourth, evaluator does not appreciate or understand that this behavioral strategy is a learning technique that I have employed for four years. It teaches the students that good behavior leads to positive interactions among students and teachers. My scholars quickly learned this when they realized that it was better to do right than do wrong.

- Fifth, evaluator argues that by punishing the whole class for misbehaving with the substitute teacher, that this proves that I discipline unfairly and inequitably. Wilson, again, never addressed the nature of this allegation with me in any meetings. Had she done so, she would have learned that the whole class was punished because NO ONE would give the names of the perpetrators. The class to which she refers is the same unruly and harassing class that I had trouble with for nearly three months. Furthermore, the whole class would often receive a punishment/consequence because the majority of the class committed the wrong act. (There were at least 7-8 students in a class of about 30 who readily caused trouble and anxiety for me and the other students.) Wilson's allegations in this portion of the evaluation suggest that I mistreat my students, and that as a teacher, I am not meeting the standards in this area. Had Wilson done a thorough investigation, including discussing the situation with me, and conducting another investigation with my students now, she would have learned that not only are her allegations false, but misconstrued. If there were any complaints among the parents and students, Wilson never directed them to speak to me in a meeting to address their concerns, which is the protocol that they follow with other teachers. Furthermore, Wilson and other administrators have provided behavioral conferences with other teachers, students and parents when there were serious issues in the class. This option was not provided to me by Wilson at any moment during this school year.

- My students received teacher consequences based on the severity of their negative behavior. When considering "inequitable treatment," how "fair" is it that teachers and substitutes have to be harassed by students? How "fair" is it that a teacher is punished by administration for how she handles student behavior? And how "fair" is it that administrators provide strategies and support to some teachers, but not to others.

- Fifth, Wilson's allegation to this portion of the evaluation would cause the reader to infer that I unfairly and inequitably punish <u>all or most of</u> my students. This cannot be so considering that four of my five sections were entirely respectful and behaved very well. Not a single complaint came from those students or their parents. Rather, any and all complaints came from the harassing 2$^{nd}$ period class. To assess my performance on this particular group is unfair and inequitable. In fact, this harassing class became so fed up with the disrespect and punishments that they changed their behavior dramatically. For the past <u>SIX</u> months, there has not been a single complaint from a student or a parent.

- Sixth, during this school year, there have been reports from teachers that when we need to send students out or suspend them from our classes, administration over turns our requests, and sends the student back because of the District's pressure to reduce the suspension and expulsion rates. This factor is very present at RHS. In my case, I did not receive any support when I had requested that a student be removed from my class permanently because of his unruly behavior. His constant racial jokes made it severely uncomfortable for me as a teacher, and made it especially difficult when I needed to establish community in my class. This is inequitable.

- Seventh, promoting equity in the class is the foundation of my educational philosophy. The District and Rodriguez' administration are well aware of this by my actions of reporting the inequitable, racist incidents that were exhibited on our campus in April 2008. The discipline rates among students of color were severely inequitable when compared to White students, and this was proven by the actions of Amy Gillespie-Oss and her administration. Treating students fairly is a reality for me. When I do come hard on students, it does not to make them weaker, but shapes their character and enhances their morality. These students were beyond disrespectful. Some of the things they said and did were harassing to me, but my devotion and commitment to them as scholars would not allow me to let them remain this way. The effects of my "hard" discipline produced countless days and lessons that have been enjoyable, amiable, and equitable, especially in the 2$^{nd}$ period class.

- Eighth, if my discipline was "inequitable" and "unfair," it should be on the administrator's part to observe the disruptive, unruly class in order to alleviate the tensions between the students and teacher. No administrator ever observed my 2$^{nd}$ period class, and cannot attest to the "inequitable" treatment that the evaluator accuses me of.

- I contend that this discrepancy is a form of administrative "nit-picking" and discrimination, and there is not validity to the evaluator's statement in the final evaluation.

## Discrepancy #3—Standard 2.3—Promoting social development and group responsibility

On September 25, 2009, evaluator reported in the first observation that I "meet or exceed CSTP." She underlines that I "engage student in individual and group work that promotes responsibility to the classroom community." On December 7, 2009, evaluator reported nothing on the observation for this category. Neither did she highlight or underline any portion in this category. On the evaluation, Wilson reports that I "meet or exceed CSTP;" however she marks me one level below. She underlines that I "promote positive student interactions as members of large and small groups." Based on these ratings, I raise the following question/concern:

- If there was no markings on the December observation, then on what grounds does the evaluator feel that I have dropped a level in this category?

### Discrepancy #4—Standard 2.4—Establishing and maintaining standards for student behavior

On September 25, 2009, evaluator reported in the first observation that I "meet or exceed CSTP." She underlines that I "equitably reinforce expectations and consequences." On December 7, 2009, evaluator reports in the second observation that I "do not meet CSTP" and am "progressing towards CSTP." Evaluator underlines that "students are confused about what the standards are" and that I "establish basic standards for behavior." Evaluator also reported that there were "off-task conversations." Based on these ratings, I raise the following questions and concerns:

- At my first observation, students were extremely quiet in the class. In comparison, at the second observation, my students were talkative while working on their project assignments. In my class, talking is an accepted behavior as long as students demonstrate completion of work, which my scholars performed by the end of the session. It is apparent (based on Wilson's observation reports and evaluation) that "good behavior" is signified by quietness among the evaluator; however, I identify good behavior as abiding by my class rules, which center on respecting peers and teacher. These standards have been established from the beginning of the school year, and have been reinforced throughout the year. Because of my standards of respect, I have never severe complaints about the bad or "basic" behavior of my students, again except for that harassing class.

- As far as students being "confused about the standards," my students were asking clarity questions regarding a project that they were required to complete. This assignment, in particular, was not only new to the students, but also to me as the teacher. This was my first time creating this project, and I welcomed their questions. Having and receiving them helped me to provide clarity to its content, which I can then use should I decide to repeat the project.

- Students had been participating in a study of the Salem Witch Trials and the concept of scape-goating in American history. When Wilson came to observe, my students were engaged in a "Work Day" session, in which they were provided class time to work exclusively on their projects. Evaluator makes the assumption that because students ask for clarity regarding certain aspects of the project instructions (i.e. "how do we do want ads") that this means they are confused about the standards of the project. (The standards were to develop a comprehensive understanding of the Salem Witch Trials, and to analyze how scape-goating is a recurring theme in American history. They would then demonstrate their understandings and analyses in the form of a newspaper. No student questioned this. Rather, it was a question about how to make want ads for their newspaper.)

- Wilson reports on the evaluation that "classroom procedures and routines were not enforced." According to my classroom rules and procedures poster, which is displayed on a large portion of the wall, all students must "be respectful, be on time, be ready to learn, and be a scholar." In addition, the procedures for every class is that students be on time and be prepared to work. This is something that has been reiterated to the students throughout the year. On the day that Wilson observed for the second time, my students were on time, they worked on their projects, and they showed their progress by the end of the class period. Wilson was not there to observe them turn in their product; and while it is true that some students did talk during this class session, she has no evidence to prove that they did not work.

- Evaluator reports in the evaluation that while "some students worked productively...many students engaged in off-task, loud conversations." Evaluator does not indicate that when the students seemed to be getting too loud that I instructed them to be more quiet and return back to work. Neither does the evaluator state that students who were loud did return to completing their work. Wilson's lack of thorough analysis causes any reader of this evaluation to assume that I allow "off-task" behavior and discussions to dominate my class; any reader could also assume that I allow my students to do what they want while not completing any assignments. Had the evaluator conducted an update on her "observation," she would have seen that while the students were talking during this session, the students also completed their work by the end of class. In fact, because of this "Work Day," I received a good turn-in rate for the newspaper project that my scholars completed on the Salem Witch Trials. The products can be seen inside my classroom, posted on the walls, and also on the outside walls of my class. (Another element that proves that my displays are related to learning activities.)

- Evaluator reports in the evaluation that I provided "no direct instruction" regarding the assignment that the students were supposed to complete. In the post observation meeting regarding the December 7, 2009 observation, the evaluator never discussed this issue with me. On what grounds does the evaluator make this observation? Contrary to her allegations, the students did receive direct instructions regarding the project, as they made references to them when they asked their clarity questions. If this was not an element of discussion in the post-observation meeting, or at any other meeting regarding my teaching, then why is it included as a negative reference in my evaluation?

- I contend that this discrepancy is a form of administrative "nit-picking" and discrimination, and there is not validity to the evaluator's statement in the final evaluation.

## Discrepancy #5—Standard 2.5—Planning and implementing classroom procedures and routines that support student learning

On September 25, 2009, evaluator reported in the first observation that I "meet or exceed CSTP." She underlines that I "assist and encourage students in developing and maintaining equitable routines and procedures." On December 7, 2009, evaluator does not report if I do not meet, progress, meet or exceed CSTP. She does not underline any areas of this standard. On the evaluation, Wilson reports that I "do not meet" and am "progressing towards CSTP." She underlines that I "have not enforced classroom procedures and routines;" but that I "develop procedures and routines." Based on these ratings, I raise the following questions and concerns:

- During the December post-observation meeting, the evaluator made no mention of me dropping from exceeding to not meeting this category of the standard. If such is the case, on what grounds does Wilson argue that I do not meet this standard?

- On what basis does she make this allegation if she marked nothing on this standard in the December observation?

- In addition, what evidence does the evaluator provide that would suggest that I do not enforce procedures and routines? My students have not only learned my procedures and routines, but readily exercise them. If they did not, I would have an excess of referrals and disciplinary reports that would suggest my students misbehave. My students understand that not only do I "develop" my routines and procedures, but I have also "encouraged and assisted my students in developing and maintaining" the routines and procedures. It is because of the good rapport and respect that I readily enforced in my class that allows my students to trust me and to work well with me.

- I would question why the evaluator makes the report that I "do not meet" this standard on the evaluation report (which is the document that is placed in my personnel file) when it is clearly evident that I do, especially as can be identified on my first observation and the continual good rapport that I have with my scholars.

- I contend that this discrepancy is a form of administrative "nit-picking" and discrimination, and there is not validity to the evaluator's statement in the final evaluation.

## Discrepancy #6—Standard 5—Assessing Student Learning

- According to the observations conducted on September 25th and December 7th, I "meet or exceed CSTP." On the evaluation, Wilson reports that I am only "progressing towards CSTP."

On September 25, 2009, evaluator reports in the first observation that I "meet or exceed CSTP." She underlines that I "establish clear and appropriate goals based on student content standards." On December 7, 2009, evaluator reports in the second observation that I "meet or exceed CSTP." She underlines that I "use subject matter standards from district, state, and other sources to guide establishment of learning goals for all students that reflect the key subject matter concepts, skills, and applications." On the evaluation, Wilson reports that I am "progressing toward CSTP." She underlines that I "inconsistently use adopted material to establish learning goals for students." Based on these ratings, I raise the following questions and concerns:

- During the post observation meetings, the evaluator never discussed any negative aspect of communicating learning goals for all students. On what grounds do I drop another level?

- Evaluator reported on the evaluation, "From February 24-March 17, 2010, posted objective for English 11 was "students will recognize media's projection of racial and ethnic stereotypes. Students were to meet this objective by watching and taking notes on a series of films including, but not limited to, <u>Stand and Deliver</u>, <u>Breakfast at Tiffany's</u> and <u>Bruce Almighty</u>.

  - o At no time during the school year does the evaluator address my cultural image in mass media unit, which was an extensive study of how media project negative images of all ethnic groups.

  - o The evaluator makes the assumption and allegation that in order to meet the learning objective, students only watched movies.

  - o Had the evaluator discussed this unit with me, she would have learned that not only did the students have several objectives and learning goals relating to this unit, but that there were substantial ELA standards that supported the unit.

  - o On one of the days that the evaluator came to my class, she and another individual (whom I assume was from West Ed), stayed in the classroom for no more than 5 minutes. (From what I understand, observations made with West Ed staff are not to be used for teacher evaluations.) During this visit, she observed my students watching <u>Stand and Deliver</u>. Students were required to take notes on the film, and identify the stereotypes that were in the film. What Wilson does not address, because she never asked about the unit, is that the students had already engaged in extensive readings and lectures concerning Latino culture and history. Had Wilson discussed this unit with me, she would have also learned that the film they were watching was used as an example of how media project stereotypes.

  - o Reader will refer to the numerous reading excerpts that students were required to engage in and take notes on. Reader will also notice the class work packet that students completed in relation to the unit. Reader will see that not only did the students engage in a lecture, but took several notes on it. Reader will also notice the film notes that students were required to take.

  - o Reader will also notice the Cultural Image Packet that was distributed to students at the beginning of the second semester, which outlines the goals, objectives, and class work requirements. There is an array of sources used in the unit, as is always the case with all thematic units I teach.

- o   This evaluation would cause one to believe that my lessons consisted solely of videos and had no other sources for students to use.

- o   I contend that this discrepancy is a form of administrative "nit-picking" and discrimination, and there is not validity to the evaluator's statement in the final evaluation. Neither has this administrator accurately analyzed this unit, and therefore cannot judge me as not meeting the standard, especially when there was never a discussion of this element.

### Discrepancy #7—Standard 5.2—Collecting and using multiple sources of information to assess student learning

On September 25, 2009, evaluator reports in the first observation that I "meet and exceed CSTP." Wilson underlines that I use "a variety of assessment tools" and I "collect, select, and reflect upon evidence to guide short-term and long-term plans and support student learning." On December 7, 2009, evaluator makes no indication if I meet or do not meet the standards. Neither does she underline any aspect of this standard. On the evaluation, Wilson reports that I am "progressing toward CSTP." She underlines that "the teacher uses limited sources of information to assess student learning and one or more assessment strategies to monitor student progress." Based on these ratings, I raise the following questions and concerns:

- Evaluator never addresses the elements of this standard during any observation meeting. On what grounds did I move from exceeding the standard to only progressing?

- At the December observation, I used a variety of assessment tools, which included completed work, oral discussions, and group collaboration.

- Evaluator makes no mention of my standing on the December observation notes. How then can the evaluation suggest that I am only progressing when there was neither a discussion to allow improvement, nor any discussion to show how I decreased in performance?

- Reader will refer to the subsequent student work, which suggest that I use multiple sources of information to assess student learning (i.e. quick writes, summative tests, class projects).

- On the September observation, Wilson observed ONE form of student assessment (student essay), and yet identifies from the observation chart that I provide a "variety" of tools, which are used to plan and support student learning.

- At the time of the first observation, I was on good terms with this evaluator. When the second observation and the following evaluation occurred, I was not on good terms with the administration, and had in fact filed a complaint against them for discrimination and retaliation. The results of both negative reports appear to be in direct correlation to my allegation charges.

- I contend that this discrepancy is a form of administrative "nit-picking" and discrimination, and there is not validity to the evaluator's statement in the final evaluation.

## Discrepancy #8—Standard 5.4—Using the results of assessment to guide instruction

On September 25, 2009, evaluator reports in the first observation that I "meet and exceed CSTP." Wilson underlines that I "include assessments as a regular part of instruction to plan and revise lessons." In this category, she asks "how does this happen?" In the post-observation meeting, I discuss that based on the students' essays and how well or poorly they performed, I determine my next steps for a lesson. On December 7, 2009, evaluator indicated no rating for this standard. On the evaluation, Wilson indicated no rating for this standard. Based on these ratings, I raise the following question:

- Why has this standard not received a rating for this category if I demonstrated/explained to the evaluator how I meet or exceed the standard in the first observation meeting? This should be included in the evaluation.

## Discrepancy #9—Communicating with students, families, and other audiences about student progress

On September 25, 2009, evaluator reports in the first observation that I "meet or exceed CSTP." Wilson underlines that I "engage students, families, and support personnel in regular discussions regarding student progress," and "involve students and families as partners in the assessment process." On December 7, 2009, evaluator reports that I "meet or exceed CSTP." Wilson underlines that I "provide students with timely information about their current progress and how to improve their work." On evaluation, Wilson reports that I am only "progressing towards CSTP." Wilson underlines that I "provide students with information about their current progress." Based on these ratings, I raise the following questions and concerns:

- If I have met or exceeded in this area as proven by my observations, on what grounds does the evaluator have in stating that I only "progress towards" the standards?

- If there was a drop in performance, this should have been indicated/discussed during post-observation meetings.

- On both observations, the evaluator watched as I discussed student progress with the students. On the first observation, Wilson saw the lesson plan, which asked the students to engage their parents in their assessments. In the second observation, Wilson saw that I discussed individual grades with my students.

- The evaluation should have included the same ratings as was observed in September and December.

- I contend that this discrepancy is a form of administrative "nit-picking" and discrimination, and there is not validity to the evaluator's statement in the final evaluation.

### Concerns regarding evaluator's comments:

Evaluator mentions that "the posting of grades online was discusses during post-observation conferences...at which time Ms. Killings set a goal of having grades posted online by January 15, 2010. As of March 26, 2010, grades still not posted online. Based on this statement, I raise the following questions and concerns:

- Why is this element even a part of the evaluation? This is not a requirement for RHS teachers.

- This evaluation would infer that I disobey and exercise insubordination when given directives.

- When evaluator first discussed posting grades online, I was under the impression that the teachers were required to do so. Because of the business of my schedule, I did not complete this task by December. When we had the second observation meeting, I indicated that I would push to have them posted by semester 2. In January, after receiving the Notice, I was deeply disturbed by how administration chose to handle things with me. Because I was dealing with that situation, I had no time or energy to post grades online, which is a long process for teachers to complete. I immediately asked Betsy Hall if this was something that teachers were required to do, and she reported that administration can only suggest posting grades, but that they cannot require that we do so. With that said, I did not make an effort to post grades because all my time was devoted to working on my case, instructing my students, and dealing with a hostile working environment. However, parents and students were made aware of students' progress. If parents wanted to know grades, they regularly emailed me, and I responded in a timely manner.

Conclusion: Based on the discrepancies that I identified in this evaluation, it is evident that there are personal biases that negatively affected my evaluation. I have identified several contradictions that support the fact that this evaluator has not accurately assessed my performance as an educator. It also seems highly circumstantial that as another Black instructor under her administration, I, too, have been a recipient of a negative evaluation, which profoundly affects my personnel file. It is also highly suspect that I would receive a "progressing" evaluation (which I identify as a poor evaluation) when I have clearly demonstrated that I meet or exceed the standards, not only as a fourth year teacher, but even when I was a first year teacher. This evaluation leads me to believe that RHS administrators continue to exercise retaliatory and discriminatory actions against me by denigrating my competence and excellence as an instructor. Furthermore, I argue that since this administration did not support me as their instructor, that it is a clear indication of their unprofessional conduct, especially when they reprimand and discredit me for attempting to handle my own classes. Finally, Lisa Wilson's unwillingness to address any negative aspect of my teaching during both meetings violates my rights as an instructor to change any "wrongful" areas, and improve on my teaching before the evaluation. As such, I should not be given a poor evaluation under these circumstances. Because Wilson indicated that I meet or exceed the standards in the majority of the categories (as evident by the observation reports), I contend that my evaluation should reflect this, and not as "Progressing Towards CSTP."

I suppose the reason I fought so hard against these injustices was because I never wanted them to think that everyone would cave under their lies. Plus, I knew that my service in the District was to my children, their parents, and the community. And as long as I had that, then there was a reason to fight to stay.

I want to point out here that while I had to deal with the harassment and discrimination from my employers, I was still dealing with some issues in my class. It was no secret on campus that the District and administration were doing everything they could to destroy my career and reputation. And although some students were changing their negative behavior towards me, there were others who still wanted me destroyed. This includes the student that I have been charged with for sexual misconduct. While Part 1 of this story does not go into the details of the matter, I think it is important that the reader understands that everything that emerged in November 2010 was a direct result of what I have already shared. And the threats to my job security as well as my personal freedom had also come at the same time that the District launched their attacks. When your whole way of life is being threatened by so many, it is no wonder why anyone wouldn't do things under duress.

By February of 2010, I could tell that this was the end of me as a public school teacher. In the back of my mind, I knew that this would be the turning point to bring all things to a close. I knew that my days in this District and the school were numbered, and I had indeed had enough. The overwhelming stress of the last four years had taken its toll on me, and when I was at the lowest point in my life, when the school and District had me at my breaking point, I was then confronted with the biggest fear of losing everything I had worked so hard for. This time, it would not come at the hands of the administrators or District officials. It would come from my very own student.

# My Spiritual Thermostat

*"Do not neglect the gift which is in you, [that special
inward endowment] which was directly imparted to
you [by the Holy Spirit] by prophetic utterance when the
elders laid their hands upon you..."*
*(I Timothy 4:14 AMP)*

There is a point that I want the reader to notice. At no time
during my discussion of the professional backlash did I mention
anything about the Lord; and there's a reason for it. Because I
had been going through so much at the job and in my personal
life—including my spiritual one—it was as if my trust in God had
wavered. There was no doubt that I was in love with the Lord, but I
felt like He had let me down when He allowed so much devastation
to come my way. All my life, I only knew success—only good things
happened to me; and I attributed that to the grace and blessing of
God. So when things began to turn against me, I felt like He had
abandoned me when I had never left Him, and had agreed to fight for
others as He instructed me. Even though I knew that God was with
me, I couldn't feel Him fighting for me. Every time I would make

progress in one area, I was met with immediate hostility in another; it seemed like Satan had beaten me to the brim, and I literally lost myself in it all. I lost my peace and happiness, my willingness to do anything for my children, and my hunger for more. Slowly, but surely, my soul was dying, and it did not help that so many people that I thought were for me were actually against me. It was a trying time, one of immense betrayal and disloyalty. This was something that I had never experienced before, and it killed me. And I wanted God to save me from it all; yet it seemed like He was so far away.

I felt like Job, who had been a loving husband, father, and neighbor to his community; who had given to the poor and helped the needy. But in one instance, everything he had was taken from him, including his health. Although he cried out to the Lord to save him from his troubles, it seemed like the Lord was far from him, and he couldn't understand why. Although Job had a small group of friends who were supposed to comfort him, instead these same individuals ridiculed and criticized him. No matter what his defense was, he could not prove to others that he did not deserve it, because to people like Job's friends (yes, I'm talking to you Church folks), anytime calamity hits a Believer, the first thought is "God must be mad at them for their heinous and atrocious sins."

It's a sad state to be in when one area of life takes a downward turn because of your stand for righteousness. It's an even harder dilemma when your spiritual thermostat drops because of the treatment you receive for God's people. But that is exactly what I was dealing with in 2009-2010.

The following section is written to give you an understanding of what was going on with me spiritually so that you can know that when Satan attacks you, he comes with his best shots and hits you in every area of your life. To this day, I cannot figure out what it is that God sees in me that would make Him think that I could stand in the midst of all this; but I pray that in the end, the reward is double what I had lost.

This section is really aimed at addressing people in the church. And I hope as they read this, they understand that often times, they have a hand in causing their brother or sister to fall simply through their critical, judgmental behavior. While I would not say that I blame them for everything I went through, I do argue that their lack of concern, compassion, and care was a part of the reason why I made many of the decisions I did. Whether or not it is "correct" to specifically address them in this format, I could care less. Perhaps we will begin to open our eyes and see how our actions have a way of hurting the ones that are suffering the most, even those in the Body of Christ.

The tumultuous storm that I experienced at the job was also experienced in my spiritual walk. Sometimes when it seems like everything around you is crumbling, you may tend to think that something is strangely wrong with who you are. That's how I felt. Not only was I dealing with hell at my job, but things were falling for me, even in the area that I expected to always work well: the church.

For years, I had been extremely active in the ministry, doing all

I could to help push the vision of my father. As mentioned prior, I led the youth ministry because I had a strong heart for the young generation. In 2009, God allowed for another opportunity to push the youth ministry further. I was so excited about it because there is nothing like having a fresh, new anointing to get a ministry going higher. The anticipation and excitement stirred things in my spirit once again, and I strongly believed that God would do even greater works than I had seen when I was younger. Unfortunately, not everyone that I worked with in this area wanted that same push that I did, and things slowly began to fall apart. I remember asking myself, *Has God abandoned me? Why are these things happening to me?* But I also remember thinking, *Lord, I know what You can do and what You desire to do in this generation, but I can't do anything without that same zeal and enthusiasm from others.* Needless to say, in spite of all the prodding to get that particular group to want what God wanted for that ministry, it would not go any further under my direction. Without exposing too much of *why* it didn't go higher, I became increasingly frustrated and discouraged. It affected my heart so profoundly because I could tell that there was no heart for my children from my generation. My thing is this: If you don't want to help my kids spiritually, then sit down. It's too difficult trying to pump up others when I also have to minister to the ones that are supposed to be ministering to my kids. It's a waste of my time, and everyone that knows me understands that I hate wasted time.

Other things that had happened to me and Sister in the church really affected my spiritual walk. I became increasingly angry and bitter by what God's people had done to us. What people seem to NOT understand is that no matter how old Pastors' daughters become, the pressure from "church scrutiny" is too difficult to handle, especially when the Church is supposed to operate in love. In my heart, I felt as though the things that God's people had done to us was so overwhelmingly distressing that I could not take it anymore, and I needed to leave. The problem was that the anointing, the power, and the Spirit of God was and is so heavy in my father's ministry that it's rare to find that same thing in any other congregation. The Word of God was and is so rich, and what rests on my father is something that I want to flow on my life as well. But sometimes when things are so tense and so heated because of people's attitudes, perceptions, and behaviors, it becomes almost unbearable to stay. At that time in my life, I needed peace where I fellowshipped. The last thing I needed to deal with was drama with God's people. I already had to deal with that in the world and in my job. I had to cope with people trying to destroy my life; and when I felt like God's people were mistreating me or Sister, I had to escape it all. My heart was dying; my soul was crushing; and I knew before long my body would surely have a breakdown. To make matters worse, I was also dealing with the harassment and mistreatment of my student. The problem is I didn't know what to do. I didn't feel like I had someone who I could talk to about everything, and that's what I felt I needed. There was not a day that I did not call upon the Lord to help me, especially because I could not understand WHY He had allowed so much to happen to me all at the same time. I knew one thing for sure: I needed to get out and figure out what was happening to me. Sometimes when we have so many things going on and they all seem to be going insane, we just need to "get away." I knew I couldn't simply quit my job because I had bills to pay. I couldn't leave to work at another school because my personnel file was damaged. And because I expected Church to be that one place that I should have experienced peace yet it wasn't there for me, I decided to break from that for a while.

I would never suggest or encourage anyone who is dealing with a lot to leave the Church or the place of worship. But sometimes there are situations and circumstances that happen, which ultimately cause people to leave the ministry. Sometimes, the Church can be harsher, more critical, and least forgiving than the people in the world. It becomes increasingly harder when you are the Pastor's child, and your business is ALWAYS in the spotlight. What I desperately needed at that moment was not what I was receiving by attending the ministry, and so I left. I didn't attend another church, however. Sundays were spent reading the Word and fellowshipping with God on a very personal level. I needed God to do a work inside of me, something that could and would be permanent. I needed the issues in my life to come in alignment with His Word, and I needed all this to happen without any pressures from His people or any ministerial commitments. I just needed the presence of the Lord, just me and Him.

I stayed away from church for about three or four months, but I didn't abandon my dependence on the Lord. Some people who leave the ministry also leave the Lord. That was not the case for me. The Holy Ghost ministered to my heart every day. He was so patient with me as I continuously divulged my hurts and pain to Him. I knew I needed Him to deliver me from so much, ESPECIALLY the issues I had at the job and with that student. In it all, I was always grateful that God was always watching me and watching over me. During the course of those months in 2010 (between May and August), I knew that as I continued to be honest and pour my heart out to the Lord, He was going to deliver me from the trials and tribulations that I endured. It was during those months that God showed me in a vision that I would be arrested on charges of rape. It was during those months that God was preparing my heart for what would later happen in November. It was during those months that my heart became soft and pliable to His Word and His Spirit. And I told the Lord that if He would continue to work with me and be patient towards me, then I would return to Him and never look back.

Before the day of my arrest, I had come back to the church. My father really helped me to deal with the hurt from God's people, and as he ministered to me, my heart became softer. Forgiveness was the key to making that happen. I had repented. I had forgiven. I had released the pain experienced at the church; and for the first time in many, many months, I had sensed joy and happiness.

Before the new school year began in August 2010, I met with my principal to try and make peace. Back in July, I had sent her an email, informing her that I had no intentions of coming back to the school, and that I wanted to possibly move to Los Angeles and find work there. I told her my reasons were because I wanted "something new," but the truth is I was growing tired and frustrated with my harassing student; however, because I could not find work in time for the new school year, I had to return to RHS. (For the most part, readers can Google my name to find out a general idea of what happened between the student and me, including extortion and blackmail, which finally resulted in my arrest. Because the nature of my case is not fully complete, I cannot discuss many details except that which has already been reported in the courts. I will say this, however: When I told the police and prosecutor what had happened to me, none of them believed me. For months, I had endured a lot of threats from this student to do what he wanted or else risk losing my life and career. While he will not admit to the direct threats, this student, a year after the entire November 2010 fiasco, sent a message to me through a mutual source, indicating how sorry he was for everything he had done to me. He even offered to help me with my case in order to get the charges dropped because he knew that he was wrong for what he did. The way I see it, if you did nothing wrong, then there is nothing to apologize for; neither should you feel intense guilt for something that you never did. And even though he will never admit to threatening my life in exchange for the things he wanted, God knows the truth, and that truth will prevail. At this point, it is unclear as to whether or not his apologies are legitimate. What the messages do infer is that there was something that he had not been truthful about from the beginning; and as he watched my life quickly become a national story, he could no longer handle the guilt that dwelt in him. As the second book, *Fear, Faith, and Patience: Letters to my Lord,* will reveal, he and his friend has a prominent hand in demolishing my career to simply cover what they had done to me. In all the months that I had to patiently wait for the court's decision, I was not allowed to say anything to anyone about the matter. That proved especially hard as I read the comments and reports from people about how sick and twisted I was to do such a thing; and that I deserved every consequence that the courts issued. It was hard to deal with, especially in the public eye. But I am grateful that God never let me lose my mind. Now, at the closing of my case, I can honestly say that God did a wonder that is too extraordinary for me to comprehend. Who would have thought that in a million years, this student, under the weight and pressure of that guilt, would ever see fit to admit to his wrong, and seek a way to help me win my case? I'm anxious to see how this will all eventually turn out.)

When I realized that returning to RHS was my only option, I wanted to do everything I could to have a peaceful school year, even if I could not escape that student. I wish I could say that these efforts proved to be successful, but they weren't. You can never expect wicked people to side with you when they are hell-bent on destroying you. Even though I had done everything right up until that point, I was foolish to think that the District and the administrators would suddenly have a change of heart. Nevertheless, I knew that in order to be prepared for the greatest fight of my life, I was going to need the power of God to be with me. And as hard as it has been, especially to go through it with the world watching, I am grateful that He has not left me.

# Conclusion

The Word of the Lord is here for all who will listen. When all hell is breaking loose in every aspect of our lives, the Lord is ever ready to be there with us, for in our weakness He is made strong. We come to know the Lord for real when everything around us is gone. We must always see ourselves as being desperate for His power and His presence. The Lord is a jealous God, and He will not allow anything or anyone to take His place in our hearts. He must be first and foremost. When we become desperate for Him, He comes through for us.

"But now [in spite of past judgments for Israel's sins], thus says the Lord, He Who created you, O Jacob, and He Who formed you, O Israel: Fear not, for I have redeemed you [ransomed you by paying a price instead of leaving you captives]; I have called you by your name; you are Mine. When you pass through the waters, I will be with you, and through the rivers, they will not overwhelm you. When you walk through the fire, you will not be burned or scorched, nor will the flame kindle upon you. For I am the Lord your God, the Holy One of Israel, your Savior...Because you are precious in My sight and honored, and because I love you, I will give men in return for you and people in exchange for your life. Fear not, for I am with you. "(Isaiah 43:1-5 Amplified)

I had to trust that once I returned to the Lord by doing what He wanted me to do that He would be with me no matter what happened to me. We would be foolish to think that Satan will leave us alone just because we want to do what's right. No, instead, he intensifies the fire! But we have a promise from God that even when we go through the fire, not only will He be with us, but He will not allow us to be burned. What a great Word to have when things are incredibly tense and heated! God not only promises to be with us during this time, but He promises to bring us out. Once we are out, that which we lost in the fire, we will receive double for our trouble. The only way that we will come out unscathed is if we allow the fire to burn and remove all the things that God displeases. This is how we can see God using what Satan created to destroy us as actually working for us. Satan wants to kill us with the fire. God wants us to be purged by the fire. At least when we come out, we will be pure and holy *if* we continue to place our faith in Him.

I love the Lord. And in spite of the troubles that I am experiencing, I would never exchange this spiritual growth and revelation for a single moment of the past. I am grateful that the Lord delivered me from a terribly abusive situation at the hands of a student and an entire school district, even if I may have disliked the manner in which it came.

What I intend to share with the reader in the second book is not to make anyone in particular look bad. We all make mistakes, and have to give an account for the actions we commit on earth. Rather, I hope that it will bring healing to others who are going through a similar situation. For me, the second part of this story is for my children that I left behind. I can't begin to tell you how much my heart misses you, and I wish I had told so many of you the truth before the lies became so public. I feel that if there is anyone who deserves to know what happened, it should be you. And hopefully through this story, you will come to see that no matter who tries to destroy you, no one can annihilate you unless you give them that power. For so long, I had relinquished that might out of my fears; but I regained my strength when I began to trust God and not myself. You, too, must exercise that same kind of faith as you take your journey through life. I've never been one to make up excuses because those are for the weak; but I have always been real, and that helps me be strong. If there is any lesson to learn through this story, it is this: When you are destined for greatness, you must earnestly push beyond the confines of your shortcomings. You must become stronger and wiser than your enemies. And you must ever be ready to fight to obtain your destiny because there will be plenty of people who will try to assassinate what you know you should be.


But you must never let them win.

Made in the USA
Monee, IL
01 October 2020

43722368R00138